# EVOLUTION AND

# MORMONISM

T0307732

# EVOLUTION AND

## A Quest for Understanding

# MORMONISM

Trent D. Stephens

D. Jeffrey Meldrum

with Forrest B. Peterson

Foreword by Duane E. Jeffery

Signature Books • Salt Lake City

*To those who search for understanding*

Jacket design by Ron Stucki

∞ *Evolution and Mormonism: A Quest for Understanding*
was printed on acid-free paper and was composed, printed,
and bound in the United States of America.

© 2001 Signature Books. All rights reserved.
Signature Books is a registered trademark of
Signature Books Publishing, LLC.

07   06   05   04   03      6   5   4   3

www.signaturebooks.com

Library of Congress Cataloging-in-Publication Data
Stephens, Trent D.
     Evolution and Mormonism : a quest for understanding /
by Trent D. Stephens and D. Jeffrey Meldrum ;
with Forrest B. Peterson ; foreword by Duane E. Jeffery.
      p. cm.
    Includes bibliographical references and index.
    ISBN 978-1-56085-142-4 (pbk.)
     1. Evolution—Religious aspects—Church of Jesus Christ
of Latter-day Saints. 2. Church of Jesus Christ of Latter-day
Saints—Doctrines. I. Meldrum, D. Jeffrey, 1958- II. Peterson,
Forrest B., 1947- III. Title.

BX8643.E94 S74 2000
231.7'652'088283—dc21
                                 00-055615

# Contents

Foreword by Duane E. Jeffery, *vii*
Introduction, *xv*
Acknowledgments, *xxi*

1. The Wonder of It All, *1*
2. The Bottom Line, *7*
3. The Truth Shall Make You Free, *15*
4. When the Prophet Speaks, *31*
5. The Evidence of Things, *59*
6. What about Darwin? *81*
7. DNA on the Witness Stand, *101*
8. Our Place in Nature, *119*
9. The Body as a Temple, *131*
10. Written in Stone, *139*
11. Genesis Revisited, *165*
12. In God's Image, *187*
13. Eternal Evolution, *203*

Appendix. Three Official LDS
      Statements on Evolution, *209*
References Cited, *219*
Index, *231*

# Foreword

Duane E. Jeffery

There is a certain irony in the fact that the twentieth century in Mormonism begins and ends with the teachings of Joseph F. Smith. He became president of the church in 1901, and from then until his death in 1918, he presided over a major consolidation of doctrines that, up to that time, had not been particularly well defined. This consolidation—or reconstruction, as historian Thomas G. Alexander has called it—was driven primarily by three prominent Mormon writers and doctrinal commentators whose roles in this area have not been fully recognized by the church at large: B. H. Roberts, James E. Talmage, and John A. Widtsoe.

These three were far more sensitive to the life of the mind than were many of their religious contemporaries; they believed deeply that the gospel was too precious to be defended with anything but the best scholarship and honesty the Saints could muster. They believed in an ultimate synthesis of truth, and that God reveals his truths through both prophets and academicians. And their names have come to symbolize that commitment. Talmage's two seminal works —*Jesus the Christ* and *Articles of Faith*—remain the foundations of Latter-day Saint doctrinal study. Roberts's *Comprehensive History of the Church* still stands as the church's official history for its first century; his priesthood manuals for the years 1907-12 still constitute the high-water mark of our organized doctrinal study courses. Widt-soe's long history of doctrinal writings (*Evidences and Reconcilia-tions*) in the church's official magazine continues to exert consider-able influence.

Not to be ignored or forgotten is Nels L. Nelson, an English pro-fessor at Brigham Young University who during the early years of the twentieth century enjoyed an unusual relationship with church pres-ident Joseph F. Smith. President Smith was known to send drafts of his speeches to Nelson for editing and suggestions, and it was Nelson who produced Mormonism's first book on that most controversial of issues: science and religion.

The book appeared in 1904 and was considered a missionary tract by both its author and by the church's governing First Presi-dency. Nelson envisioned it as the first of at least two books aimed at making Mormonism noticed—and noted—by the world's academic fraternity. He titled it *Scientific Aspects of Mormonism*, and aimed to show that not only was Mormonism compatible with then-current scientific thought, but that indeed it had arrived at many of the basic philosophical positions before science did. Of particular interest is his teaching of a rather thorough-going brand of organic evolu-tion—he saw it as fully compatible with Mormon teachings and revelations.

Demonstrating such a consilience of science and religion was necessary, Nelson believed, because "a religion which is not scien-tific is scarcely worth the credence of our enlightened age." And while he recognized that he could not deal with all concepts of sci-ence, he insisted that he could show that Mormonism's "basic data are not out of keeping with those general laws of nature on which all the conclusions of scientists rest," and that "science and Mormonism see things in this world primarily in the same way, and also reason as to the purpose of things in the same way." For him, the "book of na-ture" is (like scripture) a direct revelation of God; the laws of the uni-verse are nothing more than the general divine laws of God. Mortal-ity was meant to be "a glorious university—the only real univer-sity—for the development of (God's) sons and daughters."

Unfortunately, Nelson was not trained in science and his treatise suffers from that fact. His overall outlook was laudatory but ultimately flawed, both by his own limitations and those of the science of the day. For evolution is surely the most controversial philosophical concept of the modern world, and its mechanisms were only dimly seen in 1904. The entire process is founded on the science we now call genetics—but that word was not even coined until the year after Nelson's book appeared. In 1904 we did not even know if the laws of genetics applied to human beings—the first demonstration of that came also the year after Nelson's book was published.

So Nelson's effort was doomed despite the soundness of his overall conceptual scheme that religion must progress along with science or it will quickly become irrelevant for anything other than social niceties. I fear that subsequent developments in the twentieth century have validated that point of view.

Ultimately religions can do only about three things with science. They can, of course, attack it, and many religious concepts now lie in the dust bin of history from that approach. They can ignore it—in which case they progressively become incapable of addressing modern and future problems. Or they can engage it and incorporate the demonstrated truths found thereby into a more productive view of their overall universe.

This latter path is difficult, and to many people of faith it sounds like selling the store, given the past history of science/religion relationships. But that is so only if one takes the view that God reveals himself solely through revelation and scripture, and that scripture is doctrinally complete—or, if not complete, at least sufficient. And that has not been the position of historical Mormonism.

The angel Moroni had spelled that out to church founder Joseph Smith, citing the ancient prophecy of Joel: "And it shall come to pass afterward, that I will pour out my spirit upon all flesh; and your sons and your daughters shall prophesy, your old men shall dream dreams, your young men shall see visions" (Joel 2:28; JS-H 1:41). This scripture has been consistently understood by Mormon commentators to refer to the rise of science. Apostle Joseph Fielding Smith (son of President Joseph F. Smith) probably stated this interpretation most succinctly:

*... the Lord has already commenced to pour out his Spirit upon all flesh,* and we do find even now that the sons and daughters prophesy; the old men dream dreams, and the young men see visions.

Now, my brethren and sisters, *I am not going to confine this prophecy to the members of the Church.* The Lord said he would pour out his Spirit upon *all* flesh ... (p. 176)

*There has never been a step taken from that day to this, in discovery or invention, where the Spirit of the Lord ... was not the prevailing force, resting upon the individual, which caused him to make the discovery or the invention ... nor did the Lord always use those who have faith, nor does he always do so today. He uses such minds as are pliable and can be turned in certain directions to accomplish his work, whether they believe in him or not.* (*Doctrines of Salvation,* 1:176, pre-1954; emphasis in original.)

I suppose that Joseph Fielding Smith may not have meant to include Charles Darwin and evolution in this sweeping idealism, though in this particular passage he did not qualify his sentiment at all.

But in President Joseph F. Smith's day, the church began to deal with Darwin and evolution fairly directly. The Nelson book was a beginning. In 1908 President Smith and his counselors in the First Presidency took note of the rising tide of international discussion regarding the implications of evolution for religion and morals. They appointed a committee to formulate a position statement for the church, to be released in November 1909. This was a double anniversary—fifty years to the month since Darwin had published his fundamental work, *On the Origin of Species,* as well as the centennial of Darwin's birth.

The committee's work appeared over the signatures of Joseph F. Smith and his counselors. It has been reprinted many times by critics of evolution in the church, for it is easily interpreted as having an anti-evolutionary tone. Its major argument is that man is composed of both body and spirit, and it labors long to establish that the human spirit results from a spirit birth to a Heavenly Father and a Heavenly Mother. The origin of the human body is less clear, however. After stating that Adam, "like Christ, took upon himself an appropriate body," the statement turns briefly to other matters, then dismisses evolution and concludes by saying that humans are capable of evolving into Gods.

Numerous questions from church readers prompted a clarification just five months later. In April 1910, in their official columns in the church magazine, the First Presidency took a more detailed stance. They identified three possible options for the origin of the human body, listing evolution by "natural processes ... through the direction and power of God" as one acceptable view. No First Presidency since then has ever clarified the details of this issue any further. I find it regrettable that the church's study manual for 2000-2001 includes only the 1909 statement, with no context whatever nor any evidence of the subsequent clarification.

Commentary on evolution continued cautiously from that time on. The next major LDS book dealing with the subject was written by geologist Frederick J. Pack in 1924 and is decidedly pro-evolution. As this present book details, that guardedly favorable attitude in the church continued for some time. A major discussion among the general authorities in 1931 resulted in a First Presidency ruling that the church had no doctrinal position on *either* side of the two most controversial issues: whether there were human-like beings on Earth before the time generally ascribed to Adam, and whether there was death on Earth prior to the fall of Adam. So for several decades, beginning with Joseph F. Smith's administration, the church remained open on the subject of evolution, though aware of possible pitfalls. The chosen course was one of minimal engagement, little attempt at accommodation, but certainly not one of rejection.

All that changed, however, at mid-century, as a couple of books claiming to be authoritative took a decidedly antagonistic stance toward evolution. That story is well known. Less well known is that those works have not found substantive support from church history, and none whatever from ever-advancing science. A careful study of the subject clearly demonstrates that the anti-science position espoused by some in the church is untenable. Perhaps consequently, some recent writers have decided to take refuge in the third option outlined above and ignore science altogether. Lacking the training and discipline to adequately study science, they have asserted that science is irrelevant to matters of interest to religion. If we give scientists any credence at all, they argue, we would be making them into rival prophets—a clearly intolerable thought.

What does this new stance do to Mormonism's long history of claiming that "no man can be saved in ignorance," or that "man can be saved no faster than he gains knowledge"? What, to be more precise, does it do with Nelson's view that mortal life is a "glorious university—the only real university"? Perhaps Nelson and his sponsoring First Presidency were simply wrong. Mortality, says the new wisdom, is really not a university in which we learn divine natural laws. Rather it is a testing center where we learn ordinances and obedience, not science and natural laws.

Of course, this is self-defeating. It produces a mentality ever more incapable of dealing with modern issues, a people progressively "irrelevant" to discussing and resolving society's challenges. For if science is irrelevant to religion, perhaps religion is equally irrelevant to science. And since science is incontestably the force that shapes modern society, both by its technology and its increasing understanding of natural laws, we clearly run the danger of defining ourselves right out of relevance to modern life.

So, as a new century dawns, we find ourselves studying once again the teachings of the prophet who opened the twentieth century. And the present book serves as a fine introduction to the idealism found in the broader church literature of that earlier day.

Trent Stephens and Jeff Meldrum are both established research scientists. Their undergraduate careers at Brigham Young University exposed them early to the details of Mormonism's history with science and religion. Their own interests in the field were evident even then to members of their faculty. Some students in biology "muddle through," while others do well but with their sights set either on technical details of research or on a disciplined preparation for professional careers in, say, medicine or dentistry or wildlands management. Rare indeed are those who address the broader philosophical issues, who want to "engage" the issues rather than shrink from the fray. Trent and Jeff were clearly members of this latter group.

After completion of their own doctorate training, both joined the faculty of a state university whose student body is largely composed of Latter-day Saints. These students' predictable questions forced continued consideration of the issues by Trent and Jeff. Their active church involvement brought additional questions and insights to bear on the topic. One of their students, Forrest Peterson, eventually convinced them that it was a worthy effort to share their thoughts with a broader LDS audience. Thus the present book was born.

This work should not be seen as a final synthesis of Mormonism and science, much less of science and religion in general. We Latter-day Saints have fallen too far behind the discussion to envision any such synthesis; the first thing we need to do is a lot of catching up. We have no significant ecclesiastical tradition dealing with the substance of either science or scripture on the majority of science/religion issues.

In December 1910 President Joseph F. Smith and his counselors laid down a critical criterion to guide church members in discussions of this sort. "Our religion is not hostile to real science," they attested. "That which is demonstrated we accept with joy." *Demonstrated.* A key requirement. What in evolutionary science can be said to be "demonstrated"? This book attempts some initial answers.

Beyond these concepts from the First Presidency, the authors return to the philosophical stance of traditional Mormonism, to Nelson's insight that mortality is a glorious university. They have labored hard to render the fundamentals of modern genetic and evolutionary science understandable to anyone willing to expend a modicum of serious effort. "Thy mind, O man!" exclaimed Joseph Smith, "if thou wilt lead a soul unto salvation, must stretch as high as the utmost heavens, and search into and contemplate the darkest abyss, and the broad expanse of eternity" (qtd. in Smith, *History of the Church,* 3:295).

Exaltation is not, said Joseph and traditional Mormonism, a matter of marching lockstep through mortality; it is instead a conscientious, dedicated, disciplined, and rigorous search for truth, for an understanding of the laws that make this world and universe run. And the study of those laws need not be seen as a threat to one's religious commitment. Quite the contrary. God himself seems to have asserted that a study of nature's laws leads only to a greater understanding and appreciation of him and his ways: "all things are created and made to bear record of me, both things which are temporal, and things which are spiritual; things which are in the heavens above, and things which are on the earth, and things which are in the earth, and things which are under the earth, both above and beneath: all things bear record of me" (Moses 6:63).

This book is a much-needed attempt to get us back on the road to pursuing that ideal. It was that ideal that fired Nelson, Roberts, Talmage, and Widtsoe in the early years of this century. Now, a century later, we have come, in a sense, full circle, with a book that stems from the same commitment. But where they (Nelson particularly) struggled with high ideals but inadequate science, the present authors have at their command a century of the most spectacular advances in knowledge—*demonstrated* knowledge—ever to be possessed by the human race. To the extent that knowledge fulfills the prophecy of Joel, it is God's knowledge and is an integral part of our religion. It is clear that the twenty-first century will bring even more of that type of knowledge, knowledge which takes us right to the fundamental principles of life itself and the management of those principles both in humans and in other organisms. Such knowledge most certainly is "relevant" to religious concerns. Knowledge of the natural laws is essential to the wise stewardship of God's creations and creatures. We must bring ourselves into a position to deal with this massive outpouring of truth. In my opinion, we can no longer afford to ignore it. Active, honest, and rigorous engagement is the only response worthy of those who would uphold the ideals that fired the Restoration. The present book is a major step in that direction.

# Introduction

Over the past few hundred years, a variety of issues has created seeming conflicts between science and religion. One of the major points of disagreement has to do with the origin and nature of humankind. On one side is the revealed word and particularly its interpretation, which indicate that humans were created by God, in his image, and are unique and separate from Nature. On the other side are the scientific data and their interpretation, which indicate that we evolved from other preexisting life forms by random processes, and that we are related to all of Nature. Church leaders and other members have sometimes expressed strong opinions on both sides of the issue. Some members of the church have even alleged that a person cannot be in good standing in the church and "believe" in human evolution. Yet LDS students are presented with compelling data and persuasive arguments in their biology, geology, and anthropology classes that support the theory of evolution. Can a person acknowledge these data and accept these arguments while remaining an active member of the church? Can the theory of organic evolution and the doctrines of the LDS church be reconciled?

There is a relatively common experience among LDS students who enter colleges and universities. Some, perhaps many, of these students have been taught that evolution is false and, even more, that it is evil and not God's way. Enrolled in a college biology course, these students become confused when faced with a body of well-established evidence that supports the theory of evolution and seemingly contradicts previous religious education. Students who pursue a health-sciences profession or attend a graduate biology program often major in biology as undergraduates. They are required to take advanced courses in genetics and evolution and become acquainted with even more compelling evidence for evolution. Such a student is then faced with a difficult dilemma: "Do I believe what I've been previously taught in spite of what seems to be convincing evidence, or do I accept the evidence of science and discount the ideas of my family and former teachers? If I discount what they have told me about evolution, what about other church teachings?" Must students be forced to choose between science and their faith? We think not.

Every year students come to us when they discover we are active members of the LDS church and also evolutionary biologists and ask, "How do you reconcile your faith with the theory of evolution?" We discuss our opinions with these students, but when our discussion has ended, we have found that we cannot refer them to any good book on the subject because most are at least twenty years old, very dated, and often out of print. (An exception is a short but well-written section on evolution and the church in Paul, *Science, Religion, and Mormon Cosmology*, 180-81.) We have written this book to fill that void. We attempt to resolve the apparent discrepancies between the theory of evolution and the concept of the creation as taught in the LDS church.

In one of only two official First Presidency statements concerning the origin of Adam, President Joseph F. Smith and his counselors stated in November 1909: "The Church ... declares man to be the direct and lineal offspring of Deity. ... Man is the child of God, formed in the divine image and endowed with divine attributes." (This statement, which remains the official church position, is reprinted in this book's appendix; see also chap. 2.) This statement has been interpreted by some members of the church to mean that our physical bodies, as well as our spirit bodies, are the lineal offspring of deity. Because the 1909 First Presidency statement stimulated "several High Priests' quorums" to wonder, "In just what manner did the mortal bodies of Adam and Eve come into existence on this earth?" an editorial in the *Improvement Era* entitled "Priesthood Quorum's Table" addressed the issue in April 1910. "Whether the mortal bodies of man evolved in natural processes to present perfection, through the direction and power of God," it stated; "whether the first parents of our generations, Adam and Eve, were transplanted from another sphere, with immortal tabernacles ...; whether they were born here in mortality, as other mortals have been, are questions not fully answered in the revealed word of God." (The entire editorial is also reprinted in the Appendix.) Even though many people continue to debate the issue of Adam's origin, the *Improvement Era* editorial clearly allows for the possibility of a natural process employed by God in the physical creation of humankind.

Two major problems contribute to the perceived rift between evolution and some commonly held LDS beliefs: (1) If evolution is an entirely random process, as many evolutionary biologists say, how then can there be order in the universe? How could God have been in control of the process if the outcome was unpredictable? How could we have been created in God's image as the result of a random evolutionary process? (2) If Adam and Eve came into being as the result of evolutionary processes, how then could they have been immortal? If they were not immortal, how do we explain the Fall? If there was no Fall, what was the mission of Jesus? If there was no Fall and Atonement, is there then no Christianity?

In this book we hope to discuss these and other questions in a way that will benefit students and other members of the church. We also hope to compare science and faith as ways of knowing about the universe and our place in it. Science is limited to questions that can be addressed through observations; conclusions and theories must be consistent with those observations. Faith, on the other hand, is based on revelation. We are confident that religious truth and scientific truth do not conflict. Our opinions are based on years of study, both in the fields of theology and biology. We recognize the distinct but complementary roles that knowledge in each field plays in our understanding of life. We believe that God created the earth, but we also believe that as scientists we can begin to understand some of the processes God employed and interpret the prehistoric record of "creation." We believe we are the spirit children of God, but we also believe that we can discover the laws of Nature which brought our bodies into being. We believe that by gaining greater knowledge and understanding, the perceived rift between evolution and LDS theology can be bridged and disagreements dispelled.

When Charles Darwin introduced the theory of evolution by natural selection, the mechanisms of inheritance (genetics) were a mystery. The subsequent discovery of Gregor Mendel's work explained the mechanism of inheritance but did not seem to allow for variations, which Darwin's theory required. During the first three decades of the twentieth century, many scientists viewed Darwin's theory of natural selection as having been supplanted by the newly discovered principles of Mendelian genetics, with its precise statistical assortment of discrete genes. However, in the 1920s H. J. Muller demonstrated the principle of mutation, which provided the variations necessary for natural selection. The combination of Darwin's natural selection, Mendel's genetics, and Muller's mutation theory in the late 1930s and 1940s has been called by biologists the "modern synthesis" (sometimes called Neo-Darwinism). The modern synthesis has reaffirmed the integral role of evolution by natural selection in the biological sciences. Many statements made by scientists during the decades of skepticism regarding evolution were quoted by critics of evolution for many years after their obsolescence, and they are repeatedly cited by some individuals (mainly fundamentalist) to this day.

An impressive amount of new scientific data has accumulated in the past twenty-five years, data that were unknown when the previous generation of science and religion books was published. Many writers addressing the subject of evolution and creation have not considered the modern synthesis and its implications, let alone the more recent molecular evidence. The entirely new field of molecular biology has added its enormous weight to the discussion.

Concerning Adam's origin, the First Presidency under Heber J. Grant stated in a meeting of general church authorities in 1931, "Our mission is to bear the message of the restored gospel to the world.

Leave geology, biology, archaeology, and anthropology ... to scientific research" (reprinted in the Appendix). As scientists who are also active in the church and have strong faith in the gospel of Jesus Christ, we, in the spirit of that admonition from the First Presidency, present this book in the hope that it will help readers in their quest for understanding.

# Acknowledgments

We wish to thank several of our colleagues at Idaho State University, whose advice and encouragement have been greatly appreciated: Edwin W. House, Rodney Seeley, Charles Trost, and Larry Farrell. We have also valued feedback from Duane Jeffery and several of his students at Brigham Young University. In addition, we have had several long discussions with members of the LDS church's Institute of Religion adjacent to the campus of Idaho State University, and are grateful for their input: Val Clark, Kim Johnson, and Roger S. Porter. We also appreciate Mike Powell, pastor of ISU's University Bible Church, for several important discussions. We express thanks to C. Ross Belnap, former bishop, and Cornelius Hofman, former president of the Pocatello East Stake, and William S. Godfrey, current president of the Pocatello East Stake, for their support and guidance. We wish to thank the many graduate and undergraduate students with whom we have discussed these issues over the years; without their stimulating questions, this project would never have been initiated. We especially thank Bradley J. Fillmore, a graduate student with Dr. Stephens, whose encouragement has been strong throughout this entire project. We also wish to acknowledge the fifty or so students at ISU who participated in our experimental course, "What about Darwin," which explored issues of evolution and religion.

We are grateful to the numerous fireside participants who stimulated considerable discussion about science and religion as well as the relation between evolution and the LDS church. We want to thank our many friends and acquaintances (in addition to many listed above) who read drafts of our manuscript and provided valuable feedback: Christy Smith and Chris Conklin (both of whom read extensively and made many valuable comments), Elden Lott, Carl Hogg, Dan and Jean Petmecky, and Tony Christensen. We greatly appreciate the editorial assistance of Marjanna Hulet. Finally, we are especially grateful to our wives: Kathleen Stephens, Terri Meldrum, and Carol Peterson; and to our children for their patience during the years we spent working on this book.

# 1.
# The Wonder of It All

Who among us has never gazed into the expanse of heaven and marveled at its wonders? Who has never asked who we are and how we fit into the vastness of the cosmos? Over 3,000 years ago, the Hebrew psalmist, overwhelmed by the majesty of the night sky, inquired of God, "When I consider thy heavens, the work of thy fingers, the moon and the stars, which thou hast ordained; What is man that thou art mindful of him?" (Ps. 8:3-4) From earliest history, humans have searched the heavens and sought to understand their place within God's eternal scheme.

Today theologians, scientists, philosophers, and others are seeking to understand the mysteries of the universe and to find our place within it. Scientists around the world are probing the heavens at every hour of the day and night, gathering data on profound cosmic questions. From these hundreds of thousands of observations, astronomers and physicists are piecing together a picture of our solar system, galaxy, and the universe beyond. They are revealing a universe more diverse, more wonderful, and more mysterious than ever before imagined; a universe too grand, too intricate, too marvelous for mortals to comprehend fully.

Four hundred years ago, people believed that if we are the focus of God's creation, we must be at the center of his universe. The calculations of Copernicus and the observations of Galileo demonstrated that the earth is not the center of the universe. Today most people recognize Earth's place within the immensity of space and time. Even at 25,000 miles per hour, astronauts must travel several days to reach the moon. At the same speed, they would have to travel 80,000 years to reach the nearest star outside our solar system. And there are 100 billion stars organized into the great pinwheel stellar system we call the Milky Way galaxy. As vast as our own galaxy is, there are billions of other galaxies hurtling through space at the very limits of the most powerful telescopes and beyond reach of the fastest spaceships. Even if humans could travel at the speed of light (186,000 miles per second), it would take four years to reach the nearest star, and 100,000 years to travel across our own galaxy.

In addition, some scientists believe that there are other inhabited worlds throughout the universe. Those of us who are members of the Church of Jesus Christ of Latter-day Saints have been told that such is the case. As God explained to Moses: "Worlds without number have I created" (Moses 1:33). For what purpose has God placed us in a universe of incomprehensible expanse and separated by unfathomable distance from other worlds such as our own? In this vastness of creation, how can one person's presence count for anything at all? No wonder that as we probe the depths and magnitude of space we are led to question how a god of such power and majesty can be concerned with each of us individually. Again we are led to ask, along with the psalmist, "What is man that thou art mindful of him?"

Can God, with such infinite power, have the attributes of parenthood—love, mercy, forgiveness, justice, etc.—and consider each of his children important? The Lord assured Joseph Smith, "Remember the worth of souls is great in the sight of God" (D&C 18:10). If we, as frail, finite mortals, are capable of developing computers that can process hundreds of billions of calculations per second, it is not difficult to believe that God, with infinite knowledge, can be aware of each of us and be interested in each of us individually. We believe that the Spirit of God quietly confirms that God loves us, and that he is concerned with our welfare. Each man, woman, and child is great and precious in the sight of the Lord. We are not merely accidents, but children of God, created in his image, not to be forgotten or lost in space. He, who notes even the sparrow's fall, must be especially mindful of his children. In his face-to-face conversation with Moses, he explained the grand purpose behind his magnificent creation when he said, "For behold, this is my work and my glory—to bring to pass the immortality and eternal life of man" (Moses 1:39). LDS apostle James E. Talmage added: "What is man in this boundless setting of sublime splendor? I answer you ... he is greater and grander, more precious in the arithmetic of God than all the planets and suns of space. For him they were created. They are the handiwork of God. Man is his son. In this world man is given dominion over a few things. It is his privilege to achieve supremacy over many things. ... Incomprehensibly grand as are the physical creations of the earth and space, they have been brought into existence as a means to an end" (qtd. in Brown, *LDS Conference Reports,* 50).

According to LDS teachings, this world was created for God's children to experience a mortal existence, one very different from and yet patterned after our pre- and post-mortal estates as intelligences, spirits, and resurrected beings, with each realm of existence operating within a different set of eternal laws. In the books of Genesis, Moses, and Abraham, the creation of this mortal realm is beautifully described. This magnificent creative process resulted in the proliferation of plants, animals, men, and women on earth. Life, abundant, oozed from every crack of the earth's crust to create, over billions of years, the more than 30 million living species, and over twenty times that many now-extinct species.

The poet Emmeline B. Wells penned the following words: "Where-e'er we pass, The hand of God we see, In leaf and bud and tree, Or bird or humming bee, Or blade of grass. The streamlet, flow'r, and sod Bespeak the works of God; And all combine ... With most transporting grace, His handiwork to trace, Thru nature's smiling face, In art divine" (*Hymns,* no. 33). Stuart K. Hine stated in his powerful song, "How Great Thou Art": "O Lord my God, when I in awesome wonder Consider all the works thy hands have made, ...

Then sings my soul, my Savior God, to thee, How great thou art! How great thou art!"

As we walk down the road of life, we are in awe of the beauties and complexities around us. We have a deep reverence and appreciation for the grandeur of the mountains, the nobility of the giant redwoods, the power of the great blue whale, and the gentle intricacies of a flower. We see a sunrise, we feel the wind and rain, we watch a squirrel scamper up a tree, we view in appreciation as a thoroughbred gallops across a blue-green pasture. We appreciate, but do we really comprehend the immensity and complexity of what we see? Do we see the individual blade of grass? Do we contemplate the soil, water, and photosynthesis that harmonize to produce that blade of grass? We don't often see the ant on the blade of grass, or think of the bacterium on the surface of the ant, or the virus attached to the bacterium. Do we think, for even a moment, about the DNA—the common thread of life that holds us all together, from viruses, through bacteria, ants, and grass, to humans? Do we pause to contemplate the creative process on this earth, and the laws and principles that produce the face of nature, which reflect the handiwork of God? Are we impressed and excited by the wonder of it all?

At the conclusion of each creative period, God said, "It is good." In reference to this statement, LDS president Gordon B. Hinckley commented, "The earth in its pristine beauty is an expression of the nature of its Creator ... the creation continued until 'God saw everything that he had made, and, behold, it was very good.' (Gen. 1:31) I interpret this to mean that it was beautiful, for 'out of the ground made the Lord to grow every tree that is pleasant to the sight.' (Gen. 2:9) I believe in the beauty of nature—the flowers, the fruit, the sky, the peaks, and the plains from which they rise. I see and believe in the beauty of animals" ("I Believe," 4). If God and his prophets consider the world, newly created as well as in its present state, to be good and beautiful, who are we to disagree?

This earth, like other realms of existence, is fulfilling its particular destiny by harmonizing matter and laws applicable to this mortal state. God is in control but may not sit upon his throne dictating the activities of every atom, molecule, and cell within the universe. The growth and development of a tree, a bee, a bear, a whale, or a human being may operate by godly mandate, the laws of the universe interacting with matter to fulfill God's purposes. It isn't difficult to imagine a god who allows natural processes to work within the parameters of a mortal, temporal condition.

Does the concept that our planet evolved over billions of years to reach its present degree of preparedness somehow compromise God's supremacy? God, with infinite power, can allow eternal law to work automatically, naturally in concert with matter so he can devote his attention to dealing with his children as a loving father, rather than watching over the functioning of each individual atom and cell.

LeConte expressed similar sentiments:

So long as we knew not how worlds were made, we ... concluded they must have been created, but as soon as science showed *how* it was probably done, immediately we say we were probably mistaken ... Is this so when the question is concerning a work of man? Yes, one kind—viz., the work of a magician. Here, indeed, we believe in him and are delighted with his work, until we know how it is done, and then all our faith and wonder cease. But in any honest work it is not so; but, on the contrary, when we understand how it is done, stupid wonder is changed to intellectual delight. ... [T]he mission of science is to show how things are done. ... [I]f God is an honest worker, according to reason—i.e., according to law—ought not science rather change gaping wonder into intellectual delight—superstition into rational worship? (*Evolution*, 354.)

We confess to being caught up in the "wonder of it all" and to worshipping a God who uses the processes of this world to fulfill the designs of a mortal existence, all the time respecting the functions of nature, the abundance of beauty, and the complexities of this earthly existence. The discovery of natural laws governing our mortal condition only deepens our profound appreciation for the beauties and wonders around us.

# 2.
# The Bottom Line

In preparing to write this book, we approached the question of the LDS church's current position on evolution through the appropriate channels. First, one of us conferred with his local ward bishop; then all of us met with our mutual stake president, outlining our objectives and desire to know the church's current position. The stake president in turn contacted his area president. We received approval for the bishop to ask for an "official declaration of doctrine" from the First Presidency. We sought this clarification so that it would not be necessary for readers to do so individually. In response, the bishop received a letter from the First Presidency and a copy of the complete text of the official statement issued in 1909 on "The Origin of Man" (qtd. in *Encyclopedia of Mormonism*, 4:1665-669, and in this book's appendix). The secretary to the First Presidency concluded his letter to the bishop by emphasizing that any attempt to interpret or elaborate upon the 1909 statement must be considered personal opinion and not the position of the church.

The First Presidency's 1909 statement, under President Joseph F. Smith (see Appendix), is excerpted below:

"The Origin of Man"

Inquiries arise from time to time respecting the attitude of the Church ...

We are not ... putting forth anything essentially new ... "God created man in his own image. ..." In these plain and pointed words the inspired author of the book of Genesis made known to the world the truth concerning the origin of the human family. ...

The creation was two-fold—firstly spiritual, secondly temporal. This truth, also, Moses plainly taught ... [They then quoted Moses 3:4-7]. ...

The Father of Jesus is our Father also. ... Jesus, however, is the first-born among all the sons of God—the first begotten in the spirit, and the only begotten in the flesh.

"God created man in His own image." This is just as true of the spirit as it is of the body, which is only the clothing of the spirit. ... The spirit of man is in the form of man, and the spirits of all creatures are in the likeness of their bodies.

Adam, our progenitor, "the first man," was, like Christ, a pre-existent spirit, and like Christ he took upon him an appropriate body, the body of a man. ... The doctrine of the pre-existence ... pours a wonderful light upon the otherwise mysterious problem of man's origin. It shows that man, as a spirit, was begotten and born of heavenly parents ... prior to coming upon the earth in a temporal body.

It is held by some that Adam was not the first man upon this earth, and that the original human being was a development from lower orders of the animal creation. These, however, are the theories of men. The word of the Lord declares that Adam was "the first man of all men" ... and we are therefore in duty bound to regard him as the primal parent of our race. It was shown to the brother of Jared that all men were created in the *beginning* after the image of God; and whether we take this to mean the spirit or the body, or both, it commits us to the same conclusion: Man began life as a human being, in the likeness of our Heavenly Father.

True it is that the body of man enters upon its career as a tiny germ embryo, which becomes an infant, quickened at a certain stage by the spirit whose tabernacle it is. ... There is nothing in this, however, to indicate that the original man, the first of our race, began life as anything less than a man, or less than the human germ or embryo that becomes a man.

The Church of Jesus Christ of Latter-day Saints, basing its belief on divine revelation ... proclaims man to be the direct and lineal offspring of Deity. ...

Man is the child of God, formed in the divine image and endowed with divine attributes, and even as the infant son of an earthly father and mother is capable in due time of becoming a man, so the undeveloped offspring of celestial parentage is capable, by experience through ages and aeons, of evolving into a God.

The *Encyclopedia of Mormonism* is not presented as "official" church doctrine (see the editor's preface). However, our inquiries to the First Presidency concerning evolution (and we assume the same would be true for inquiries from anyone else through the appropriate channels) were answered with a copy of the 1909 statement on "The Origin of Man" from the *Encyclopedia of Mormonism*. Thus this statement is as close to an "official" position as there is at present. Under the heading "Evolution" in that book, the following entry is found:

EVOLUTION

The position of the Church on the origin of man was published by the First Presidency in 1909 and stated again by a different First Presidency in 1925:

The Church of Jesus Christ of Latter-day Saints, basing its belief on divine revelation, ancient and modern, declares man to be the direct and literal offspring of Deity. ... Man is the child of God, formed in the divine image and endowed with divine attributes (*see* Appendix, "Doctrinal Expositions of the First Presidency").

The scriptures tell why man was created, but they do not tell how, though the Lord has promised that he will tell that when he comes again (D&C 101:32-33). In 1931, when there was intense discussion on the issue of organic evolution, the First Presidency of the Church, then consisting of Presidents Heber J. Grant, Anthony W. Ivins, and Charles W. Nibley, addressed all of the General Authorities of the Church on the matter, and concluded,

Upon the fundamental doctrines of the Church we are all agreed. Our mission is to bear the message of the restored gospel to the world. Leave geology, biology, archaeology, and anthropology, no one of which has to do with the salvation of the souls of mankind, to scientific research, while we magnify our calling in the realm of the Church. ...

Upon one thing we should all be able to agree, namely, that Presidents Joseph F. Smith, John R. Winder, and Anthon H. Lund were right when they said: "Adam is the primal parent of our race" [First Presidency Minutes, Apr. 7, 1931].

WILLIAM E. EVENSON

We accept the First Presidency's statements, as reiterated in the *Encyclopedia of Mormonism*, that human beings are the sons and daughters of our Heavenly Father. We agree that we were created in the image of God. We also agree with the 1931 First Presidency statement that geology, biology, archaeology, and anthropology are best left to scientists. Beyond these official statements, however, we find still unanswered questions and differing opinions among church members concerning organic evolution. For example, whereas we all agree that our spirits are the offspring of Deity, many believe that Jesus Christ was the only begotten Son of God in the flesh and that, for the remainder of God's children, our physical bodies are prepared by natural processes; however, others insist that the natural body is also the direct offspring or a "special creation" of Deity. Some Mormons propose that the natural body could have been prepared through the process of evolution. Others insist that the church opposes the theory of evolution, although there has never been an official statement to that effect.

Even with a modern, living prophet, and with continued revelation, there remain many questions that God has chosen not to resolve for us at the present time. One such question concerns the origin of our physical bodies. Throughout the history of the Church of Jesus Christ of Latter-day Saints, there has been a variety of opinions as to the origin of Adam and Eve (this history is briefly outlined in chap. 4). The bottom line is that most of the statements that have been made concerning human origins have been in the form of opinions and personal interpretation of scriptures. Only rarely have official statements been made by the First Presidency defining the position of the church. Many of the unofficial statements concerning evolution were products of their time. However, it is important to understand that scientific progress has been enormous in this area over the past thirty years. Even statements made as late as the 1960s and 1970s are dated in terms of the science they respond to in light of the recent explosion of new knowledge in biology and anthropology relative to the theory of evolution. The conclusions of scientists are now corroborated by vast amounts of molecular (DNA) data, which did not exist before 1970, and by a greatly expanded fossil record.

One of our principal objectives in this book is to present some of the newer data about modern evolutionary synthesis and to offer some solutions as to how the perceived gulf between the theory of evolution and Mormon doctrine may be bridged. However, it should always be borne in mind that these "solutions" are expressions of our own opinions. Only the prophet can interpret scripture and speak for the LDS church. The prophet commanded the church in 1931 to "leave geology, biology, archaeology, and anthropology ... to scientific research" (*Encyclopedia of Mormonism*, 1669-70). This statement suggests that science is capable, at least in part, of discovering the mechanisms employed by God to create our physical bodies.

We, the authors of this book, have a combined experience of forty years in the fields of biology and anthropology. We hope we are some of those scientists of whom the prophet spoke in 1931. We are also active members of the church and believe that God is the author of creation. However, as scientists, we also believe that we can discover how at least a portion of that creative process occurs. There are hundreds of faithful Latter-day Saint scientists who actively pursue research dealing with the nature and development of life. The vast majority of us sees no conflict between the scientific evidence for the process of evolution and the official teachings of the LDS church.

Richard T. Wootton spent much of his career as a social scientist dealing with issues of science and religion. As part of his research, he conducted two major surveys—one in 1955, the other in 1992—in which he solicited responses to a number of questions regarding science and religion from Utah-born or Utah-educated LDS scientists.

Dr. Wootton concluded his study by stating, "Mormonism was in a class by itself as a science supportive religion. ... The results of the 1992 study of scientist graduates of Utah universities confirmed every part of the 1955 study. ... The Utah Mormon culture is still the most highly productive of scientists, first place among the states, leading by 21 percent the second place." (The second place state was Idaho, which also had the second largest LDS population.)

The LDS scientists responding to Dr. Wootton's survey "cited many distinctive religious doctrines which encourage mental development. They showed that it produced the kind of value system, family solidity, and healthy living style that are known to facilitate achievement." Of the 65 percent responding to the survey (approximately 1,400 scientists, 282 of whom were biologists), 83 percent had no difficulty harmonizing science and religion, and an additional 15 percent believed the two could be at least partially harmonized. In responding to the survey statement that "man's body did not evolve in any fashion from simpler species and is not biologically related to them," only one biologist out of 282 agreed. Dr. Wootton continued, "While most Utah biologists are Strong Mormons, we found [almost] none who believe in Special Creation as against evolution." The LDS scientists who supported the notion of a special creation (12 percent of the total surveyed) were "engineers and others whose fields have almost nothing to do with knowledge of the facts supporting evolution." He stated, "We suppose that almost everyone learns to reason well in his or her own field. But some seem to slight the rules of reason when forming opinions about conclusions in someone else's field." The belief among active LDS scientists that evolution was "apparently God's method of creating species ... was close to 100 percent true of those in the fields that study the earth and its creatures, it was also true of many Mormon scientists, no matter what their fields."

Dr. Wootton also surveyed a number of LDS seminary teachers with the same questions. Of the members of that group responding to the survey, 67 percent believed in a special creation of humans, and 62 percent believed in a special creation of other animals. However, it should be noted that 21 percent of seminary teachers surveyed disagreed with the statement, "Man's body did not evolve in any fashion from simpler species and is not biologically related to them." According to this survey, a number of seminary teachers apparently did not have a problem with God having employed evolution in the creation process. (Wootton's study is in *Saints and Scientists*.)

If the vast majority of active LDS biologists (about 400 of us, according to Wootton's study), not to mention a number of seminary teachers, are able to reconcile the theory of evolution with official church doctrine, then what is the basis of this reconciliation? Why are some church members, whose expertise is not in the biological or geological sciences, opposed to such a reconciliation? Some church members have gone so far as to say that the theory of evolution is evil and that those who teach it have been tricked by Satan. Are LDS evolutionary scientists (geologists, biologists, anthropologists), many of whom are or have been bishops, stake presidents, mission presidents, etc., dupes of Satan? We believe that there has been a great misunderstanding on the part of some members of the church concerning this theory, which is so central to modern biology, anthropology, and geology.

We have heard asserted many times that these issues are not critical to our salvation. This is correct. What is critical to our salvation is adhering to the first principles and ordinances of the gospel, obeying God, and enduring to the end. To a member of the church who is a banker, a lawyer, a carpenter, a farmer, or even a physician, these issues do not arise often during their professional experience, and, when they do, they are usually of only academic interest. However, for those of us who work in the fields of geology, biology, or anthropology, and for students in these fields, whether long-term or short-, these issues are a vital part of our daily lives. Each day we have either to reconcile our beliefs in science and religion, and ignore the apparent discrepancies, or reject either science or our religion. God has told us to seek learning by study and by faith (see D&C 88:118). We believe that all truth is part of the gospel and that the laws of Nature that are discovered through scientific research are part of God's universe (see D&C 88:42). We believe that as we gain a greater understanding of these laws we come closer to understanding God, his works, and our place in the eternities. We believe that part of God's eternal plan is to allow his children to gain a greater understanding of his glorious works by faithful study (see D&C 88:118). We also believe that in the latter days the light of knowledge will be poured out upon the Earth to benefit and bless all humankind (see D&C 121:26-33), and that scientific and technological advances are part of the fulfillment of that divine promise. We believe that the knowledge we gain by scientific research harmonizes with the knowledge that we gain through divine revelation through God's prophets.

# 3.
# The Truth
# Shall Make You Free

J esus said to his disciples, "Ye shall know the truth, and the truth shall make you free" (John 8:32). We are taught that the gospel of Jesus Christ embraces all truth and that all truth can be organized into one great whole. Conflicts only exist when all truth is not known or when we misunderstand what is true. In relation to this concept, Henry Eyring, a prominent Mormon scientist, stated, "Since the Gospel embraces all truth, there can never be any genuine contradictions between true science and true religion. ... I am obliged, as a Latter-day Saint, to believe whatever is true, regardless of the source" (*Faith of a Scientist*, 12, 31). Brigham Young added that "religious teachers ... advance many ideas and notions for the truth which are in opposition to and contradict facts demonstrated by science, and which are generally understood. ... In these respects we differ from the Christian world, for our religion will not clash with or contradict the facts of science in any particular" (in *Discourses of Brigham Young*, 397-98).

### Science as a Way of Knowing

The enormous advancements that have occurred in our civilization over the past 100 years or so attest to the power of science and technology. Whether you are a scientist or not, you benefit every day from these advancements. Our homes are lit and made comfortable by electricity and/or natural gas. We are entertained in our own living rooms with just the flip of a switch by the best musicians and actors who have ever lived. Through our computers and the Internet, the knowledge and wisdom of the ages is at our fingertips. Because of automobiles and airplanes, travel is virtually unlimited and distance on the earth is increasingly meaningless. The wonders of medical science have made our lives longer and more comfortable than ever before. Because of the discoveries of science, our knowledge of the world around us is expanding at an ever-increasing rate.

Nearly all of the modern conveniences we take for granted did not exist a hundred years ago. Before that, life had changed very little for centuries. From the time when the wheel and fire were discovered in antiquity until the modern era, transportation, heating, and lighting techniques changed very little. Travel was limited by the speed that an animal or person could walk or run. The dissemination of knowledge was limited by the speed at which a book could be printed and read. No king who has ever lived, no matter his wealth, could break through those technological barriers. No amount of money could transport him any faster than the fastest horse or fastest ship. No amount of money could buy an incandescent light, a television, or a computer before they were invented.

Today more new scientific knowledge is being accumulated daily than was gathered during the entire eighteenth century. It takes us only two weeks to publish as much new scientific data as were published during the entire nineteenth century. Scientific information is accumulating five times more rapidly than it was in 1950. The information explosion is a reality. It was possible in the seventeenth century to read every scientific journal published, to keep up with every scientific advancement. It was possible in the sixteenth century to have read everything that had ever been written in the sciences. It has been estimated that in the United States alone there are over 12,000 scientific and technical journals. If each journal is published on the average of once per month, nearly 150,000 separate issues appear annually. That number equals nearly 400 issues of scientific journals published every day. (These estimates are from Taylor, *Managing the Serials Explosion,* 3.) If each journal were 100 pages long (and most are longer than that), you would need to read three pages a minute, twenty-four hours a day, seven days a week, just to keep up. That number counts only U.S. journals; most scientists keep track of several foreign journals on a regular basis. Today scientists have to become highly specialized in a small part of one field of science to keep abreast of and contribute to those advancements.

The amount of new information that is accumulating is staggering. Furthermore, most of this new information does not replace the old—it merely augments it. Most of the past literature still exists and scientists still refer to it. Therefore, modern scientists not only have to keep abreast of new developments, we have to be familiar with what has gone before. For a new science student, the task seems almost overwhelming: to keep up with the over 400 journals published daily plus grasp the millions of volumes that already exist.

Therefore, when someone says, "There's not enough data to fully test the theory of evolution," and you see that the publication date for that statement is, say 1960, perhaps the statement was true then. However, this is not the case today. Over 90 percent of the evidence that we have available to test the theory of evolution today did not exist in 1960. The hominid fossil record barely existed forty years ago; today it is enormous. In 1960 the molecular era had not yet dawned; none of that evidence existed. Today the molecular evidence, which is probably the strongest and most voluminous support for evolution, is immense. In fact, on 22 October 1996, Pope John Paul II declared to the Pontifical Academy of Sciences in Rome: "Today ... new knowledge has led to the recognition of more than one hypothesis in the theory of evolution. It is indeed remarkable that this theory has been progressively accepted by researchers, following a series of discoveries in various fields of knowledge. The convergence, neither sought nor fabricated, of the results of work that was conducted independently is in itself argument in favor of the theory" (see origins.org/mc/resources/pope).

Science is a powerful way of knowing about the world around us. It is based on observation and experimentation. There are millions of questions that can be answered by observation. How high is the tallest mountain? How deep is the deepest ocean? We need simply to measure them. If you cannot measure them directly with a tape measure, then you can devise some means to measure them indirectly. You can then report your measurement. If someone doubts you, that person can make independent measurements. Some other measuring technique can be employed and the two techniques can be compared. The power of science stems from the fact that observations are repeatable, verifiable, and self-correcting.

Science is methodical. As many people as desire can measure the highest mountain as often as they wish for as long as they want. All the measurements can be reported and compared. The measuring techniques can be analyzed and tested. By experimentation, some measuring techniques may be found to be inaccurate and are abandoned. As a result new techniques can be devised to give increasingly accurate measurements. By making hundreds or thousands of measurements, comparing them, and continually modifying the measuring devices, we can eventually arrive at the most accurate data possible, given the current technology.

Concerning research into evolutionary biology, British scientist Richard Dawkins states, "It is like a detective coming onto the scene of a crime after it has happened and piecing it together, and saying that all the clues point to a certain conclusion. Well, millions and millions of clues point to the truth of evolution" (qtd. in Ridley, *Evolution*).

However, science has limitations. No matter how accurately we measure the highest mountain, we can never find its "true" height. First of all, our measurement can never be absolutely accurate. If we stand atop the highest mountain, where exactly do we take the measurement? If you are standing at the highest point on the mountain, you have already trampled down the snow there so that the mountain is no longer as high as it was before you came to measure it.

Furthermore, if you measure the height of the mountain today, it will not be exactly the same tomorrow. All mountains are either growing or shrinking; no mountain is static. The highest, Mt. Everest, is still growing.

In addition, when you use a device to measure something—say a measuring tape to determine the length of a table—exactly what part of the tape marks do you use? If the lines on the tape measure are 0.1 mm thick, then you can never measure the length of the table more accurately than within 0.1 mm. Therefore, the "true" length of the table can never be known. As a result of the limitations of measurement, we say that science can never discover absolute truth. We can never state the absolute height of the highest mountain. We cannot even give the exact length of a table sitting in front of us. This lack of precision in scientific measurement has been distressing for many people, especially non-scientists, who do not understand the nature of these limitations. To say that we cannot measure a 2 meter-long table more accurately than within 0.1 mm is to say that we *can* measure the table to within 99.9999 percent of its "actual" length.

This "uncertainty" has lead many non-scientists to question or attack science on the basis that it is always changing and never certain. Both of those criticisms are correct, but it is important to recognize the degree of uncertainty involved. An error of 0.0001 percent is well within the tolerance of most human functions, even if we want to build another table "exactly like" the table we measured. Many people are aware of the concept that the law of gravity has been in some ways superseded by the theory of relativity because the latter is more accurate. The differences in accuracy are of the order that we have been discussing in the measurement of the table. For most purposes, referring to the effects of gravity is plenty accurate, even though we know that there are more accurate measurements. The more precise measurements take too long and are too complicated for most purposes. This is like saying that I will no longer use a tape measure for building tables because I know that it is accurate to only 0.1 mm. I can use a laser measuring devise that can measure the table accurately to within 0.001 mm. However, because I cannot cut a table that accurately, there is no practical advantage to measuring it more accurately. Even if I could cut a table more accurately, such a cut would not make it more functional.

Another limitation of science is that it deals only with something that can be either directly or indirectly observed. Science cannot deal well with issues such as faith, love, morals, etc. We can evaluate the consequences of apparent faith, love, morals, etc. We can analyze, for example, the health and longevity of people who claim to have faith in something or someone. We can determine from the results of such analysis, within the limits of our measurement, if there is any significant difference between those people and others who claim not to have such faith. However, science cannot analyze faith itself.

We cannot analyze the motives of God. We cannot answer questions concerning his purposes in or for the universe. Therefore, we cannot analyze, through science, the purpose of our being here. Why are we here? Where are we going after this life is ended? How can we find peace? These and similar questions are outside the realm of science and require other methods of knowing.

### Faith as a Way of Knowing

For many people, faith is also a way of knowing. Throughout history, there have been people of faith who have found personal peace and reassurance that they have a purpose in life and that some part of themselves will continue after their body no longer functions. This reassurance can be a source of great satisfaction and serenity. In the midst of the greatest personal or global conflicts, people of faith can be at peace with themselves and all of humanity. Even when forced to participate in war, people can have personal inner peace and can love their enemy. Even if victims of great atrocity, people of faith can forgive those who abuse them. This personal strength and moral fortitude imparted through faith can be tremendous. (We should add that people having no religious faith can also find immense peace, happiness, and joy, and that religious faith alone does not guarantee a life without problems, challenges, or sadness.)

Through faith and revelation, we can know of things to come, which are outside the capability of science to determine. Joseph Smith learned of certain health benefits that were not yet fully known to science (D&C 89). In addition, God's spirit leads us to do good (D&C 11:12) and to love our neighbor; while the scriptures also teach us how to live in peace and harmony with our fellow humans and with all of nature. By the Spirit, we can know the truth of all things (Moro. 10:4).

However, knowledge through faith has limitations. Faith can only be understood by faith. "The things of God knoweth no man, but the Spirit of God" (1 Cor. 2:11). The scriptures say that we can be misled by false spirits (D&C 50:2). Personal revelation may be subjective, and virtually all substantive faith requires prior discipline and study (D&C 8, 9). Only the prophet can receive revelation for the entire church. According to D&C 9:7-8, the prophet should first examine the "data," come to his own thoughtful conclusion, and then go to the Lord for confirmation or refutation.

Furthermore, there are apparently many bits of information that God has not yet revealed to us and we are left to discover them on our own by conventional, scientific means. Take, for example, the measurement of the highest mountain. If we want to know its height, is it legitimate to ask God to reveal to us the exact height? Should we expect an answer if we asked? Did God directly reveal to humankind how to build a steam engine or a television or a computer? Apparently we should not expect revelation to cover information of this type, which we can obtain through other means.

## The Roles of Science and Religion

The roles of science and religion are distinct but complementary in providing us with a complete picture of the universe. If we examine any object in the universe, from a galaxy to a planet, a person, or a pebble, we may ask *how* and *why* that object came into existence. The how's and why's of a thing's existence have been defined in terms of "causes."

Aristotle (384-322 B.C.E.) was, without doubt, one of the most important and influential philosopher-scientists who ever lived. One of his greatest contributions to Western thought, among his some 170 separate works, was his categorization of human thought and reason. He laid the foundation for empirical science and speculative thought. In his book *The Generation of Animals*, he reasoned that there are four causes which describe the existence of any object in the universe. For example: How can we explain the existence of a rock? What causes a rock to exist? What causes a building to exist? What causes a plant or animal to exist? What causes us to exist? This important concept allows us to put the relationship between science and religion into perspective.

Aristotle stated:

> To know, is to know by means of Causes. A thing is explained when you know the Causes. And a Cause is that which is responsible, in any of four modes, for a thing's existence. The four Causes are:
>
>> 1) The Material Cause, or Matter, out of which the thing is made. What is the thing made of?
>> 2) The Motive (or Efficient) Cause, the agent which is responsible for having set the process going; it is that by which the thing is made. How was the thing made?
>> 3) The Formal Cause, or Form, which is responsible for the character of the course which the process follows (this is, what the thing is, or is to be). The plan by which the thing is made.
>> 4) The Final Cause, the End or Object towards which a formative process advances, and for the sake of which it advances, the rational purpose. The purpose for which the thing is made.

An illustration may be helpful to explain what Aristotle means. Consider, for example, a building. The *material cause* of the building is the stone, cement, steel, fabric, wood, plastic, all the things that the building is made of. When a construction crew comes to a building site, they bring in a whole pile of building material. That pile looks quite similar, no matter what the building is to be made of. You would see a pile of bricks and a pile of lumber for a residential home or for a university building or for a church. The major differences in building material are determined by the size of the building to be constructed. Wooden rafters and joists are adequate for small buildings, but steel beams and girders are required for larger buildings.

The *motive cause,* in the case of the building, is the construction crew itself, those people who put the building materials together to form the building. The construction crew provides the force necessary to construct the building from the raw materials.

The third cause is the *formal cause*. This "cause" is the set of blueprints that the crew uses to construct the building. It is easy for a person who knows a little bit about blueprints and construction to look at those blueprints and have a good idea what the building is going to look like.

The fourth or *final cause*—the ultimate cause, the reason for the building's existence—is the functional purpose of the building. Why was the building built? Is it to be a classroom building, or a house, or a factory, or a church? Actually, when an architect draws a set of blueprints, the reason for the building, its function, its purpose, the final cause of the building, is already in mind. Because of this relationship, the last two causes, the formal and final, often merge into each other. As a result, they are characteristically very difficult to separate completely.

There are numerous other examples of the four causes. In fact, one can list the causes for every object in the universe. One of the best known and most commonly used examples is that of a chicken. The material that makes up the chicken egg is the first, or material, cause of the chicken. However, a fertilized chicken egg, left to itself, will not develop into a chicken. It will not begin to develop until it is placed under a hen or in an incubator. The heat, then, is the second, or motive, cause necessary to produce the chicken. The third cause, the formal cause, determines that the egg will hatch out a chicken as opposed to a dog or a frog or another type of bird. The third cause, then, could be thought of as the determination of "kind." To the Greeks and most other people since them, this determination of "kind" has been a great mystery. Although we as yet do not know all the details, it appears that the determination of kind comes from the genetics of the egg, the DNA (deoxyribonucleic acid) inside the egg. DNA is the information inside each cell, which, interacting with cellular and extracellular factors, ultimately directs cell structure and function. It also appears that much, although not all (see chap. 12), of the motive force that causes a plant or animal to develop is also encoded in the DNA, and is not just a simple matter of adding heat as once thought. Therefore, for modern scientists, there is a close relation between the motive and formal causes. In the case of the chicken, the fourth, or final, cause is the purpose for which the chicken is created. Why is it here? For what purpose did God create chickens?

Likewise, we can go through the same exercise for ourselves. What we are made of—the chemicals that form us—constitutes the material cause. The motive and formal causes are determined by the DNA in our cells. That DNA, along with the nurturing environment of a mother's womb, provides the motive force that allows us to develop as an embryo and fetus. The DNA also determines that we will become a human rather than a chicken or frog. This is the formal cause. The final cause, then, is the reason for our being. Why are we here?

It is very interesting to examine what happened to the thought processes of humanity after Aristotle. Aristotelianism was transported, translated, interpreted, and misinterpreted from Greek to Latin, Syriac, Arabic, and Hebrew, and then into Italian, French, German, and English. Aristotle and other Greek philosophers had an enormous influence on the thinking of people in the late Middle Ages and early Renaissance. They adapted Aristotelian thought hook, line, and sinker. Almost anything that Aristotle said was taken as gospel. Early Renaissance Europeans considered themselves to be mental dwarfs compared to the giants of Greek and Roman history. They did not believe that they could contribute anything intellectually new to what had already been said.

During this time there was an inordinate focus of "Christian scientific thought" in Europe on the final cause. This was considered to be the most important of the causes and, therefore, should be the ultimate focus of research. Because most Christian scientists of this era were also monks, the answers to the ultimate cause often came from the Bible. What is the purpose of an ant? To teach man industry: "Go to the ant, thou sluggard; and consider her ways, and be wise: which having no guide, overseer, or ruler, provideth her meat in the summer, and gathereth her food in the harvest" (Pro. 6:6-8). Because the final cause was considered to be supreme, little attention was paid to the material and motive causes, and little progress was made in these fields of discovery. It was not considered to be important to know how the ant came into existence as long as it was known why the ant was here.

### Dividing the Causes

Francis Bacon (1561-1626) changed that concept. He directly addressed the issue of the philosophy of science and what needed to be done to get people out of the intellectual rut they had been in during the Middle Ages. He directly addressed the issue of the Four Causes. What Bacon proposed is critical to our current thinking about the interaction between science and religion. Here are some selected quotes to try to give you a feeling for what Bacon was proposing. He said: "We divided Natural Philosophy in general into the Inquiry of Causes. ... The one part, which is Physic, enquireth and handleth the Material and Efficient [or Motive] Causes; and the other, which is Metaphysic, handleth the Formal and Final causes. ... Natural History describeth the *variety of things*; Physic the causes, but *variable or respective causes*; and Metaphysic, the *fixed and constant causes*. Metaphysic is the inquiry of *final* causes, which I am moved to report not as omitted, but as misplaced. ... This misplacing hath caused a ... great inproficience in the sciences themselves. For the handling of final causes mixed with the rest in physical inquiries, hath ... given men the occasion to stay upon these satisfactory and specious causes, to the great arrest and prejudice of further discovery. [The final causes are] well enquired and collected in Metaphysic; but in Physic they are impertinent" (*Philosophical Works*, 94-96).

Bacon says that the function of "Physic," which corresponds to what we now think of as modern science, is to deal with the first two causes: what something is made of, how it functions, how it comes into being. The last two causes, Bacon says, are relegated to the area of Metaphysics, what we think of today as philosophy and religion. If we invoke the final cause when trying to discover scientific principles, our research becomes blocked. By jumping to the final cause, we propose an answer, and we no longer sense a reason to do research. This, Bacon argued, was the problem in the Middle Ages. People had an answer, therefore they stopped asking questions. For example, if we look only for final causes, and we know that ants were placed here on Earth to teach us industry, according to Bacon, we tend to not think about ants at any other level. We tend not to ask what they are made of and how they function. It is important to understand what Bacon says next: "I say this, not because those final causes are not true and worthy to be inquired in metaphysical speculations; but because their excursions ... into the limits of physical causes has bred a waste and solitude in that track" (*Philosophical Works*, 472).

Bacon is not suggesting, then, that the final causes are not true or unimportant. He is stating that because of the limitations of science, these final causes are outside its realm of investigation; they cannot be seen or measured. Furthermore, because science cannot deal with the final cause, invoking the final cause in scientific matters hinders scientific progress. This concentration on final causes is actually injurious to the progress of science, because science is incapable of addressing them. Science is capable of addressing the question of what something is made of, the material cause. We can also, hopefully, understand the action which brought the thing into being, the efficient or motive cause. Thus science can address the "how" but must leave to religion the "why." Science and religion both have their places in the search for truth. Only when someone asserts there is no God because we can discover the secrets of Nature ourselves and realize that they are controlled by natural laws, or when someone tells us that in spite of what we discover those natural laws are incorrect, do the two come into conflict.

## The Modern Reconciliation

There is evidence that a reconciliation between science and religion is occurring in some quarters, and that the classic animosity between the two concerning the theory of organic evolution is beginning to fade. More and more scientists are openly acknowledging the limitations of science as a way of knowing and recognizing the potential of the spiritual dimension. At the same time, religious leaders are acknowledging the power of scientific inquiry in helping to establish truth.

In an insightful and timely commentary, Matt Cartmill, past president of the American Association of Physical Anthropologists, observed: "Science has nothing to tell us about moral values or the purpose of existence or the realm of the supernatural. That doesn't mean that there is nothing to be said about these things. It just means that scientists don't have any expert opinions. Science looks exclusively at the finite facts of nature, and unfortunately, logical reason can't carry you from facts to values or from the finite to the infinite. ... But science's necessary silence on these questions doesn't prove that there is no infinite cause—or that right and wrong are arbitrary conventions, or that there is no plan or purpose behind the world. And I'm afraid that a lot of scientists go around saying that science proves these things" ("Oppressed by Evolution," 78-83).

Cartmill continued by acknowledging a tendency of many scientists, and especially evolutionists, to claim that evolution is purposeless and undirected. He pointed out that until recently, the "Statement on Teaching Evolution" from the National Association of Biology Teachers described evolution as "an unsupervised, impersonal, unpredictable, and natural process." Cartmill noted: "The broad outlines of the story of human evolution are known beyond a reasonable doubt. However, science hasn't yet found satisfying law-based natural explanations for most of the details of the story. All that we scientists can do is admit to our ignorance and keep looking. Our ignorance doesn't prove anything one way or the other about divine plans or purposes behind the flow of history. Anybody who says it does is pushing a religious doctrine. ... Fortunately evolutionary biologists are starting to realize this." In October 1997, the National Association of Biology Teachers deleted the words *unsupervised* and *impersonal* from its description of the evolutionary process ("Oppressed," 78-83).

It appears that increased recognition is being afforded scientists who fully acknowledge the complementary, yet distinct, roles of science and religion and embrace a world view that may include a spiritual dimension. One of the leading scientific journals, *Nature*, published in 1997 a poll conducted by Edward Larson and Larry Witham which found that 40 percent of physicists and biologists hold strong spiritual beliefs. In August 1997, another leading journal, *Science*, published an article by Greg Esterbrook, entitled "Science and God: A Warming Trend?" with the subtitle "Can rational inquiry and spiritual conviction be reconciled? Although some scientists contend that the two cannot coexist, others believe they have linked destinies." In that article Francis Collins, director of the Human Genome Research Institute (NIH), is quoted as saying, "I am unaware of any irreconcilable conflict between scientific knowledge about evolution and the idea of a creator God. ... Why couldn't God have used the mechanism of evolution to create?" (890-93).

On 22 October 1996, Pope John Paul II addressed the Pontifical Academy of Sciences in Vatican City. He stated that the group had been assembled sixty years earlier to

> inform the Holy See in complete freedom about developments in scientific research ... to serve the truth. I again extend this same invitation to you today, certain that we will be able to profit from the fruitfulness of a trustful dialogue between the church and science. ... We know, in fact, that truth cannot contradict truth. ... During this plenary session, you are undertaking a "reflection on science at the dawn of the third millennium," starting with the identification of the principal problems created by the sciences and which affect humanity's future. ... It is necessary to determine the proper sense of Scripture, while avoiding any unwarranted interpretations that make it say what it does not intend to say. ... A theory's validity depends on whether or not it can be verified; it is constantly tested against the facts; wherever it can no longer explain the latter, it shows its limitations and unsuitability. ... Consideration of the method used in the various branches of knowledge makes it possible to reconcile two points of view which would seem irreconcilable. The sciences of observation describe and measure the multiple manifestations of life with increasing precision and correlate them with the time line. The moment of transition to the spiritual cannot be the object of this kind of observation. ... But the experience of metaphysical knowledge, of self-awareness and self-reflection, of moral conscience, freedom, or again of aesthetic and religious experience, falls within the competence of philosophical analysis and reflection, while theology brings out its

ultimate meaning according to the Creator's plan. ... Theories of evolution which, in accordance with the philosophies inspiring them, consider the spirit as emerging from the forces of living matter or as a mere epiphenomenon of this matter, are incompatible with the truth about man. Nor are they able to ground the divinity of the person. (See www.origins.org/mc/resources/pope.)

While Mormons revere their prophet as God's spokesman on Earth, we recognize and accept every person's words of wisdom when we find them. The pope's statements are certainly appropriate to the issue of the interaction between science and religion. Furthermore, those of us who are scientists and embrace the Christian gospel may benefit from the example of the Pontifical Academy of Sciences, and reflect on the value of science in the third millennium.

Henry Eyring, one of Mormonism's best known scientists, said: "It is just as important to keep fact and fancy separated in religion as in science. ... One of the problems of the Church is the unsound arguments sometimes used in its defense. People examine such arguments, find they won't hold water, and say, 'My, the gospel must be unsound.' The conception that the gospel should only be defended on the right ground is of utmost importance, since otherwise one may choose a position to defend which is indefensible; and in [its] defeat it may be mistakenly supposed that the gospel is at fault" (*Faith of a Scientist*, 10, 22).

This sound advice pertains directly to issues of human origins. If we take, for example, the notion proposed by some LDS church members that humans were placed upon the earth by special creation or that they were transplanted from another planet and are not, as a result, related to the animals of this planet, we should be able to find ample scientific evidence for this human uniqueness. On the other hand, if, as proposed by the theory of evolution, humans are closely related to all life on this planet, there ought to be scientific evidence for this similarity. These two ideas pose simple, testable, alternative scientific hypotheses: either humans are unique or they are similar to the rest of creation. These hypotheses have been tested thousands of times at the levels of anatomy, physiology, developmental biology, biochemistry, genetics, paleontology, and molecular biology. The data overwhelmingly indicate that humans are not unique but are related to other animals. In fact, this similarity is so close that, at the cellular level and below, humans are largely indistinguishable from other mammals. There is no scientific evidence supporting the notion that humans are physically unique. In spite of these data, many people continue to claim, in the name of religion, that humans are physically unique. As Brother Eyring pointed out, some members' determination to employ indefensible and unsound arguments to defend what they incorrectly believe to be church positions is not helpful to the church, because "in defeat it may be mistakenly supposed that the gospel is at fault."

We see this tendency among students of science. Often, young Mormons enter colleges and universities having been told that evolution is false and, perhaps, evil, and that if they "believe" in it, they jeopardize their eternal salvation. Then those students take a college biology course where even a small portion of the overwhelming volume of evidence that supports evolution is presented. The student is faced with a difficult dilemma—to believe parents or teachers in spite of such evidence or to accept the evidence and disbelieve parents and former teachers. If the student disbelieves what parents and teachers have said about evolution, other teachings might come into question. Must our students be forced to choose between science and God? We think not.

# 4.
# When the
# Prophet Speaks

I n this chapter we present a brief but representative selection of declarations, statements, and commentaries by LDS prophets, general authorities, and other members of the church on the subject of organic evolution. The only *official* statements made by the church concerning human origins were quoted in chapter 2 of this book. The church has never taken an official stand on the broader question of evolution, although a number of individuals, including some church leaders, have formulated and, on occasion, voiced their interpretations of the scriptures and of the official statements concerning the Creation. The opinions and interpretations opposing evolution expressed by these individuals have sometimes been treated as official doctrine. In contrast, the First Presidency's temperate statements do not imply such a position.

These statements are presented chronologically and in historical context to illustrate their relationship to the social issues of the times. We emphasize that much of what was said in the past was reasonable considering the context, reflected the best scientific and theological understanding of the time, and was often motivated by a sincere conviction. Some, however, simply reflect personal opinion or unofficial interpretation of scriptural passages. It is not our intention to discuss the soundness or the implications of individual points or opinions, nor should this selection be taken as a poll or tally that would tip the scale of opinion in one direction or another. These quotations are a matter of record and we have attempted to present them accurately. We hope that this presentation will demonstrate the diversity of individual viewpoints on this matter among church members as well as among the general authorities themselves.

Prophets are by definition those who speak for God, but this does not exclude their right to also express personal opinions. Joseph Smith rejected the notion of prophetic infallibility, saying, "A prophet is a prophet only when he is acting as such" (qtd. in *History of the Church*, 5:265). Henry Eyring remarked, "A prophet is wonderful because he sometimes speaks for the Lord. This occurs on certain occasions when the Lord wills it. On other occasions, he speaks for himself, and one of the wonderful doctrines of the Church is that we don't believe in the infallibility of any mortal" (*Faith of a Scientist*, 23). Individual expression of opinion should be distinguished from official declarations of church doctrine. Brigham Young stated, "No member of the Church has the right to publish any doctrines of the Church of Jesus Christ of Latter-day Saints, without first submitting them for examination and approval to the First Presidency and the Twelve. There is but one man upon the earth, at one time, who holds the keys to receive revelations for the Church, and who has the authority to write doctrines by way of commandment unto the Church" (*Messages of the First Presidency*, 2:239).

The revelations associated with the restoration of the gospel provided members of the church with new information concerning the nature of God and the process of creation. Even before the commencement of the Darwinian debate during the mid-nineteenth century, the ultimate, or final, cause of the creation and human origins had received particular emphasis and innovation in Mormon theology. Modern revelations shed new light on Old Testament scriptural passages. The unfolding of doctrines concerning the nature of the members of the Godhead and their relationship to humankind had a significant impact on the interpretation of the Genesis account of Adam, and eventually on members' attitudes toward scientific hypotheses of human origins.

In June 1830, the prophet Joseph Smith received a revelation entitled "The Vision of Moses" which eventually became the first chapter of the Book of Moses in the Pearl of Great Price and may have been the catalyst for the Joseph Smith Translation of the Bible (see "The Remarkable Book of Moses," 15-21). The portions comprising the creation account (corresponding to Gen. 1 and 2) were recorded in Sidney Rigdon's hand, dated 10 December 1830 ("Remarkable," 21). The traditional imagery, as presented in Genesis, of Deity forming Adam from the dust of the ground was retained: "And I the Lord God formed man from the dust of the ground and breathed into his nostrils the breath of life; and man became a living soul, the first flesh upon the earth, the first man also" (Moses 3:7). The genealogy of Adam, however, as recounted in the King James New Testament, was modified in Joseph Smith's revision from "Adam, who was the son of God," to "Adam, who was *formed* of God, and the first man upon the earth" (JST, Luke 3:45, emphasis added).

In spite of the fact that the Joseph Smith Translation retained the imagery of man being formed from the dust of the ground, most of the early brethren did not take literally the image of Adam's body being molded from clay. Brigham Young said, "You believe Adam was made of the dust of the earth. This I do not believe ... I never believed that portion of the Bible as the Christian world does. I never did. I never want to" (*Journal of Discourses* 2:6). An understanding of this concept is suggested by a reading of Job, wherein Job says, "Thine hands have formed me and fashioned me as clay; and wilt thou bring me into dust again?" (10:9). Job's companion Elihu also remarks, "The breath of the Almighty hath given me life ... I also am formed out of clay" (33:4, 6). Commentator John D. Davis noted, "Each knew that he had been conceived in the womb and born. It may seem strange, but it is a fact, that the language which the writer of the second chapter of Genesis uses to describe man's creation is found in the mouth of these men when speaking of ordinary human conception and birth. And it may well be asked whether they did not believe that

God in forming the first man wrought in a manner essentially like that which he adopts in bringing every man into the world" (*Genesis and Semitic Traditions*, 45-46). From modern revelation, the passage "Ye were born into the world by water, and blood, and the spirit, which I have made, and so became of dust a living soul" (Moses 6:59) is further evidence of a process analogous to natural childbirth. Commenting in this vein, Elder B. H. Roberts said, "And though it is said that the 'Lord God formed man of the dust of the ground'—it by no means follows that he was 'formed' as one might form a brick, or form the dust of this earth. We are all 'formed' of the dust of the ground, though instead of being molded as a brick we are brought forth by the natural laws of procreation; so also was Adam and his wife in some older world. And as for the story of the rib, under it I believe the mystery of procreation is hidden" (*Gospel*, 280).

To the vision of Moses and the Joseph Smith Translation of Genesis was added a creation account recorded by Abraham and received by revelation to the prophet Joseph Smith. In the Abrahamic account, the days of creation are replaced by unspecified periods of "time." President Brigham Young, who apparently espoused a *literary*, rather than *literal,* interpretation of Genesis, stated: "As for the Bible account of the creation we may say that the Lord gave it to Moses, or that Moses obtained the history and traditions of the fathers, and from them picked out what he considered necessary, and that account has been handed down from age to age, and we have got it, no matter whether it is correct or not, and whether the Lord found the earth empty or void, or whether he made it out of nothing or out of the rude elements; or whether he made it in six years or in as many millions of years, it will remain a matter of speculation in the minds of men unless he give revelation on the subject" (*Journal of Discourses* 14:115-17). Discussing this issue in the *Ensign*, Brother Robert Woodward observed, "We therefore learn that periods of time may have lasted 24 hours each, 1,000 years each, or even millions of years. The periods of time are indeterminate in length; as one phase of the creation was finished, the next began. Therefore the age of the earth before Adam and Eve could have been very great indeed" ("In the Beginning: A Latter-day Perspective," 12-19).

According to the Abrahamic account, instead of the objects of creation being produced directly, the conditions were prepared which would bring about the end result: "And the Gods said: Let us prepare the waters to bring forth abundantly the moving creatures that have life. ... And the Gods saw that they would be obeyed and that their plan was good" (Abr. 4:20-21). Commenting on this, noted LDS scholar Hugh Nibley remarked, "What they ordered was not the complete product, but the process to bring it about, providing a scheme under which life might expand. ... Note the tense—it is future potential: the waters were treated that they will have the capacity to bring forth—'That they might bring forth'" ("Before Adam," 49-85).

The nature and character of the Godhead have significant implications for the interpretation of the pronouncement in Genesis that humans were created "in the image of God." It was revealed to Joseph Smith that "The Father has a body of flesh and bones as tangible as man's, the Son also" (D&C 130:22). In his famous King Follett discourse, delivered near the end of his life, Joseph Smith laid out the ultimate implications of the plan of exaltation and the celestial order of the Gods: "God himself was once as we are now, and sits enthroned in yonder heavens." He declared that Jesus did those things that he had seen the Father do, and that the Father of Jesus Christ also had a Father and on and on—"Where was there ever a father without being a son? Whenever did a tree or anything spring into existence without a progenitor? And *everything* comes in this way" (*History of the Church*, 6:476; emphasis added).

Brigham Young asserted that Adam descended from a physical father, and argued against the origin of Adam's body from the dust of the earth. He proposed a transplantation process, suggesting that Adam and Eve came from a distant celestial sphere, placed here to produce physical bodies for their offspring. He suggested that they would "eat and drink of the fruits of the corporeal world, until this grosser matter is diffused sufficiently through their celestial bodies to enable them, according to established laws, to produce mortal tabernacles for their spirit children" (*Journal of Discourses* 6:275). In 1926 B. H. Roberts commented further on the notion of transplantation, saying, "As vegetation was created or made to grow upon some older earth, and the seeds thereof or plants themselves were brought to our earth and made to grow, so likewise man and his help-meet were brought from some other world to our own, to people it with their children" (*Gospel*, 279-80).

The idea of Adam and Eve having been transplanted from another world eventually became entangled with the controversial so-called "Adam-God Doctrine" (see Buerger, "The Adam-God Doctrine," 14-58). This teaching was disavowed by later presidencies, first in 1912, when President Joseph F. Smith stated, "Speculations as to the career of Adam before he came to the earth are of no real value. We learn by revelation that he was Michael, the Archangel, and that he stands at the head of his posterity on earth (D&C 107:53-56). Dogmatic assertions do not take the place of revelation, and we should be satisfied with that which is accepted as doctrine, and not discuss matters that, after all disputes, are merely matters of theory" (*Improvement Era*, 417-18; see "Adam" in *Encyclopedia of Mormonism*, and references therein).

The year 1859 marked the publication of Charles Darwin's *On the Origin of Species by Means of Natural Selection*, in which he proposed the mechanism of natural selection to explain the unity and diversity of life on earth. In the second and all subsequent editions, he concluded, "There is grandeur in this view of life, with its several powers, having been originally breathed by the Creator into a few forms or into one; ... from so simple a beginning endless forms most beautiful and most wonderful have been and are being evolved" (1876 ed., 447). Anticipating the controversy that would ensue, Darwin stopped just short in this book of discussing human origins, stating simply that much light would be shed on the question. But the implications were unmistakable and resounded widely long before the publication of his later book, *The Descent of Man*, in 1871. The full impact of *Origin* was not felt in America for some decades, but initial reactions from Mormon members and leaders were immediate.

In 1861 George Q. Cannon said, "[Brigham Young] unmistakably declare[d] man's origin to be altogether of a celestial character—that not only is his spirit of heavenly descent, but his bodily

organization too,— that the latter is not taken from the lower animals, but from the originally celestial body of the great Father of Humanity. ... 'Look at this picture'—Man, the offspring of ape! 'And on
this'— Man, the image of God, his Father" (*Millennial Star*, Oct.
1861, 654). Elder Cannon himself taught: "Adam was no gorilla, no
squalid savage of doubtful humanity, but a perfect man in the image
of God. When placed on the earth, he was immortal. Eve was no de-
graded, loathsome creature, but a lovely admirable being—a suitable
partner for an immortal man. ... The most perfect men and women
on earth today are physically far beneath their great progenitors,
Adam and Eve. We are not the offspring of monkeys, but are the children of God, and Jesus is our brother" (*Juvenile Instructor*, qtd. in
Bankhead, *The Fall of Adam*, 30). Orson Pratt, one of the few early
brethren who maintained a literal interpretation of the creation of
Adam "from the dust of the earth," said in 1874, "We have the general characteristics of the human form, and we do not look like the
original of man according to Darwin's idea; we do not look like the
monkey or baboon from which Darwin said we originated" (*Journal
of Discourses* 17:32).

A further example from this period is provided by Elder Erastus
Snow who remarked in 1878: "The theory of evolution, that man in
our present state upon the earth is but a sequence and outgrowth of
steady advancement from the lowest order of creation till the present
type of man ... [is] in short that our great-grandfathers were apes and
monkeys. And how much satisfaction these philosophers have in the
contemplation of their grandfather monkeys, we are left to conjecture. ... But we find nothing on the earth, or in the earth, nor under
the earth, that indicates that any of these monkeys or apes ... ever accomplished any great exploits. So far as the history of the earth is
known, whether written or unwritten ... or whether found impressed
in the rocks, neither geologist nor any other scientists have ever been
able to show us any great exploits of any of these inferior grades of
being ... as to develop in their future progress the present order of beings we call man" (*Journal of Discourses* 19:270-71).

George Q. Cannon stated in 1896, "Doubt has been thrown upon
the Mosaic account of the creation, the whole religious world has

been agitated and in many instances faith in the scriptures has been destroyed by this theory of the eminent philosopher, Charles Darwin" (*Collected Discourses*, 5). It is interesting to note that in these last two quotations, Darwin is depicted not as a scientist who has collected data and drawn conclusions, but as a philosopher who has drawn conclusions *without* data.

The year 1909 was seminal in both scientific and LDS history. Not only did that year mark the centennial of Darwin's birth and the 50th anniversary of the publication of *On the Origin of Species*, it also yielded the first, and most important, official statement of the church on human origins. In the wake of public discussion associated with the celebration of *Origin* and the implications of organic evolution, numerous inquiries were directed to the First Presidency concerning the church's position. In response, the First Presidency, under Joseph F. Smith, appointed a committee consisting of Orson F. Whitney (chair), James E. Talmage, and others to prepare a statement which was issued in November of that year as the first official declaration on the topic, entitled "The Origin of Man" (rprtd. in *Encyclopedia of Mormonism*, 4:1665-69). This statement remains a benchmark of doctrinal exposition on this subject and, as stated, remains the "official" position of the church at the present time (see chap. 2).

The main points of that statement are:

1. "God created man in his own image. ... All men and women are in the similitude of the universal Father and Mother, and are literally the sons and daughters of Deity."
2. "The creation was two-fold—firstly spiritual, secondly temporal."
3. "The spirit of man is in the form of man."
4. "Adam was the first man of all men ... and the primal parent of our race."
5. "True it is that the body of man enters upon its career as a tiny germ or embryo, which becomes an infant, quickened at a certain stage by the spirit whose tabernacle it is, and the child, after being born develops into a man. There is nothing in this, however, to indicate that the original man, the first of our race,

began life as anything less than a man, or less than the human germ or embryo that becomes a man. ... The Church of Jesus Christ of Latter-day Saints, basing its belief on divine revelation, ancient and modern, proclaims man to be the direct and lineal offspring of Deity."

This statement implicitly distinguishes between the *spiritual* origin and distinctness of man (i.e., man as the literal spiritual offspring of Deity) and the framing of man's *physical* tabernacle. The statement does say, "It is held by some that Adam was not the first man upon this earth, and that the original human being was a development from lower orders of the animal creation. These, however, are the theories of men." But what appears unequivocal becomes more ambiguous within the same paragraph: "all men were created in the beginning after the image of God; and whether we take this to mean the spirit or the body, or both, it commits us to the same conclusion: Man began life as a human being, in the likeness of our heavenly Father."

The emphasis seems to be that the spirits of "Adam's race" are the "literal sons and daughters of Deity." This sentiment is evident in the remark by Elder Charles W. Penrose: "It is an eternal principle that every seed produces its own kind and not another kind. And as we are the children of God, we can follow out the idea and perceive what God our Father is, the being who is the progenitor of our spiritual existence, the being from whom we sprung" (*Journal of Discourses* 26:21-22).

The 1909 First Presidency statement that "The Church ... declares man to be the direct and lineal offspring of Deity. ... Man is the child of God, formed in the divine image and endowed with divine attributes" has been interpreted by some members of the church to mean that our physical bodies, as well as our spirit bodies, are the lineal offspring of Deity. The 1909 statement stimulated "several High Priests' quorums" to ask of church headquarters, "In just what manner did the mortal bodies of Adam and Eve come into existence on this earth?" In reply, an April 1910 *Improvement Era* editorial stated, "Whether the mortal bodies of man evolved in natural processes to present perfection, through the direction and power of God; whether the first parents of our generations, Adam and Eve, were transplanted from another sphere, with immortal tabernacles ...; whether they were born here in mortality, as other mortals have been, are questions not fully answered in the revealed word of God" (13:570). This clarification has seldom been mentioned in reference to the 1909 First Presidency statement (see Jeffery, "Seers, Savants and Evolution," 61).

In a 1911 editorial, President Joseph F. Smith said, in relation to the teaching of evolution in the church's schools: "There are speculations which touch the origin of life and the relationship of God to his children. In a very limited degree that relationship has been defined by revelation, and until we receive more light upon the subject we deem it best to refrain from the discussion of certain philosophical theories. ... Some of our teachers are anxious to explain how much of the theory of evolution ... is true, and what is false, but that only leaves their students in an unsettled frame of mind. They are not old enough and learned enough to discriminate, or put proper limitations upon a theory which we believe is more or less a fallacy. In reaching the conclusion that evolution would be best left out of discussions in our Church schools we are deciding a question of propriety and are not undertaking to say how much of evolution is true, or how much is false. ... The Church itself has no philosophy about the *modus operandi* employed by the Lord in His creation of the world, and much of the talk therefore about the philosophy of Mormonism is altogether misleading" (*Juvenile Instructor* 46:208-09).

Earlier in the same editorial, President Smith stated: "It is the mission of our institutions of learning to qualify our young people for the practical duties of life. It is much preferred that they emphasize the industrial and practical side of education. ... If our Church schools would confine their so-called course of study in biology to that knowledge of the insect world which would help us to eradicate the pests that threaten the destruction of our crops and our fruit, such instruction would answer much better the aims of the Church school, than theories which deal with the origin of life." This comment was probably appropriate considering the knowledge of evolution, the debate among biologists over evolution and genetics, and the technical-vocational approach to education employed at that time.

A lot has changed since 1911, however. First, our church schools are no longer just vocational technical institutions. Vocational institutions serve an important training function, and academic institutions address other issues. There are now topics, such as eradicating insect pests, which require more complex solutions than ever imagined, far beyond the scope of industrial and practical education. Addressing such questions is the function of schools such as Brigham Young University. Second, we have come to learn, by wrestling with many intricate questions, that controlling insect pests without eradicating ourselves in the process is not a simple issue. We now know that managing insects requires a knowledge of their life cycles, chemistry, genetics, and *evolution*. Most other practical questions in biology, such as preventing crop failures and preventing or correcting birth defects, require the same multifaceted approach. Third, the decision to avoid teaching evolution in the church schools was abandoned at least by the fall of 1971, when a formal class in evolution was instituted at BYU. (One of the authors, Trent Stephens, was a student in that first class.) It has been the case for many years that all the biology classes at BYU teach evolution as the foundation of the discipline, and that students graduating from BYU in the biological sciences take a formal course in evolution as part of their core curriculum.

Even though President Joseph F. Smith said that he personally believed the theory of evolution to be "more or less a fallacy," and even though many people in the church continue to debate the validity of the theory and the issue of Adam's origin, President Smith's statement allows for the possibility of a natural process in the creation of humankind. It is important to remember that even in the context of discouraging the teaching of evolution, President Smith stated, "We ... are not undertaking to say how much of evolution is true, or how much is false. ... The Church itself has no philosophy about the *modus operandi* employed by the Lord in His creation of the world."

During the 1930s and 1940s, the writings of Elder John A.

Widtsoe appeared monthly in the *Improvement Era* as a regular column entitled, "Evidences and Reconciliations." (Selections were combined in a single volume, *Evidences and Reconciliations*, arranged by G. Homer Durham and published by Bookcraft.) With credentials in both science and church leadership, Elder Widtsoe believed science to be a part of Mormonism. The column he wrote entertained an array of subjects, including a number of essays on science and religion. Frequently, he addressed issues surrounding evolution and human origins. While lauding the accomplishments of technology, and championing the harmony of the gospel and true science, Elder Widtsoe echoed the prevailing tone of the period: the contemporary scientific community views Darwinism as an inadequate explanation for biology, let alone human origins.

It must be remembered that in the decades preceding the Modern Synthesis, it was the specific evolutionary *mechanism* proposed by Darwin—natural selection—not the *fact* of evolution itself that was called into question. But to many religionists, this criticism of natural selection was taken as a sign of serious equivocation, if not outright capitulation. In one essay entitled "Men and Monkeys" (*Science and Your Faith in God*, 265-67), Elder Widtsoe quoted at length a speech delivered in 1929 by Henry Fairfield Osborn, then president of the American Association for the Advancement of Science. Implied in Osborn's remarks is the notion that past theories are overturned by new discoveries; that "science has pushed back into an unknown period the time of man's emergence, and denies the descent of man from progenitors of any existing forms of life." Although this speech was critical of Darwinism, it supported an evolutionary origin of humankind.

In another column, "Were There Pre-Adamites?" Elder Widtsoe alluded to the inferences made regarding the fragmentary fossil evidence of human-like beings pre-dating Adam. While acknowledging the existence of such, he pointed out that knowledge of the nature of such fossils remains in the region of hypothesis. However, he concluded with the statement, "The mystery of the 'creation' of Adam and Eve has not yet been revealed" (*Improvement Era* 51:305). In response to the question "To What Extent Should the Doctrine of

Evolution Be Accepted?" Elder Widtsoe enumerated several "well-established observations" in support of evolution:

> First, the fossil remains of prehistoric life on earth show that in the oldest rocks are remains of the simplest forms of life; and as the rocks become younger, more complex or more advanced life forms seem to appear. The scale of life seems to ascend from amoeba to man, as the age of the particular part of the earth's crust diminishes.
>
> Second, each group of living things has much the same bodily organization. In the case of mammals, all, including man, have similar skeletons, muscular arrangements, nervous systems, sense organization, etc. In some species the organs are rudimentary—but they are there.
>
> Third, the embryos of man and the higher animals, in earlier stages, are identical, as far as the microscope can reveal. This is held to mean that embryonic development summarizes or recapitulates the stages of man's development through the ages past.
>
> Fourth, all organic creatures may be so grouped, according to structure and chemical nature, as to show gradually increasing relationships from the lowest to the highest forms of life. Similarities in blood composition are held to indicate nearness of kinship. The blood of the great apes is very similar to the blood of man.
>
> Fifth, it has been possible, within historic times, to domesticate many animals, often with real changes in bodily form, as the various breeds of cattle, sheep, or dogs. Besides, isolated animals, as on the islands of the sea, have become unique forms, differing from those on connected continents. (*Evidences and Reconciliations*, 159.)

He then cited two notable weaknesses of the theory. The first was his impression that the reported similarities are "far-fetched and not well enough established." The second was his sense that the theory "fails to explain the emotional, reasoning and religious nature of man." He concluded that the whole squabble about evolution centers on the question of whether life came by chance or by divine will.

Similar expressions were made by Brother Frederick J. Pack, University of Utah geology professor. In 1924, as an "outgrowth of numerous conversations with young people," Pack published a book entitled *Science and Belief in God*. Selections from it were included in

*Science and Your Faith in God,* compiled by Paul R. Green in 1958. It pointed out the distinctions between the separate yet complementary roles of science (answering the how's) and religion (answering the why's). The scientific understanding of the time was accurately represented and lent an enlightening perspective on that understanding. For example, in a discussion of the "present status of Darwinism" (ca. 1924), Professor Pack noted, "Today there are but few scientists of prominent standing who regard the doctrine [of natural selection] as an adequate explanation of the operating principle of evolution" (*Science and Belief in God,* 113). He summarized the perceived shortcomings of the theory: "Darwinism as a sufficient explanation to account for evolution of life has, therefore, not made good. In the first place, natural selection cannot originate new variations, and, in the second place, it cannot preserve variations long enough to give rise to new species. Moreover, its postulation of non-directed development is out of harmony with the findings of paleontology."

In July 1925, the issue of evolution and creation was thrust onto the national center stage when a young high school science teacher, John Scopes, was tried by the state of Tennessee for teaching the theory of evolution in public school. The "Great Monkey Trial," as it came to be known, polarized the nation. Once again the First Presidency, under President Heber J. Grant, responded with an official statement entitled, "'Mormon' View of Evolution" (*Improvement Era* 11:1090-91; see also *Encyclopedia of Mormonism,* 4:1669-70). It featured an abbreviated version of the 1909 statement and reiterated the position that humans are the literal sons and daughters of Deity, that the pre-existent spirit of Adam took upon him an appropriate body to become a living soul. Of note are the omissions from the 1909 statement: the discussion of the two-fold creation—spiritual and temporal (other than humankind's spiritual birth to heavenly parents), theories concerning the first man as a development from lower orders of the animal creation, the embryonic development of Adam's body, and the perfection and perpetuation of animal creation. Thus the 1925 First Presidency statement removed what had been construed by some as implicit anti-evolution sentiments in the 1909 statement.

In 1930 Elder Joseph Fielding Smith, then a junior member of the Quorum of the Twelve (and son of the late President Joseph F. Smith), delivered a talk at the Utah Genealogical Society Conference spelling out his disbelief in "pre-Adamites." He went on to assert that there was no death before the fall of Adam, that the earth was young, and that Adam was created in an immortal state. His remarks were published in the October 1930 issue of the *Utah Genealogical and Historical Magazine* as "Faith Leads to a Fullness of Truth and Righteousness" (21:145-58). Such statements stood in contrast to the circumspect positions adopted in the 1909 and 1925 First Presidency statements and drew a request, by Elder B. H. Roberts, for clarification from the First Presidency. There was intense discussion on the issue of organic evolution. After several months of deliberation, the ensuing unambiguous instructions from the First Presidency to the general authorities read: "Upon the fundamental doctrines of the Church we are all agreed. Our mission is to bear the message of the restored gospel to the people of the world. Leave geology, biology, archeology and anthropology, no one of which has to do with the salvation of the souls of mankind, to scientific research, while we magnify our calling in the realm of the Church. ... Upon one thing we should all be able to agree, namely, that Presidents Joseph F. Smith, John R. Winder and Anthon H. Lund were right when they said: 'Adam is the primal parent of our race'" (qtd. in Jeffery, "Seers, Savants and Evolution," 41-75; see also *Encyclopedia of Mormonism*, 2:478).

Elder James E. Talmage, who had worked with the First Presidency on the 1909 statement, when discussing this controversy in his journal, related on 7 April 1930: "The decision reached by the First Presidency, and announced to this morning's assembly, was in answer to a specific question that obviously the doctrine of the existence of races of human beings upon the earth prior to the Fall of Adam was not a doctrine of the Church; and, further, that the conception embodied in the belief of many to the effect that there were no such Pre-Adamite races, and that there was no death upon the Earth prior to Adam's fall is likewise declared to be no doctrine of the Church."

To balance the public record of opinion on the matter, Elder

Talmage delivered an address entitled "The Earth and Man," which, by First Presidency direction, was published in the *Church News* and as a separate pamphlet. In it Elder Talmage pointed out that the fossilized remains of plants and animals were the remains of organisms that had "lived and died, age after age, while the earth was yet unfit for human habitation." He continued: "In speaking of the origin of man we generally have reference to the creation of man's body; and of all the mistakes that man has made concerning himself, one of the greatest and gravest is that of mistaking the body for the man. The body is no more truly the whole man than the coat is the body. ... Notwithstanding the assumption that man is the culmination of an evolutionary development from a lower order of beings, we know that the body of man today is the very form and fashion of his spirit. ... I'd not regard Adam as related to—certainly not as descended from—the Neandertal, Cro-Magnon, the Peking, or the Piltdown man. Adam came as divinely directed, created and empowered, and stands as the patriarchal head of his posterity. ... He is born in the lineage of Deity, not in the posterity of the brute creation" ("Church News," *Deseret News*, 21 Nov. 1931, 7-8; the speech was published in pamphlet form by the church on the same date and has been more recently republished in the *Instructor*, Dec. 1965, 474-77, and 15 Jan. 1966, 9-11).

In 1933 elders Talmage and Roberts died, followed in 1952 by elders Widtsoe and Joseph F. Merrill, the latter being the last of the early brethren with secular training in the sciences. The following year, 1953, Elder Joseph Fielding Smith delivered a speech at BYU entitled "The Origin of Man" and in 1954 published his book manuscript, *Man: His Origin and Destiny*, emphasizing scriptural literalism and labeling evolution as a plan of Satan: "It has been truthfully said that organic evolution is Satan's chief weapon in this dispensation in his attempt to destroy the divine mission of Jesus Christ" (*Man*, 184). Mormon historian E. Robert Paul traces many of the fundamentalist Creationist ideas in *Man: His Origin and Destiny* to the evangelical Christian "geologist" George McCready Price, whose influential books *New Geology*, *The Phantom of Organic Evolution*, and *The Geological-Ages Hoax* contributed significantly to the Creationist

Movement. (Interestingly, Price based his religious scientism on the views of the Seventh-day Adventist prophetess Ellen G. White, who claimed to have been present when God created the world. For further discussion of this topic, see Paul, *Science, Religion, and Mormon Cosmology*, 180-81.)

Numerous inquiries were made of the First Presidency for clarification on the points made by Elder Smith. President David O. McKay reiterated that the only official declaration of the church regarding the origin of man was the 1909 statement of Joseph F. Smith et al. and that the church's position had not changed since then. It is unclear precisely why President McKay did not mention the 1925 statement. He further made the distinction that the church had no official position concerning the theory of evolution. Joseph Fielding Smith's book, *Man: His Origin and Destiny*, said President McKay, "expresses the views of the author, for which he assumes full responsibility. The book was not published, approved, or authorized by the Church, nor did the author intend that it be." In addition to the 1909 statement, he offered James E. Talmage's sermon "The Earth and Man" for "further information on the subject" (copies of this correspondence are in our possession).

To further clarify the church's position, President McKay's counselor, J. Reuben Clark, delivered an address by assignment entitled "When Are the Writings or Sermons of General Authorities Entitled to the Claim of Scripture?" (*Church News*, 31 July 1954, 2f). President Clark counseled:

> In considering the problem here, it should be borne in mind that some of the General Authorities have had assigned to them a special calling; they possess a special gift; they are sustained as prophets, seers and revelators, which gives them a special spiritual endowment in connection with their teaching of the people. They have the right, the power, the authority to declare the mind and will of God to his people, subject to the over-all power and authority of the President of the Church.
>
> Here we must have in mind—must know—that only the President of the Church, the Presiding High Priest, is sustained as Prophet, Seer

and Revelator for the Church, and he alone has the right to receive revelations for the Church, either new or amendatory, or to give authoritative interpretations of scriptures that shall be binding on the Church, or change in any way the existing doctrines of the Church.

When any one except the President of the Church undertakes to proclaim a new doctrine of the Church we may know that he is not moved upon by the Holy Ghost, unless he is acting under the direct authority and direction of the President.

When any man, except the President of the Church, undertakes to proclaim one unsettled doctrine, as among two or more doctrines in dispute, as the settled doctrine of the Church, we may know that he is not moved upon by the Holy Ghost, unless he is acting under the direction and by the authority of the President.

Even the President of the Church, himself, may not always be "moved upon by the Holy Ghost," when he addresses the people. This has happened about matters of doctrine (usually of a highly speculative character) where subsequent Presidents of the Church and the people themselves have felt that in declaring the doctrine, the announcer was not moved upon by the Holy Ghost.

President McKay never issued a more specific official pronouncement on the topic. Elder Paul H. Dunn related a personal remark that President McKay made to him. President McKay reportedly said, "The day the mantle fell on me, 1951, April, it became very conscious in my mind that we had now arrived on the world scene and I took a silent oath and covenant not to speculate publicly" (qtd. in Dunn, *Truth or Speculation*, audiotape). Elder Marion D. Hanks also reported an exchange with President McKay in which the president said, "It would do no violence to my faith to learn God had formed man in one way or another" ("An Attitude, the Weightier Matters," 70).

In February 1953, the *Improvement Era* published an article by Brother Frank B. Salisbury, a botanist at Utah State University, entitled "Science and Religion, Their Basic Positions." It is a lucid treatment of the distinctions between revelation and the "scientific method" as ways of knowing. "If man exists as part of some master plan such as the ultimate perfection of the human soul, science alone can neither affirm nor deny it. Science may study the *how* of man's existence, but can say nothing about the *why* [emphasis in original]. There should be no conflict between science and religion, but, on the contrary, these two fields should complement each other to the end that man might find peace and satisfaction in his quest for both spiritual and material knowledge" (56:80ff). Again, in 1965, the *Improvement Era* reiterated the roles of science and religion and the contrasting methods for revealing truth by presenting a series of discussions with a physician, a sociologist, a physicist, and a chemist (no biologist was represented) ("Science and Religion," 860-98).

In contrast, in 1958 Elder Bruce R. McConkie of the Seventy echoed the beliefs of his father-in-law, Elder Joseph Fielding Smith, regarding a young earth, paradisiacal creation, pre-Adamites, and evolution in his book *Mormon Doctrine*. He concluded, "There is no harmony between the truths of revealed religion and the theories of organic evolution" (256). However, at least in relation to the age of the earth, Elder McConkie later revised his opinion, suggesting that the earth was perhaps 2.5 billion years old (*Mortal Messiah*, 29).

President McKay privately disavowed Elder McConkie's book, which was written without approval of or direction from the church. The First Presidency concluded that the book was "full of errors and misstatements, and it is most unfortunate that the book has received such wide circulation" (Paul, *Science, Religion, and Mormon Cosmology*, 179).

Additional balanced viewpoints appeared in the *Improvement Era*, in 1964, on the subject. "How Old Is the Earth?" (67:828), by Paul Cracroft, presented the "young earth" viewpoint of Melvin Cook, a professor of metallurgy at the University of Utah. Brother Cook would eventually co-author a popular book, *Science and Mormonism*, published by Deseret Book in 1968, which presented an unorthodox geological account in support of the neoliteralist tenants of a young earth. The Cook article was followed by "The Gospel and the Age of the Earth" (*Improvement Era*, 68:608), by Henry Eyring, then dean of the Graduate School, University of Utah, which presented evidence for an ancient earth. An editorial note introducing the article explicitly stated, "As far as is known The Church of Jesus Christ of

Latter-day Saints has never taken an official stand on the age of the earth."

President Harold B. Lee addressed the issue of science and religion in December 1972's *Ensign* First Presidency message. He stated:

> I was somewhat sorrowed recently to hear someone, a sister who comes from a church family, ask, "What about the pre-Adamic people? ... Aren't there evidences that people preceded the Adamic period on the earth?" I said, "Have you forgotten the scripture that says, 'And I, the Lord God, formed man from the dust of the ground, and breathed into his nostrils the breath of life; and man became a living soul, the first flesh upon the earth, the first man also ...'" (Moses 3:7). ... She wondered about the creation because she had read the theories of the scientists, and the question that she was really asking was: How do you reconcile science with religion? The answer must be, If science is not true, you cannot reconcile truth with error.

Four years later, in 1976, Frank Salisbury, a plant physiologist at Utah State University, published a book entitled *The Creation*, in which he examined the origins of life from the perspectives of science and religion (225). He stated, "There are tentative ways to reinterpret and reconcile science and/or the revealed creation accounts, yet a total reconciliation must await future knowledge." For several years, this was the only commercially published book in print available to LDS students on evolution and the church.

Beginning in 1978, a generation of BYU students received a thin blue booklet entitled *The Fall of Adam, the Atonement of Christ and Organic Evolution*, written and published by Reid E. Bankhead. Brother Bankhead, a religion instructor at BYU, distributed it widely to students. It contains a brief introduction in which the reader is encouraged to accept "the words of the latter-day prophets (including *Man, His Origin and Destiny*, by Elder Joseph Fielding Smith) and the living oracles today." It presents a selection of remarks by church leaders, including Joseph Fielding Smith, Bruce R. McConkie, Mark E. Petersen, Marion G. Romney, George Q. Cannon, James E. Talmage, and John A. Widtsoe, addressing the creation and fall of Adam and their relationship to the atonement of Jesus Christ. The carefully

selected remarks are uniformly critical of hypotheses of human evolutionary origins. For example: "According to this theory of primor-
dial life, man at one time developed from an ancestor which, as one
writer described him, was 'a hairy, four-legged beast which had a tail
and pointed ears and lived in trees.' Which requires more faith—to
believe that God is our Father, or that some monkey-like ape gave us
birth? And which would you rather have as your father—a creeping
ape or Almighty God?" (*Way of the Master*, qtd. in Bankhead, *Fall of
Adam*, 31).

In 1979 a presentation by Keith H. Meservy, an associate professor of ancient scripture at BYU, entitled "Evolution and the Origin of
Adam," was delivered at the Third Annual Church Education System
Religious Educators' Symposium. Parts of that presentation were
published by the Church Educational System. Despite official assertions to the contrary, Brother Meservy suggested that the church did
in fact "have a doctrine on Man and his origin that is based on the
scriptures as interpreted by the living prophets" (219). Basing his
opinion on the 1909 First Presidency statement, he alleged that "the
prophets have taught that the spiritual as well as the physical procreation of their own species by the gods is the true explanation of the
origin of man." This "doctrine" was attributed to founding church
prophet Joseph Smith by way of an unpublished third-party letter.
When considered in context, the quotations from Brigham Young in
Meservy's treatise actually refer, not to evolution, but to the now-
repudiated Adam-God theory. However, the idea that Adam's physical body was begotten by Heavenly Father was clearly advocated by
some individuals and indirectly attributed to others. At the root of
the issue of Adam's origin seemed to lie the presumption that "like
begets like." For example, President John Taylor stated in 1882, "The
primitive organisms of all living beings exist in the same form as
when they first received their impress from their maker ... and every
living creature, including man, propagates its own species and per-
petuates its own kind, so does God perpetuate His" (*Mediation and
Atonement*, 164-65). A number of the brethren were further quoted as
opposing the suggestion that man's physical body evolved "from
lower forms of life." Citing undated personal correspondence from

Elder Marion G. Romney, Meservy quoted: "The General Authorities of the Church are, of course, like all other men, different in their personalities. However, on the fundamentals they are in accord, and one of those fundamentals upon which they are in accord is that Adam is the Son of God, that neither his spirit nor his body is the product of biological evolution."

Elder Bruce R. McConkie, while a member of the Quorum of the Twelve, remained a vocal critic of evolution. A prominent example occurred on 1 June 1980 in a fourteen-stake BYU fireside address he delivered entitled "Seven Deadly Heresies." Under Heresy #2, Elder McConkie said, "There are those who say that revealed religion and organic evolution can be harmonized. This is both false and devilish." At publication, however, the tone of the speech was considerably softened (see *BYU Speeches of the Year* [1980], 74-80). Carrying on the legacy of Elder Joseph Fielding Smith, Elder McConkie established the "Pillars of Faith" —interlocking concepts relating the Creation, the Fall, and the Atonement. Elements of this paradigm have been included in church curriculum materials for Old Testament Studies as recently as 1998.

In 1981, while presiding over another fourteen-stake BYU fireside, Elder McConkie stated that he had received numerous letters concerning the church's position on evolution and prepared a form letter that basically said: "The Lord has revealed enough about the creation so that we can understand the Fall and he has revealed enough about the Fall so that we can understand the Atonement. Beyond this, we don't know. We do know that Adam was the first man upon this earth and that he was created by God and is the image of God, he did not descend from an inferior being" ("Elder McConkie Addresses BYU Stakes," *7th East Press*). The next year, the *Ensign* carried an article by Elder McConkie in which he said, "Before we can even begin to understand the temporal creation of all things, we must know how and in what manner these three eternal verities—the Creation, the Fall, and the Atonement—are inseparably woven together to form one plan of salvation" ("Christ and the Creation," June 1982, 9).

Three years later, at the church's October 1983 general conference, Elder McConkie said that rejection of the "pernicious doc-trine of organic evolution" was one of the "tests of true believers" ("What Think Ye of the Book of Mormon?" 13:72-74). Elder Boyd K. Packer's address at the same conference also included several im-plicit criticisms of evolution. For example, he remarked that hens' eggs would never hatch out as crocodiles and that evolutionists were not enthusiastic genealogists. These remarks prompted a number of written queries, in response to which Elder Packer acknowledged he had merely expressed his personal opinion on the matter. Five years later, he explained his position in an address delivered at the Book of Mormon Symposium, entitled "The Law and the Light," which was subsequently published, but with an "official disclaimer" that he was expressing personal views and not speaking for the church. Elder Packer stated:

> If man is but an animal, then logic favors freedom without account-ability or consequence. Had man evolved from animals, there could have been no fall, no law broken, no penalty, no need for a mediator. The ordinance of baptism would be an empty gesture since it is for the remission of sins. Many who perceive organic evolution to be law rather than theory do not realize they forsake the atonement in the process.
>
> And, I am sorry to say, the so-called theistic evolution, the theory that God used an evolutionary process to prepare a physical body for the spirit of man, is equally false. I say I am sorry because I know it is a view commonly held by good and thoughtful people who search for an acceptable resolution to an apparent conflict between the theory of evo-lution and the doctrines of the gospel. An understanding of the sealing authority with its binding of the generations into eternal families can-not admit to ancestral bloodlines to beasts. (In *The Book of Mormon: Jacob Through Words of Mormon*, 1-31.)

The *Ensign* and church curriculum manuals continued to wrestle with the topic. For example, in 1980 the *Ensign* published an article by Kent Nielsen, assistant professor of the history of science at BYU, entitled "The Gospel and the Scientific View: How the Earth Came to Be," in which he chronicled the rise of scientific naturalism and its perceived implications for religion. He then pointed out the limita-tions imposed on naturalistic interpretations by the restored gospel and incorporated the ideas of a pre-Fall paradisiacal world without procreation and death.

In 1983 Deseret Book published *Reflections of a Scientist*, by Henry Eyring, professor of chemistry at the University of Utah. It conveys one LDS scientist's contemplations on the relationship between science and religion. In one essay, he relates a meeting with President Joseph Fielding Smith following the publication of *Man: His Origin and Destiny*, during which President Smith explained his views conveyed in the book. Brother Eyring replied, "Brother Smith, I have read your books and know your point of view, and I understand that is how it looks to you. It just looks a little different to me" (53). They parted on the best of terms.

On the subject of evolution, Brother Eyring remarked, "Animals seem pretty wonderful to me. I'd be content to discover that I share a common heritage with them, so long as God is at the controls" (*Reflections*, 59-60). The book concludes with the following admonition:

> As parents and teachers we pass on to our children and pupils our world picture. Part of this picture is religious and part of it deals with the world around us. If we teach our pupils some outmoded and nonessential notions that fail to hold water when the students get into their science classes at the university, we run grave risks. When our proteges shed the bad science they may also throw out some true religion. The solution is to avoid telling them that the earth is flat too long after it has been proved round. Don't defend a good cause with bad arguments.
>
> So I am certain that the gospel, as taught in the Church of Jesus Christ of Latter-day Saints, is true. It's a better explanation of what I observe in science than any other I know about. There are still lots of things I don't know, but that doesn't bother me. I'm a happy muddler. The gospel simply asks me to find out what's true as best I can and in the meantime to live a good life. That strikes me as the best formula for living there could be. (*Reflections,* 101.)

In September 1987 the *Ensign* carried a response to the question, "Do we know how the earth's history as indicated from fossils fits with the earth's history as the scriptures present it?" written by Morris S. Petersen, a professor of geology at BYU and a stake president.

He noted that "among the life forms God created were apparently many species now extinct. ... As one examines the rock layers it becomes evident that there is a highly ordered pattern in the occurrence of fossils. ... From the fossil record we learn that the dinosaurs were the dominant animals on the earth between 225 and 67 million years ago. ... The existence of these animals is indisputable, for their remains have been found in rocks all over the earth. What eternal purpose they played in the creation and early history of the earth is unknown. The scriptures do not address the question."

E. Robert Paul published a book in 1992 entitled *Science, Religion and Mormon Cosmology*. One chapter of that book dealt with the issue of evolution and the church, in which he presented a chronology somewhat similar to our presentation in this chapter. Also in 1992, church educators were provided with a packet of statements approved by BYU's board of trustees addressing evolution and the origin of man. The board was then composed of the First Presidency, seven members of the Quorum of the Twelve, and a few others. This packet was intended to summarize the official church position and to be used whenever the question arose at BYU. It included the 1909 statement, the 1925 statement, and the *Encyclopedia of Mormonism* article, "Evolution." The prefatory comments concluded with the statement, "Various views have been expressed by other Church leaders on this subject over many decades; *however, formal statements by the First Presidency are the definitive source of official Church positions* [emphasis added]."

William E. Evenson, a professor of physics and dean of the College of Physics and Mathematical Sciences at BYU, was asked by the BYU administration to prepare a statement explaining the evolution packet (see "Evolution Packet Defined," *BYU Daily Universe*, 3). Brother Evenson stated that the packet was prepared because of confusion in the minds of students and the potential for controversy about the church's position. He said that BYU faculty were requested to refer students to the material in the packet, and that "when other items are distributed, they should be clearly separated and given as a supplement to this material and include a fair sampling of the diverse viewpoints among LDS leaders. For example, if one included statements by LDS apostles in a handout on evolution, the range of views would include some statements against evolution, some sympathetic to evolution, and several shades of opinion in between. We want to avoid the implication that a greater sense of unanimity or resolution of this topic exists than is actually the case. ... The process was one of constructive and harmonious effort to provide materials from which students could see clearly the foundation of LDS doctrine on this subject and distinguish it from the wide variety of opinions encountered in LDS literature."

In 1998 Joseph Fielding McConkie, a professor of religion at BYU and son of Elder Bruce R. McConkie, published a book entitled *Answers: Straightforward Answers to Tough Gospel Questions*. One chapter of the book addressed issues of science and religion. Brother McConkie stated that there are "irreconcilable differences between the theory of organic evolution and the doctrine of the Fall." He said that the theory of evolution, even theistic evolution, "is at odds both with scripture and with an official declaration of the First Presidency on the origin of man." Brother McConkie's book embraces a literal interpretation of the Creation, which includes concepts of a young earth, paradisiacal creation, and no death before the Fall.

It is clear that the official declarations of the First Presidency on the origin of humankind, let alone on evolution generally, are extremely circumspect, limited primarily to the *spiritual* heritage of mankind and the authorship of Creation. Individual commentaries and expressions of opinion have varied considerably through the years. However, in our own experience, a formal solicitation for the official position of the church on the topic evoked a reference to the 1909 statement and to entries in the *Encyclopedia of Mormonism*. It is important to remember that this initial First Presidency statement, which remains the official pronouncement today, "declares man to be the direct and lineal offspring of Deity." Some members of the church continue to interpret this statement to refer to our physical bodies in spite of the clarifying statement of 1910: "Whether the mortal bodies of man evolved in natural processes to present perfection, through the direction and power of God; whether the first parents ... were transplanted from another sphere, with immortal tabernacles ...; whether they were born here in mortality ... are questions not fully answered in the revealed word of God" (*Improvement Era*, Apr. 1910, 570). Other inquiries have been answered with only an abbreviated version of the *Encyclopedia of Mormonism*'s entry on "Evolution." Under the *Encyclopedia* entry "Origin of Man," by John L. Sorensen, it states: "Official statements indicate that the details of how Adam became 'the first man' are considered not to have been revealed clearly enough to settle questions of process" (1053-54). Furthermore, the First Presidency's counsel in 1931 to "leave geology, biology, archeology and anthropology ... to scientific research" (*Encyclopedia*, 4:1669-70) is reiterated in the *Encyclopedia of Mormonism*'s entry on "Evolution." It is with this admonition in mind that we proceed.

# 5.
# The Evidence
# of Things

S cience is empirical; it is based on observation. Its strength lies in its being founded on the collection of observable, reproducible facts or data. One scientist or group of scientists can report an observation or the results of an experiment, and other scientists can replicate the same observation or perform the same experiment to see if they obtain the same results. Scientists can also slightly change the perspective of the observation or the parameters of the experiment to determine if they will still obtain predicted results. In the case of an important theory, such as evolution, this process of replication and verification can be repeated thousands of times. The words *experiment* and *experience* share the common Latin root, meaning *to try out*. One of the beauties of science is that virtually *anyone* can try out the experiment, can challenge the current conclusions or theories by designing a particular experiment to test a new hypothesis. On the other hand, it is of no scientific merit for someone to advance or challenge a hypothesis or theory without presenting reproducible data.

   It is important for anyone considering science to understand the difference between a fact, a hypothesis, a law, and a theory, as each applies to science. A fact, or datum, is a truth that has been established by experience or observation, and many facts constitute data. A hypothesis is a proposed explanation for some phenomenon, an attempt to make sense of a set of data, which usually is advanced provisionally so that it can be tested. A law is a statement of a relationship or phenomenon that consistently occurs under a given set of conditions. Examples include the laws of motion, the laws of thermodynamics, the law of gravity, the law of definite composition in chemistry, the law of partial pressures, and the law of independent assortment in genetics. A theory, according to *Webster's Dictionary,* in scientific terms, is a coherent group of explanations for a related group of phenomena. Many people have the mistaken notion that, given enough time and evidence, a theory will eventually become a law. In reality, a theory is a much broader concept than a law. A law describes a single phenomenon, whereas a theory explains a group of related phenomena, each of which may be described by a law. Examples include the theory of relativity, the theory of quantum mechanics (which incorporates the law of gravity), the cell theory, the nuclear theory, and the theory of evolution.

*Webster's Dictionary* also presents a non-scientific definition of a theory as a guess or conjecture. It is unfortunate that this one term, theory, has two very different definitions: one is a coherent group of explanations, the other is a guess. This situation has led to many misconceptions about the strength of various scientific positions, especially concerning the theory of evolution. It is common for scientists and non-scientists alike, when speaking of non-scientific issues, to state, "Well, I have a theory about that." In this context, a "theory" often means an unstated, educated guess or explanation about some event, which may be trivial. As a result, many individuals have trivialized well-documented, well-founded unifying principles such as evolution by the casual retort, "Oh, it's *only* a theory."

The difference between a theory and a fact can be demonstrated in the following examples. Perhaps the most time-honored "fact" in our society is that the sun "rises" every morning. Given the provision that the sun only appears to rise as the earth rotates, we can state as a

fact that the sun (apparently) rose this morning, because that phenomenon can be observed by any number of people. However, when
we add the term "every morning" and state that the sun rises every
morning, the concept becomes a theory, a prediction, because there
is no way that we can observe *every* morning, forever.

Another example is the cell theory, which states that all living
things are composed of cells. That is not a statement of fact. It is a
theory. We can look at a *specific* tissue and observe for a fact that the
tissue is composed of cells, but without looking at *every* tissue from
*every* living thing, we cannot state as a fact that they are all made of
cells. The cell theory *predicts* that any tissue a person observes is
composed of cells. The long-term test is to continually determine if
the predictions of a theory are borne out by the facts. Whenever an
observation or experiment reveals a fact that is not consistent with
the prediction of the theory, and if that observation can be repeated,
then the theory must be modified to accommodate the new fact or be
replaced by a new theory.

Unlike science, which is based on repeatable observation, religion is based on faith, feelings, and subjective experience. Because of
this difference, there is a tendency for some people to accept science
and dismiss religion, whereas other people accept religion and dismiss science. This conflict is beautifully depicted in the movie *Contact*, based on the novel by astronomer Carl Sagan. In this movie, the
main characters, one a scientist and the other a theologian, debate
the issue of feeling versus observation in discovering truth. In the
end, the scientist has an experience that she can neither document
nor repeat, and only at that point comes to realize the validity of religious experiences. In contrast to the perceived conflict between science and religion, some people are able to realize a balance between
the two by recognizing that each has its place in the search for truth
(these ideas are discussed in chap. 3).

One of the greatest sources of conflict between science and religion is the concept that seeing is believing. Those who embrace science and reject religion are often of the opinion that "if I can't see it,
then it must not exist." If we examine the process of "seeing," it
quickly becomes apparent that relying on our visual senses may not

be all that it's cracked up to be. How many times do we see something that is actually quite different from the facts? In court, how many times do two witnesses testify differently of the same event? The concepts of optical illusion and sleight of hand are founded on this discontinuity between observation and fact.

There are many examples of *normal* dysfunctions in our visual systems, and no one is exempt. For example, as light enters a person's eye it is inverted 180 degrees. The image remains inverted as it passes to the brain. The brain then inverts the image to make the world "appear" right side up. Therefore, what we see is 180 degrees off from the way the world actually is. Prismatic lenses can be worn that invert the image before it reaches the eyes. For several days after a person begins wearing such glasses, the world appears upside down, but then the brain adjusts by re-inverting the image, and things are again perceived as being right side up. When the glasses are removed, the world again appears upside down, but, once more, the brain adjusts and things are again perceived as before. If we do not see the world as it is in the first place, how can we believe what we see?

As another example, look at the figure on page 63 and follow the directions in the legend. What happened? What are the facts? Did the Frenchman *in fact* lose his head? But what do you *see*? This blank spot in your visual field is called the blind spot of your eye. The blind spot occurs because there are no photo receptor cells at the point where the optic nerve exits each eye. As a result, the eye is not capable of detecting any image carried by the light striking that part of the retina. We do not normally see a blank spot for two reasons: (1) We are normally seeing with two eyes, and the blank spots for the two visual fields do not overlap. (2) If we are observing something with one eye closed, our brain fills in the missing part of the visual field by duplicating the image immediately surrounding the blank spot. As a result of the blind spot, we are not seeing the whole picture, ever. Therefore, is seeing *always* believing?

The effect of filling in the visual blank may be even more dramatically illustrated by another demonstration. Look at B in the figure below and follow the directions. As you slowly move the book toward your eye, you will notice that in this case the white area disappears and is filled in with lines. Your brain puts lines into a figure where no lines exist. Do you believe what your eyes are seeing? Do you believe what is in front of your face?

How many of us extend the concepts of this demonstration to what we read, such as when we read the scriptures? How many of us

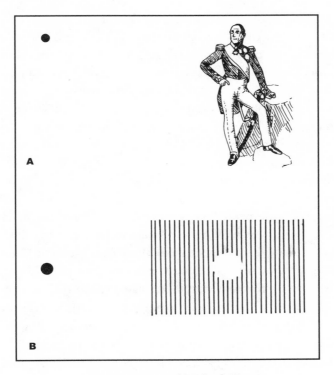

### Demonstrating the Blind Spot

*A. The French Revolution. Close your left eye, hold the book at arm's length, stare at the spot on the left side of the figure, and slowly move the book toward your right eye. You will notice that when the book is a few inches in front of your eye, the French gentleman loses his head.* **B. Filling in the spot.** *Repeat the process described in A: close your left eye, hold the book at arm's length, stare at the spot on the left side of the figure, and slowly move the book toward your right eye. You will notice that when the book is a few inches in front of your eye, the white spot in the center of the stripes fills in with stripes.*

add in words or phrases based on our preconceived notions of what we expect? Unlike the example above, we do not literally *see* words that are not there, we just impose interpretations or additional meanings in our minds. How many times have you found yourself saying, "I know that's in the scriptures, somewhere"? How many of the apparent conflicts between science and religion are the result of what we *read into* the scriptures?

Another interesting feature of vision is the speed with which we see. The action potentials—distinct spikes of electrical activity that travel along a nerve fiber—from our eyes to our brain occur at the rate of about 20 to 25 per second. Because of the physical limits of generating action potentials, we cannot be forced or trained to see any more rapidly. Because of this speed limit to vision, if we observe still pictures at a rate faster than 20-25 per second, we see only fluid movement. We think we are seeing actual movement. The reality is that our brain simply interprets this rapid input of still pictures as movement. The images are simply coming in faster than the brain can analyze them individually, and so it blurs everything together and we see smooth, flowing action. If the film is run less than twenty-four frames per second, the movement appears fast and jerky, like an "old time movie"; if it is run faster, we see "slow motion." This trick of the human brain is the basis of the entire motion picture industry. Is what we see real or interpretation?

We can push this issue of visual images even farther. We can take a picture of a person's face, cut it in half, and flash that image of half a face onto a screen for a fraction of a second (say about 1/20th of a second), so the eyes do not have time to scan the entire image. If we ask, "What did you see?," those being so examined will say they saw a person's face. If asked if there was anything peculiar about the face, they will most likely say, "Not really." Asked if there was any difference between the left and right ears, they will most likely respond that they noticed nothing particular. It is unlikely that anyone would say that one ear was missing. In reality, they only saw half the image. Their brains filled in the other half of the picture to make a complete face. Why would the brain trick them like that? The theory is that your brain is not used to seeing only half faces. When it is exposed to half a face for an extremely brief period, it assumes that it simply did not receive all the information concerning the whole picture in the allotted time, so it simply fills in the missing parts.

Another important component of "seeing" is remembering (see Begley, "You Must Remember This," 68-69). If a visual image is not placed into our memory within a matter of minutes, it is as though the thing was never seen at all. For people who have brain disorders affecting their memory, everything around them is constantly new but never recalled. Recent research has revealed that, even in people with normal brain function, the nature of memory is sometimes imperfect. According to current theory, the way we remember an event is not like recording it as a motion picture. The whole memory is not stored together like rolls of film inside the brain. Rather the brain is more like a set of pigeon holes with bits and pieces of memory stored in each. For example, a person might remember a trip his family took to Disneyland when he was a child. The information of which family members took the trip may be stored in one pigeon hole or set of pigeon holes. Some of the most "memorable" images of Disneyland may be stored in another set of pigeon holes (emotion-charged experiences are the most memorable). That Disneyland was "fun" may reside in yet another set of holes.

When a person attempts to retrieve a certain memory from storage, the pieces are pulled out of their individual pigeon holes and brought together. A common error made in such recollections is the "who was there" error. If the memory of family is stored in a given pigeon hole, it is apparently retrieved as "the whole family was there" type of memory because the whole family *was there* for so many events and because so many such memories are piled up in the pigeon hole of family memory. As you reminisce about the trip to Disneyland, you may say to a younger sister, "Remember when we went on the Space Mountain ride?" To your surprise, she replies, "No, I was too *young* to go on the Space Mountain ride. Mom and I had to wait for all of *you*." You have no memory of this family member's absence from that particular event, probably because younger sisters are quite insignificant. However, the event, i.e., being left out, was very significant to your younger sister.

In addition, a person can bring two pieces of memory together which did not occur together and come up with the wrong memory. Often the problem occurs because the emotional part and the factual part are stored separately and then are drawn out and matched to form the complete memory. However, sometimes a person can match the emotions of one memory and the "facts" of another. This becomes a "real" memory, and it can be retrieved at any future time. For example, a person might remember being lost in a shopping mall as a child and might recall the emotion of terror associated with that experience. At a later time, someone might have related to her a story of being lost in the woods. The person hearing the story had been in the woods perhaps only once and had never been lost there. For some reason, when the lost-in-the-woods memory is stored, a faulty link is made between this memory and the terror associated with being lost in the mall. When later recalled, the feeling of terror is incorrectly pulled out with it, and, *now*, the person has feelings of terror over being lost in the woods.

This type of faulty memory has caused some major problems in our society. There is now evidence that in the process of trying to draw out deeply buried, emotionally-charged memories from children, such as those associated with abuse, false memories can actually be implanted. To the child, the memory is no less real, even though the event never actually happened. The child is not lying. It should be emphasized that even though there have been instances of false memories of abuse, many such memories are, unfortunately, all too real.

In addition to problems of seeing, perceiving, and remembering images originating from outside the body, our brains are capable of generating its own images of things that do not exist or of events that never occurred. These misrepresentations are called hallucinations, and they can be induced by drugs or brain disorders. Hallucinations are real for those persons experiencing them. It is often not possible to distinguish what one sees of the outside world from what is "seen" in the mind. Because both images are generated in the brain, one type of "seeing" is perceived as no more or less "real" than the other.

Seeing what no one else can see or has seen can be a major challenge for religion. When someone says, "I've seen a vision," how can anyone be sure that what was seen was real or imagined? How can others verify the experience if it is not subject to replication? This has been a challenge to prophets. In the Book of Mormon, Lehi's own wife complained against him, telling him that he was a visionary man; saying: "Behold thou hast led us forth from the land of our inheritance, and my sons are no more, and we perish in the wilderness" (1 Ne. 5:2).

The first principle of Christ's gospel is faith—"the substance of things hoped for, the *evidence* of things *not seen*" (Heb. 11:1; emphasis added). Alma said, "Faith is not to have a perfect knowledge of things; therefore if ye have faith ye hope for things which are not seen, which are true" (Alma 32:21). Faith, therefore, unlike science, is not based on seeing and, as a result, is not to have a "perfect knowledge," which can be achieved with repeated observation, such as seeing the sun rise every morning.

While recognizing the distinctions between science and faith as ways of knowing, it is interesting to note some common principles. We have seen that faith is based on "substance," on "evidence of things." Christ admonished his followers to live his teachings to determine if they were of God, to "try it out" or, in other words, to experiment, to replicate the experience (John 7:16-17). Alma employs the very word "experiment" in his well-known allegory of faith likened to a seed. Alma 32 is a timeless example of the "scientific method" applied to faith:

> A seed may be planted in your heart ... if it be a true seed ... if ye do not cast it out by your unbelief ... it will begin to swell within your breasts; and when you feel these swelling motions, ye will begin to say ... this is a good seed ... it beginneth to enlarge my soul; yea, it beginneth to enlighten my understanding. ... Now behold, would this increase your faith? I say unto you, Yea ... because ye have tried the experiment, and planted the seed, and it swelleth and sprouteth ... ye must needs know that the seed is good. And now, behold, is your knowledge perfect? Yea, your knowledge is perfect in that thing [the knowledge that the seed is good, as explained in the latter part of Alma 32], and your

faith is dormant; and this because you know, for ye know that the word hath swelled your souls ... that your understanding doth begin to be enlightened, and your mind doth begin to expand, O then is not this real? I say unto you, Yea, because it is light; and whatsoever is light, is good, because it is discernible ... after ye have tasted this light is your knowledge perfect? Behold I say unto you, Nay; neither must ye lay aside your faith, for ye have only exercised your faith to plant the seed that ye might try the experiment to know if the seed was good. ... If ye will not nourish the word ... ye can never pluck of the fruit of the tree of life. But if ye will nourish the word ... by your faith ... it shall take root ... it shall be a tree springing up unto everlasting life.

The difference between faith and knowledge is demonstrated in the experience of Jared's brother (Ether 3): "And the Lord saw that the brother of Jared had fallen to the earth, and the Lord said unto him: Arise, why hast thou fallen? And he saith unto the Lord: I saw the finger of the Lord. ... And the Lord said unto him: Because of thy faith thou hadst seen ... for were it not so ye could not have seen my finger. ... And because of the knowledge of this man he could not be kept from beholding within the veil, and he saw the finger of Jesus ... and he had faith no longer, for he knew, nothing doubting. Wherefore, having this perfect knowledge of God, he could not be kept from within the veil. ..."

So what did the brother of Jared *know* before and after this experience? Moroni stated, "Because of the knowledge of this man he could not be kept from beholding within the veil ... having this perfect knowledge of God, he could not be kept from within the veil." In reply to the Lord's question (i.e., did he believe), the brother of Jared replied, "Yea, Lord, I know that thou speakest the truth, for thou art a God of truth, and canst not lie." *This* is what the brother of Jared *knew* before this experience, that God speaks the truth and cannot lie. This *knowledge* came as a result of the brother of Jared's *faith*. On the other hand, what did the brother of Jared *not* know without seeing the Lord for himself? He said, "I knew not that the Lord had flesh and blood." Jesus then *explained* to the brother of Jared what he had *actually* seen. He said, "This body, which ye now behold, is the body of my spirit ... and even as I appear unto thee to be in the spirit will I appear unto my people in the flesh." Therefore, before the brother of Jared saw Christ, he had the *knowledge* that God does not lie, but he had *no knowledge* as to the *appearance* of God. Faith brought him to a knowledge of spiritual issues but not to a knowledge of tangible ones. He had to *see* Jesus before he could know about his physical condition. Even then, the brother of Jared's visual experience was inaccurate. He thought that what he had seen was a body of flesh and blood. Jesus explained to him that he was looking, rather, at a spirit body, which had the same appearance of one with flesh and blood.

Those of us who believe in spiritual manifestations can seek such a manifestation concerning a given spiritual experience, such as a vision, whether our own or someone else's. For example, Lehi had a vision of the Tree of Life: "Behold, I have dreamed a dream; or in other words, I have seen a vision" (1 Ne. 8:2). Some of Lehi's sons found his vision hard to understand. They stated: "The Lord maketh no such thing known unto us" (1 Ne. 15:2-9). In contrast, Nephi said, "I, Nephi, was desirous also that I might see, and hear, and know of these things, by the power of the Holy Ghost, which is the gift of God unto all those who diligently seek him. ... For he is the same yesterday, to-day, and forever. ... For he that diligently seeketh shall find; and the mysteries of God shall be unfolded unto them" (1 Ne. 10:17-19). In addition, we can also, in some cases, examine physical confirmations. For example, the Book of Mormon is an important part of the LDS religion because for many it provides physical confirmation of Joseph Smith's claim to visions. The existence of the Book of Mormon (or the New Testament, or the Torah, or the Koran) is a *fact*. One can question its origin, but not the *fact* that it exists. People can read the book for themselves and draw their own conclusions about its origins.

The idea that our mental images are imperfect, that our senses are imperfect, and that our memories are perhaps even more imperfect emphasizes the issue that we have a basic, inherent problem with data—the very foundation of science—or with visions or other spiritual manifestations—the foundation of religion. We have a basic human problem: we cannot trust each other when it comes to perceiving reality. When it comes down to it, we cannot even trust ourselves. How do you know that what you are seeing is really there? How do you know the observation you make is not tainted by your perception and interpretation?

The brain is constantly judging new information against what it already "knows." Thus what we perceive is influenced by what we already believe. How many times have you heard someone present a piece of data and found yourself expressing doubt? For example, "I saw a UFO last night." "I don't believe that." "I saw something last night that had red flashing lights." "You might have seen something with red flashing lights, but it wasn't a UFO!" Why would you say that? Because you think you already know the answer. Randy Moore, editor of *American Biology Teacher*, stated a few years ago, "Millions of people believe in UFOs from outer space ... I've seen many UFOs, but have never suspected that any are from outer space" ("Debunking the Paranormal," 4-9). This expression of disbelief brings to mind an observation by Francis Bacon on the subject of seeing and believing: "They are ill discoverers that think there is no land when they can see nothing but sea ... the inquisition of man is not competent to find out *essential forms* or *true differences*" (*Philosophical Works*, 94).

When scientists collect data and publish them, the entire scientific community is invited to interpret them. An individual scientist may be the only one who actually made the observation. Those observations are reported and interpreted. Will other scientists believe them? What if the scientist was Gregor Mendel, the monk who discovered the first basic laws of genetics. If that scientist was Mendel, counting peas and publishing his data, are you going to believe those data or not? Mendel's observations laid the foundation for an entire field of research. However, as Mendel was out in his pea patch collecting data, he was also apparently throwing out a few wrinkled or smooth peas that did not fit his hypothesis. Modern statisticians have concluded that his data fit his predictions too well. What Mendel apparently did not know was that data cannot be perfect. Data tend to fit predictions, but if the data fit the predictions too closely, something is probably wrong.

However, this is an interpretation too. Mendel may have been completely honest out in the garden, and the statisticians may be wrong. We were not there to see if Mendel was throwing away peas. We only have the data of modern statisticians and their interpretation, which suggests that Mendel could not have gotten as close as he did to his predicted ratios without fudging. Because we cannot necessarily trust the collection of data, even by a monk, science must rely on independent confirmation until the results become unquestionable, as is the case with the gene theory.

Let us look at some other famous experiments and see what they tell us about data and interpretation. A person can drop an apple from an outstretched hand to the floor and observe the apple fall. (We use an apple in this demonstration to honor Isaac Newton, who discovered the law of gravity.) To the person watching, the apple's falling is a fact, a piece of data. The apple can be dropped in the presence of thousands of people and the demonstration can be repeated any number of times. Now that we have these data (that all the apples observed fell when dropped), we can record the observations and publish the data. Now we look for an explanation of the data. Why did the apple fall? Gravity. What is gravity? Is gravity data or interpretation? Is it a theory or a law? In *Webster's Encyclopedic Unabridged Dictionary,* gravity is listed both as a law *and* a theory.

What is gravity? It is an attractive force between two objects. Where are the data that support that notion? You can *see* the apple fall but you cannot *see* gravity. To say that there is an attractive force pulling on the apple is interpretation. If two objects attract each other (the apple and the earth), then should not the earth also move? The idea that the earth is larger and therefore does not appreciably move is an interpretation.

Perhaps the most famous experiment relative to gravity was performed by Galileo who dropped two balls of different mass from atop the Tower of Pisa. We can repeat that experiment. What if we drop two golf balls of identical diameter, one filled with air and one solid? If we drop them both at the same time, what will happen? Which will hit the ground first? Surprisingly, the solid ball lands first. It is not supposed to do that. The two balls are supposed to land at the same time. That is what Galileo observed. Galileo leaned over the Tower of Pisa and showed that two objects of the same size, irrespective of mass, fall at the same rate.

You know what is really interesting about that famous experiment? It never happened. From the time we were in kindergarten, we were told about that experiment that Galileo performed over the leaning tower. We have even seen drawings of the famous experiment. In reality, the experiment must be performed in a vacuum in order to eliminate all air resistance. It is unlikely that the people of Pisa could have put the whole tower, Galileo, and the balls into a vacuum. It was a thought experiment. Thought experiments do not require as much funding as actual experiments. Of course they are based on mathematical calculations, which can be repeated and verified any number of times. Mathematical equations can also be separately tested and verified.

Nonetheless, what does Galileo's thought experiment tell us about the nature of scientific studies? What is the difference between Galileo's experiment with the imaginary balls at the Tower of Pisa and Alma's experiment with the word and the seed? Because we are unable to travel into the deepest reaches of space and, at present, cannot even see into the deepest reaches of space, experiments about things such as black holes are also thought experiments. With such experiments, science and faith may not seem that far apart. Even though thought experiments are based on mathematical verification, they are also based on assumptions, which may be flawed.

Let us consider another experiment concerning gravity. What do you predict will happen if a rock is dropped into a glass of water? It should sink, right? The experiment can be performed any number of times. What will happen if we use a straw to blow air into the bottom of the glass? What if we then strike a match in the air above the water? After performing these experiments, we can interpret them as follows: rock is heavier than water, which is heavier than air, which is heavier than fire. Based on this interpretation, we can predict that a rock or water will fall when placed in air or fire. According to Aristotle (384-322 B.C.E.), these were the four elements, the *only* four elements: earth, air, fire, and water. From the fourth century B.C.E. until the seventeenth century C.E., all objects in the universe were thought to be made of these four elements.

We have just established experimentally the physical relationship among the four elements which constitute Aristotle's material cause (see chap. 3). So much for Physics 101 in 350 B.C.E. Now, what about the chemical relationships? Each of the four elements can be connected by lines representing the four forces of the universe: warm, cold, wet, and dry. These constitute Aristotle's second cause, the forces of nature. The four elements can be transformed from one to another by one or more of the four forces. For example, water, when heated, becomes air. Air, when cooled, becomes water. Ice is even colder, having some characteristics of water and some of earth, but it also contains some air, which allows it to float on water. This was the basis for Chemistry 101 in 350 B.C.E.

We can next approach more advanced chemistry courses in 350 B.C.E. If we consider the motive cause in greater detail, we find that we can start pushing matter up or down the force lines between the elements. If we find two material objects that are similar to each other, they would lie next to each other along the force lines connecting the primary elements. All we have to do is fiddle with them, manipulate them, add the right amount of formative cause and we should be able to tweak them a little bit up or down one branch or another. Say we're considering something like lead, which is somewhere along the line between earth and water. If you heat it a little, it becomes liquid. Gold is on the same force line, right beside lead. Why couldn't you apply the right motive force and change lead to gold? Lead was so plentiful in the Middle Ages that people used it to roof their houses. Why not transform some of that cheap lead into expensive gold? This reasoning was the basis of alchemy.

Another important idea was that some transformations require seeds. One can plant a seed in the earth, add a little water and sunlight, and, in time, a plant forms out of the mixture of earth, water, and light. The type of plant that forms is specific to the type of seed planted, and the plant then yields more seed. Therefore, following the same reasoning, why not take a little bit of gold, a seed, put it into some lead, and under the right conditions, grow more gold?

Now let's consider Cosmology 101 in 350 B.C.E. What logical conclusion about the universe can we draw from our experiment with earth, air, fire, and water? If heavy, earthy objects sink in water, what could you say about heavy objects in the entire universe? They will all be at the bottom of the universe, right? We can predict that water will be on top of land. That's easy to verify by observation; all you have to do is look at where lakes and oceans are located—they're on top of land. Sometimes you have to dig down to release trapped water and sometimes it comes out with a force trying to get out from under the ground. Where's the air? Around us, above the land and water. Where are the lights? Up in the sky. So everything's in order. The lights are the lightest, they're up at the top of the universe, the air is in the middle, the water's on top of the ground, which is at the bottom. Everything is perfectly fine. We have a well-ordered universe; no more explanation is needed.

However, Aristotle added a twist to this well-ordered universe. Based on his observations and reasoning, he concluded that the universe must be a sphere and that it goes out in all directions. This was an incredibly logical breakthrough on Aristotle's part. He concluded that in an open, non-confining universe, rather than all the heavy, earthy objects dropping to the bottom, all the heavy things will attract each other toward the center. All that solid matter will form a sphere, the earth, with water on the surface, air above, and lights in the sky. Aristotle had gone beyond the data to an ingenious interpretation of those data. His concept that the earth was the center of the universe was a logical concept; it was tight, and it was supported by an enormous amount of data.

Aristotle's description fit obvious everyday experiences. The earth, the heaviest object in the universe, is in the center, with water and air on the outside, and outside of the air, in the heavens, is where the lights, the stars and planets, are located. Beyond the stars, there is nothing, and there can be nothing because anything solid out there is now here, having been drawn to the earth in the center. When the light begins to dim in a star and cools, it becomes heavy and falls to the earth. Aristotle stated,

> There is not, nor do the facts allow there to be, any bodily mass beyond the heaven. The world in its entirety is made up of the whole sum of available matter ... and we may conclude that there is not now a plurality of worlds, nor has there been, nor could there be. This world is one, solitary, and complete. It is clear in addition that there is neither place nor void ... beyond the heaven ... void is defined as that which, although at present not containing body, can contain it ... [the earth's] shape must be spherical ... if particles are moving from all sides alike toward one point, the center, the resulting mass must be similar on all sides ... (*On the Heavens*, 91.)

Claudius Ptolemaeus (better known to us as Ptolemy, 127-151 C.E.), a Greek mathematician, astronomer, and geographer, greatly solidified Aristotle's theory of the universe. He confirmed that the earth was indeed spherical and even managed to approximate its circumference, although somewhat inaccurately.

How different is the Ptolemaic theory of the universe from the model we employ today? Newton had the same concept as Aristotle and Ptolemy: gravity is the tendency for solid objects or earthly things to attract each other. So all solid matter *should* come together in the center of the universe. What's the problem? The problem is the enormity of space. Neither Aristotle nor Ptolemy had any idea how enormous the universe actually is. The stars and planets are like dust particles when compared to the immensity of space. Carl Sagan stated, "If we were randomly inserted into the Cosmos, the chance that we would find ourselves on or near a planet would be less than one in a billion trillion trillion ($10^{33}$, a one followed by thirty-three zeros)" (*Cosmos*, 5). As a result of these great distances, the forces of gravitational attraction are overcome between the stars and planets, and there are multiple, relatively tiny gravitational foci in the immense universe. The modern data also suggest that the known universe is expanding, the galaxies moving apart by a great force that counteracts gravity.

Aristotle's universe was nowhere near big enough, and, as a

result, his model did not include the concept that there could be multiple foci for the accumulation of solid matter. This never occurred to Aristotle or anyone afterward for 2,000 years, during which time the earth was comfortably the center of the universe. Aristotle and Ptolemy had their model nailed down solidly. They had the data and a solid interpretation. Given the data they had at their command, no one could have done better. The amazing thing is that, although most people today consider the Ptolemaic universe to be completely wrong, it was not that far off. If we change one concept, that of a single focal point, to the concept of multiple points, the Ptolemaic universe becomes the modern universe. If we consider some aspects of the Big Bang theory, such as the notion that at the beginning of the universe all matter was condensed into one place in the center, the Aristotelian universe *is* the modern universe, only the central mass was misidentified.

During the Middle Ages, the physical arrangement of the four elements was retained, even though, in many cases, the notion that the earth was spherical was discarded and the idea resurfaced that heavy objects settled on the bottom of the universe. In the fourth century C.E., Lactantius referred to the absurdity of a region on a spherical earth where people would hang head down, while the Bishop of Gabala argued that the heavens are not a sphere, but a tent or tabernacle, because "It is He ... that stretched out the heavens as a curtain, and spreadeth them out as a tent to dwell in" (Isa. 40:22). He also argued that the earth is flat because "the sun was risen upon the earth when Lot entered into Zoar" (Gen. 19:23).

Aristotle's concept of the universe was also expanded to include devils and angels. Dante (1265-1321), in his *Divine Comedy,* argued that "The lightest and most holy things went up into heaven, whereas heavy, vile things went to the center; the very center is the place of the Devil and his legions." Even today many people retain this concept of heaven and hell. This model of the universe agreed with both religious and scientific views. The only debate was if the earth was round or flat. By the time of Columbus, almost everyone had concluded that the earth was round. No one debated if the earth was the center of the universe: that was a given. Only the shape was debated.

The whole universe was very orderly, and everyone was quite comfortable. Science and religion were in general agreement.

Then came Nicolaus Copernicus (1473-1543), whose observations and hypotheses upset the whole apple cart. He proposed that the earth was not the center of the universe, but that it orbited the sun. By the early sixteenth century, the movements of the known planets had been thoroughly described. The planets (a name meaning wanderer) appeared to follow zig-zag paths across the constellations. In order for the planets to orbit the earth, a complex series of orbits was required to explain their observed movements. Copernicus proposed that if all the planets and the earth revolved about the sun in concentric orbits, the observed movements become easily explainable.

Few people believed what Copernicus had to say. They already had all the data they needed and the data were explained very well by the Ptolemaic universe. Furthermore, the prevailing interpretation of the scriptures confirmed the Ptolemaic model, and Dante filled in what the scriptures seemingly had not covered. Everything was comfortable. Why rock the boat? The great Protestant reformer, Martin Luther, said of Copernicus, "The fool will turn the whole science of Astronomy upside down. But as Holy writ declares, it was the Sun and not the Earth which Joshua commanded to stand still" (Ronan, *Galileo*, 29). Most Catholic authorities took little official notice of the Copernican theory, dismissing it as a passing fad, but Copernicus' influence spread to other inquisitive minds, among them Tycho, Kepler, and Galileo.

Nearly 100 years after Copernicus, Galileo Galilei (1564-1642) turned his newly developed telescope to the heavens in 1609 and began to collect new data. To his amazement, Galileo discovered that the dark areas on the moon, previously thought to be merely variations in light intensity, were actually pits and craters, valleys and mountains. These features on the moon cast shadows, as though they were made of earth, not light! How could a body of light exhibit features of solid matter? When Galileo turned his telescope toward Jupiter, he made an even more startling discovery. Jupiter had moons! How could Jupiter have satellites if the earth was the center of the universe? The only logical interpretation was that Copernicus was correct: the sun, not the earth, was the center of the universe.

Galileo's interpretation of what he saw went against religion, it went against science, it went against logic, it went against everything that most people considered holy. What happened to Galileo because of his marvelous observations, his brilliant conclusions? Everyone was up in arms; the scientists and theologians wanted his head. Cardinal Bellarmine cautioned: "To affirm that the sun is really fixed in the center of the heavens and that the earth is situated in the third sphere and revolves very swiftly around the sun is a very dangerous thing, not only by irritating all the theologians and scholastic philosophers, but also by injuring our holy faith and making the sacred scriptures false" (Gingrich, "The Galileo Affair," 137). Galileo, a devout Catholic, stated, "Though scriptures cannot err, its expounders and interpreters are liable to err in many ways. ... Those natural effects which the experience of the senses places before our eyes ... are in no wise to be revoked because of certain passages in scripture, which may be turned and twisted into a thousand different meanings" (Brodrick, *Galileo, the Man, His Works, His Misfortunes*, 76-77). In spite of Galileo's observation, the Catholic church, under the Inquisition, threatened him with excommunication unless he retracted his opinions. He complied, but in so doing might have mused, "If the Vicar of Christ insists that I must not affirm what I happen to know, I have to obey ... [but] not even God can prevent my reason from seeing what it sees" (Santillana, *Crime of Galileo*, 322).

Of course, with Galileo's retraction, the issue did not go away. In fact, the controversy continued to rage for years. As more and more scientists turned their telescopes to the sky and made the same observations and more, they began to conclude that the only explanation was the one advanced by Copernicus and Galileo. The Copernican revolution swept through science, changing it forever. The theologians followed more slowly. They had not made the same observations as the scientists. Their interpretation of theology strongly favored an earth-centered universe. The Catholic church did not admit its error in threatening Galileo with excommunication for over 350 years. In 1992 Pope John Paul II declared that the church had been wrong in condemning Galileo. (As an interesting side note, a recent survey of scientific literacy in the United States found that "27 percent of adult Americans still believe the Sun revolves around the Earth, rather than the other way around" ["Ask Marilyn," 16].)

The pope said he did not want to wait so long in the case of Darwin. He stated in a letter to the Pontifical Academy of Sciences in 1996 that evolution is fully compatible with Christian faith. He stated that the Catholic church accepts evolution as a theory well-supported by research in a variety of scientific fields and that there was meaning in the fact that several scientific disciplines had come up with evidence of evolution independent of one another. The pope said that it is in the church's interest to develop its scientific knowledge. Speaking of the scientific method, the pope stated, "A theory proves its validity with the degree to which it submits to verification. It is constantly measured by the accumulation of facts. Where it ceases to be able to account for these facts, it shows its limits and its inability to be adapted. It must therefore be reconsidered." The pope then stated that the scientific method cannot be applied to spiritual matters, and the spiritual aspect of human life cannot be explained scientifically (see Weil, "Pope: Church accepts evolution as well-supported scientific theory," 2; Sheler, "The Pope and Darwin," www.usnews.com/ usnews/issue/4evol.htm).

The Copernican revolution began over 400 years ago. Today no educated person believes that the earth is the center of the universe. In 1969 Neil Armstrong stepped onto the surface of the moon, confirming, once and for all, Galileo's conclusion that the moon is a solid heavenly body. The scriptures have not changed, but our interpretation of them has. Henry Eyring said of Galileo and the apparent controversy between science and the scriptures, "When the smoke of battle cleared away and men looked at matters calmly, it became apparent that nothing essential had been lost. A lot of human philosophy disappeared, but it turned out to be unnecessary" (*Faith of a Scientist,* 63). This profound change in our concept of the universe came about because of the accumulation of scientific evidence. No matter how strongly established a paradigm or model may be in science or religion, new and accumulating scientific data compel us, from time to time, to change our thinking and world views. Galileo's sage advice should remain our watchword. It is "the better part of wisdom not to ... apply passages of scripture in such a way as to force them to support, as true, conclusions concerning nature, the contrary of which may afterwards be revealed by our senses."

# 6.
# What About Darwin?

Charles Darwin introduced his theory of evolution by natural selection through the publication of his book *On the Origin of Species by Means of Natural Selection or the Preservation of Races in the Struggle for Life* in 1859. His book ignited a storm of controversy much like that started by Galileo's observations of the solar system 200 years earlier. Like Galileo, Darwin made observations and then drew conclusions, but unlike Galileo, whose observations confirmed an existing theory proposed by Copernicus, Darwin's theory was new. Most scientists consider Darwin's to be brilliant deductions from the data collected. His conclusions began with simple steps and expanded to include all living things on the planet. The development of Darwin's theory, from very simple to more expansive, closely resembles the development of the law of gravity by Isaac Newton, who also drew expansive conclusions from simple beginnings.

Newton's formal education was interrupted for two years when the plague forced Trinity College in Cambridge to close. During those two years, he lived at home and spent considerable time in his mother's garden with little more to do than think. He pondered many issues, such as what causes apples to drop from trees to the ground.

The thing that is interesting about Newton's questions is that millions of people see fruit fall from trees and other such phenomena during their lives, but usually think nothing about it. He began with the simple question of why does fruit fall from trees, and expanded his thoughts to include the entire universe. He asked: "At what speed is the apple falling at any given moment?" and "What if the tree were five times as tall? How would that affect the speed of the apple?" In order to address these and other questions, he invented calculus. "What if the tree was on a high mountain? What if the tree was as high as the moon? Why is the moon, like an apple, not falling to the ground?" Today, because of Newton's questions in his mother's garden, we are able to orbit space stations around the Earth and send expeditions to Mars and beyond.

When Charles Darwin sailed on the *Beagle*, he was not much of a biologist. He had not been trained in biology at the major centers of learning of the day. However, much like Newton, he did not let apples fall unnoticed. As he found new biological curiosities, he was led to ask why. Why is there a fossil skeleton of an animal, near the beach in Brazil, which no longer exists as a living species? Why are there bird species on the Galapagos that exist nowhere else in the world? Not being extensively trained in biology, Darwin did not have pat answers to these questions. He had not been taught the conventional wisdom of the day. As a result, he had to think through the possible answers in his own mind.

The captain of the *Beagle* had hopes of finding evidence for establishing the site of the Garden of Eden on their voyage. He had a ready answer to Darwin's questions: "That's the way God made it." End of discussion. Stating that God made the earth and everything on it, and that no more questions need be asked, is the type of answer that stifled the progress of science through the Middle Ages. Unfortunately, even in Darwin's day, some people held to that answer. Yet faithful scientists then, as now, believe that God *did* make the earth but that we can, in some small degree, understand the mechanisms of that creation.

Again, Darwin's approach to scientific reasoning was much like that of Newton concerning the law of gravity. Newton did not doubt that God was the author of the law of gravity. He simply asked how it works. The easy answer for a strict "biblical literalist" is that God made it that way. As true as that answer is, it is not satisfactory scientifically; it simply appeals to the final cause and does not explain the laws and principles by which nature functions. Newton believed that even though God made gravity, we can discover how it works. Likewise with Darwin. God may have placed unique species of birds on the Galapagos for his own amusement, but Darwin believed he could discover, as a scientist, how such a feat was accomplished.

In order to better understand the theory of evolution by natural selection, it is important to understand what Darwin actually said in developing the theory. Most people today, scientists as well as non-scientists, have not read the text of *The Origin of Species*. It is important to understand that Darwin, in *The Origin*, follows a logical progression of data and interpretation of them. It is important to read his descriptions of the data he collected and his interpretations of them. As you read what Darwin said and the conclusions he drew, ask yourself, "Is there some alternative interpretation, and can I formulate such an alternative interpretation?"

Darwin states in his introduction to *The Origin*, "When on the H.M.S. 'Beagle' ... I was much struck with certain facts in the distribution of the organic beings inhabiting South America. ... These facts ... seemed to throw some light on the origin of species—that mystery of mysteries. ... On my return home, it occurred to me, in 1837, that something might perhaps be made out on this question by patiently accumulating and reflecting on all sorts of facts which could possibly have any bearing on it" (*Origin of Species* [1872], 11; the first edition was published in 1859). Darwin had observed certain facts which led him to draw certain conclusions. He continues, "In considering the Origin of Species ... a naturalist, reflecting on the mutual affinities of organic beings, on their embryological relations, their geographical distribution, geological succession, and other such facts, might come to the conclusion that species had not been independently created, but had descended, like varieties, from other species. ... I am fully convinced that species are not immutable; but ... are lineal descendants of some other and generally extinct species."

## Variation Under Domestication

Darwin devotes the first chapter of his book to issues familiar to almost everyone in the nineteenth century: variations among domestic animals. Most people living at his time had seen for themselves examples similar to those presented in his book. He begins his book by stating, "When we compare the individuals of the same variety or sub-variety of our older cultivated plants and animals, one of the first points which strikes us is, that they generally differ more from each other than do the individuals of any one species or variety in a state of nature ... we are driven to conclude that this great variability is due to our domestic productions having been raised under conditions of life not so uniform as, and somewhat different from, those to which the parent species had been exposed under nature." The data that Darwin presents here are that we see more variation in domestic plants and animals than in similar wild populations. For example, it is well known, even today, that wild roses are quite limited in color range, as well as in size and shape. However, because of the extensive work of rose gardeners, there is now a wide range of color, size, and shape among domestic varieties. He attributes this greater variation in domestic species to less uniform living conditions. This appears to be a fairly straightforward observation and a reasonable interpretation.

For his own research on domestic animals, Darwin chose pigeons. He states, "Believing that it is always best to study some special group, I have, after deliberation, taken up domestic pigeons. I have kept every breed which I could purchase or obtain." He proposes, "Each of the endless variations which we see in the plumage of our fowls must have had some efficient cause. ... Some authors ... believe that every race which breeds true ... has had its wild prototype ... I have never met a pigeon, or poultry, or duck, or rabbit fancier, who was not fully convinced that each main breed was descended from a distinct species. ... From ... several reasons, namely,—the improbability of man having formerly made seven or eight supposed species of pigeons to breed freely under domestication;—these supposed species being quite unknown in a wild state ... though so like the rock-pigeon in most respects; —the occasional re-appearance of the blue colour and various black marks in all the breeds ... and lastly, the mongrel offspring being perfectly fertile; —from these several reasons taken together, we may safely conclude that all our domestic breeds are descended from the rock-pigeon." These passages are interesting to consider today, because there are probably few people who do not recognize that varieties are all related under one species and are all derived from a common ancestor. In this regard, our concept of species has changed considerably over the past 140 years.

Darwin continues, "Let us now briefly consider the steps by which domestic races have been produced. ... The key is man's power of accumulative selection: nature gives successive variations; man adds them up in certain directions useful to him. The great power of this principle of selection is not hypothetical. It is certain that several of our eminent breeders have, even within a single lifetime, modified to a large extent their breeds of cattle and sheep." Anyone who has grown up on a farm, or has raised a garden, is well acquainted with this concept. Darwin says that only 1/1000 people are good breeders, because of their skill in the "accumulation in one direction, during successive generations, of differences absolutely inappreciable by an uneducated eye. ... We have proofs ... in several cases in which exact records have been kept; thus, to give a very trifling instance, the steadily increasing size of the common gooseberry may be quoted. [Furthermore,] ... trying to possess and breed from the best individual animals ... a man who intends keeping pointers naturally tries to get as good dogs as he can, and afterwards breeds from his own best dogs. ... This process ... would improve and modify any breed."

Darwin then presents a specific example from his own experience: "two flocks of Leicester sheep kept by Mr. Buckley and Mr. Burgess, as Mr. Youatt remarks, have been purely bred from the original stock of Mr. Bakewell for upwards of fifty years. There is not a suspicion existing in the mind of any one at all acquainted with the subject, that the owner of either of them has deviated in any one instance from the pure blood of Mr. Bakewell's flock, and yet the difference between the sheep possessed by these two gentlemen is so great that they have the appearance of being quite different varieties."

He continues, "The pear, though cultivated in classical times, appears from Pliny's description, to have been a fruit of very inferior quality. ... [The art of raising better quality pears] has consisted in always cultivating the best-known variety, sowing its seeds, and, when a slightly better variety chanced to appear, selecting it, and so onwards." Numerous additional examples could be added from modern plant and animal breeders.

Darwin adds a note concerning animal breeders: "He can never act by selection, excepting on variations which are first given to him in some slight degree by nature. No man would ever try to make a fantail [pigeon] till he saw a pigeon with a tail developed in some slight degree in an unusual manner."

Another point that Darwin makes in the first chapter of his book is the concept that there are often more visible differences between varieties within a species than there are between different species. He says, "When we look to the hereditary varieties or races of our domestic animals and plants, ... we generally perceive ... less uniformity of character than in true species." In other words, if we consider a variety to be a less rigid taxonomic division than a species, why do we see greater variability between varieties than between species? Darwin concludes his first chapter by stating, "Over all these causes of Change, the accumulative action of Selection ... seems to have been the predominant Power."

This is the essence of Darwin's first chapter in *The Origin*, his major point being that variation occurs naturally in plants and animals and that breeders can *select* for those characteristics they are interested in perpetuating within a given variety. As a result of this *artificial selection*, varieties become different from each other. Sometimes those differences become so extreme that there appears to be a greater difference between varieties than between species. None of the ideas presented in this chapter raises concerns for most modern readers.

### Variation Under Nature

In his second chapter, Darwin explains that, just as we observe variation in domestic plants and animals, there are also variations in wild plants and animals. He writes, "No one supposes that all the individuals of the same species are cast in the same actual mold. These individual differences ... thus afford materials for natural selection to act on and accumulate, in the same manner as man accumulates in any given direction individual differences in his domestic productions." He once more emphasizes, "I was much struck how entirely vague and arbitrary is the distinction between species and varieties. ... The term species ... comes to be a mere useless abstraction. ... I look at the term species as one arbitrarily given ... that it does not essentially differ from the term variety. ... The term variety, again, in comparison with mere individual differences, is also applied arbitrarily."

Even today modern biologists have some difficulty defining the term *species*. A species is often explained in terms of reproductive success of *natural* matings. For example, a dog and wolf can successfully reproduce, but they are still considered separate species because they do not *normally* interbreed. The problem of variety and species may also be emphasized by the example of dogs and wolves. A German shepherd can be successfully mated with a wolf, which is a different species, and their offspring are capable of reproducing. (This case is different from crossing a donkey and a horse to produce a hybrid mule, which cannot reproduce because of differences in horse and donkey chromosomes.) On the other hand, due to physical limitations as the result of size differences, a German shepherd and chihuahua, which are varieties within the same species, *normally* cannot successfully breed. If the wolf and dog are different species, then why are the German shepherd and chihuahua not separate species?

Darwin then takes the concept of merging varieties and species a bit farther: "I look at varieties ... as steps towards more strongly-marked and permanent varieties; and at the latter, as leading to sub-species, and then to species. ... The more important and adaptive characters ... may be safely attributed to the cumulative action of natural selection." For example, if the German shepherd and chihuahua are currently varieties, at what point should we consider them sub-species, or species? Darwin then observes, "If we look at each species as a special act of creation, there is no apparent reason why more varieties should occur in a group having many species, than in one having few. ... My tables [of plants and coleopterous insects] clearly show ... wherever many species of a genus have been formed, the species of that genus present a number of varieties."

In this chapter, then, Darwin emphasizes that variation is a natural phenomenon. Where you see a lot of variation in the species of a genus, you also see a lot more variation in the varieties. In general with fewer species, where there is less variation, each species also has less variation in that there are fewer varieties. Darwin proposes that this concept of variation follows some as yet undiscovered law of variation, and does not seem to fit the notion that each species was created independently. If each species were created separately, what about varieties? Were wolves and dogs created as two different species? Should they be considered as separate species or should they be reclassified into one species? What about German shepherds and chihuahuas? Should they be considered varieties or separate species? According to the Bible, each plant and animal was to breed after its *kind*. The term *kind*, as used in Genesis, differs considerably among animal groups (see Gen. 1:20-26): *fowl* is a modern class distinction, *great whales* is a suborder designation, *cattle* is a genus distinction, *creeping thing* is probably a kingdom designation, and *man* is a species designation.

This information suggests that it is probably unproductive to attempt to equate the term *kind* in the Bible with any scientific designation such as *species*. Rather, the term *kind* may simply be an expression of the universal observation that, allowing for slight variation, plants and animals generally produce offspring that appear similar to themselves; there is continuity from generation to generation. This concept is not different from that presented in evolutionary theory. The difference is if the slight variation is considered trivial, as was the case with scientists before Darwin, or if the slight variation is considered to be the stuff of evolutionary change, which Darwin's proposal advanced. Darwin's point in this chapter is that these slight variations, given enough time in selective breeding, can produce substantial changes in plants and animals.

**Struggle for Existence**

In chapter 3, Darwin describes what he calls "the struggle for life. Owing to this struggle, variations, however slight and from whatever cause proceeding, if they be in any degree profitable to the individuals of the species ... will tend to the preservation of such individuals, and will generally be inherited by the offspring. The offspring also will thus have a better chance of surviving, for, of the many individuals of any species which are periodically born, but a small number can survive. I have called this principle, by which each slight variation, if useful, is preserved, by the term Natural Selection, in order to mark its relation to man's power of selection [artificial selection]. But the expression often used by Mr. Herbert Spencer of the Survival of the Fittest is more accurate." Here, Darwin formally introduces the term *Natural Selection.* This is the great unifying theory for which Darwin became so famous, or infamous, depending on the judge. This is the term that has linked his name inextricably with evolution. He did not coin the term evolution. He did not invent the idea of evolution—the idea existed long before Darwin was born—but he did develop a theory that made it possible, for the first time, for biologists to understand a *mechanism* by which evolution could occur. Note also that the term "Survival of the Fittest," also often ascribed to Darwin, is here, correctly, attributed to Herbert Spencer.

In this chapter, Darwin brings all the ideas leading to his "Theory of Natural Selection" together. First, there is variation among plants and animals. Second, by artificial or natural means, certain traits can be selected. Third, because of the struggle for life, not all the offspring of a given plant or animal will survive. Therefore, any trait resulting from natural variation that gives one plant or animal an advantage over another will be naturally selected for. That, in a nutshell, is Darwin's theory. The rest of *The Origin* is devoted to evidence pertaining to the theory. Had the implications of his theory not encompassed the human species as well, it is doubtful that such a simple, logical, elegant theory would have become such a source of commotion and contention.

## Natural Selection; or, Survival of the Fittest

In chapter 4, Darwin restates and expands on the ideas presented in the first three chapters. He states:

> that if variations occur, can we doubt (remembering that many more in-
> dividuals are born than can possibly survive) that individuals having
> any advantage, however slight, over others, would have the best chance
> of surviving and of procreating their kind? ... This preservation of favor-
> able individual differences and variations, and the destruction of those
> which are injurious, I have called Natural Selection, or the Survival of
> the Fittest. ... It has been said that I speak of natural selection as an ac-
> tive power or Deity; but who objects to an author speaking of the attrac-
> tion of gravity as ruling the movements of the planets? ... Natural selec-
> tion acts only by the preservation and accumulation of small inherited
> modifications. ... Unless favorable variations be inherited by some at
> least of the offspring, nothing can be effected by natural selection. ...
> Isolation ... is an important element in the modification of species
> through natural selection ... Natural selection acts slowly through the
> preservation of variations ... species which are most numerous in indi-
> viduals have the best chance of producing favorable variations within
> any given period.

Darwin continues to compare natural and artificial selection throughout this chapter. He also points out that natural selection should involve the displacement of one variety or species by another that is more fit. He gives a historical example from his native England: "In Yorkshire, it is historically known that the ancient black cattle were displaced by the long-horns, and that these 'were swept away by the short-horns' (I quote the words of an agricultural writer) 'as if by some murderous pestilence.'"

## Laws of Variation

In chapter 5, Darwin attempts to describe the basis of natural variation, which is the basis of selection. Unfortunately, even though there is evidence that Darwin read Gregor Mendel's work on genetics (a copy of Mendel's paper exists in Darwin's library, with notes in his handwriting in the margin), he apparently did not realize its im-portance to his theory. As a result, Darwin was frustrated his entire life that he was unable to discover the basis of variation. He says, "I have hitherto sometimes spoken as if the variations ... were due to chance. This, of course, is a wholly incorrect expression, but it serves to acknowledge plainly our ignorance of the cause of each particular variation." Little did he know that mutation, the basis of variation, *is* random (the idea that mutation is random but is buffered by non-random limits is discussed in chap. 12). Darwin also notes, "A tendency to vary, due to causes of which we are quite ignorant." The later rediscovery, in the early part of the twentieth century, of Mendel's work on genetics (which, even though contemporary with Darwin's work, was not appreciated by *anyone*, and was not "discovered" until years later) and of the concept of mutation by H. J. Muller allowed modern biologists to fill in this missing link in Darwin's theory. The discoveries contributed significantly to the development of what has been called neo-Darwinism, or the Modern Synthesis. The Modern Synthesis, which completes the succession of variation, selection, and survival, has provided a powerful means of understanding all aspects of biology. As Theodosius Dobzhansky stated, "Nothing in biology makes sense except in the light of evolution" (*American Biology Teacher*, 125-29).

## Difficulties and Objections

As the titles of chapters 6 and 7 suggest, Darwin here addresses some shortcomings of his theory. He states, "Long before the reader has arrived at this part of my work, a crowd of difficulties will have occurred to him. Some of them are so serious that to this day I can hardly reflect on them without being in some degree staggered; but, to the best of my judgement, the greater number are only apparent, and those that are real are not, I think, fatal to the theory. ... First, why ... do we not everywhere see innumerable transitional forms?" This issue was a challenge to the theory for many years after Darwin first raised it. One of the major problems in addressing transitional forms is that neither Darwin nor anyone else at the time could realize how many extinct species there actually are in the fossil record. Some of the most important missing transitional forms, which were initially raised as a challenge to evolution theory, have only recently been discovered in the fossil record (many within the past ten to twenty years). Those recently discovered fossils, including so-called "missing links," were predicted by the theory of evolution, and stand as strong supports to the validity of the theory. This fossil evidence will be discussed in chapter 10.

Darwin lists additional issues: "Secondly, is it possible that an animal having, for instance, the structure and habits of a bat could have been formed by the modification of some other animal with widely different habits and structure?" Opponents of the theory of evolution still use this argument. Their claim is that it is impossible for all the characteristics of an animal such as a bat to have evolved simultaneously. This is based on the unfounded notion that each characteristic of a given plant or animal is the result of a separate, *independently functioning* gene or set of genes. Modern research is beginning to reveal that a number of characteristics originally thought to be independent are governed by developmental constraint and are actually closely inter-related (see chap. 12).

"Thirdly, can instincts be acquired and modified through natural selection?" We have learned an enormous amount about the inheritance of instinct and behavior since the time of Darwin, when virtually nothing was known on the subject. We now know that many instincts are inherited just like any other biologic characteristic. It has been recently demonstrated that instinctive behavior can be "transplanted" from an embryo of one species to that of another by simply grafting a few brain cells from one to the other (see Balaban, "Changes in multiple brain regions ...," 2001-2006).

"Fourthly, how can we account for species, when crossed, being sterile and producing sterile offspring whereas, when varieties are crossed, their fertility is unimpaired?" Once more, with the discovery of genetics, many of these issues have been resolved. Darwin knew nothing of chromosomes, which are the structures within the cell nucleus containing the genes. T. H. Morgan discovered in the 1920s that genes are associated with chromosomes. During most cell divisions, the chromosomes double in number and then half of them become associated with each new cell. Animals of different species often have different numbers of chromosomes, so that the offspring of matings between two species do not receive a balanced set. This imbalance is usually lethal because, during cell division, an unequal number of chromosomes associates with the daughter cells. However, some exciting questions associated with Darwin's original question still remain unanswered. For example, it is clear why missing a given chromosome would prove lethal, because of critical missing genes, but it is not as clear why having an extra one is also usually lethal, or at least debilitating. It is also not clear why the chromosome number is fixed in some species, with one extra or one missing being lethal, whereas in other species there may be a difference of up to twelve chromosomes between races within the species (see Sites, "Cytonuclear genetic structure of a hybrid zone ...," 379-92). (This topic will be discussed in more detail later in the book.)

Most of the problems with evolution that Darwin and others pondered in the nineteenth century have been addressed by the Modern Synthesis. However, other questions remain and new ones have been raised. Many of these are being confronted by current research (see chap. 12), and others remain for future research. Such is the nature of science. There are plenty of new (or even old), exciting questions left for future generations of scientists to address.

### Chapters 8, 9, and 10

In the latter half of chapter 7, and in the next three chapters, Darwin presents a range of odd and unusual forms and functions in biology. Although we do not have space to discuss them here, they are a delight to read and ponder. In these chapters he exhibits the patience, perseverance, attention to detail, and powers of perception that make a scientist great. He was driven to collect numerous examples from nature to test and support his theory. Many of those examples are presented in these chapters.

### On the Geological Succession of Organic Beings

Darwin states in chapter 11 that "all the chief laws of paleontology plainly proclaim ... that species have been produced by ordinary generation: old forms having been supplanted by new and improved forms, the products of Variation and the Survival of the Fittest." The body of evidence in support of this statement has grown by several orders of magnitude since Darwin. One of the greatest strengths of a scientific theory is its power of prediction. The theory of evolution by natural selection accurately predicted the results obtained over the past 140 years from geology and paleontology. Furthermore, Darwin's theory even predicted the results from fields of research unimagined in the nineteenth century. All that has been discovered in the relatively new field of molecular biology was predicted and anticipated by Darwin's simple yet elegant theory (see chap. 7).

## Geographical Distribution

Perhaps the most compelling evidence supporting Darwin's theory is the geographical distribution of species, as discussed in his chapter 12. The best place to study this topic is on an archipelago (a series of islands). The Galapagos Archipelago is inextricably connected with the memory of Charles Darwin. It stands out as the major source of inspiration in the development of his theory. Darwin states,

> The most striking and important fact for us is the affinity of the species which inhabit islands to those of the nearest mainland, without being actually the same. Numerous instances could be given. The Galapagos Archipelago ... lies at a distance of between 500 and 600 miles from the shores of South America. Here almost every product of the land and of the water bears the unmistakable stamp of the American continent. There are twenty-six land-birds; of these, twenty-one, or perhaps twenty-three are ranked as distinct species, and would commonly be assumed to have been here created; yet the close affinity of most of these birds to American species is manifest in every character, in their habits, gestures, and tones of voice ... Why should this be? Why should the species which are supposed to have been created in the Galapagos Archipelago, and nowhere else, bear so plainly the stamp of affinity to those created in America? There is nothing in the conditions of life, in the geological nature of the islands, in their height or climate ... which closely resembles the conditions of the South American coast: in fact, there is a considerable dissimilarity in all these respects. On the other hand, there is a considerable degree of resemblance ... between the Galapagos and the Cape Verde Archipelagoes: but what an entire and

absolute difference in their inhabitants! The inhabitants of the Cape
Verde Islands are related to those of Africa, like those of the Galapagos
to America.

Here is a masterful example of the geographic distribution of animals presented as a test of Darwin's theory. If the Galapagos bird species had been created as an independent species on the islands, there
is no reason to expect them to be any more closely related to each
other or to bird species on nearby large land masses than to any other
birds in the world. However, as predicted by Darwin, if the Galapagos bird species evolved from one or a few species that arrived on
the islands from the mainland, then the Galapagos birds will be more
closely related to each other and to bird species of nearby South
America than to any other birds in the world. The data are entirely
consistent with the predictions. All the evidence collected by early
biologists, such as color patterns and behavior patterns, supported
the hypothesis that the Galapagos birds are related. Darwin's theory
of common descent predicted that when the techniques became
available to collect molecular data, they would demonstrate that
these birds are related in some specific pattern.

Only during the past fifteen to twenty years has the technology
existed to test the hypothesis of species relatedness of the Galapagos
birds. These techniques have allowed us to examine the sequence of
nucleotides that make up the DNA of the birds, as well as thousands
of other species in similar conditions. In each case where such an
analysis has been conducted, and there have been hundreds to date,
they all support Darwin's prediction in this case that the birds on the
Galapagos are related to each other and to those in western South
America. Furthermore, the analysis can demonstrate which species
are the oldest and which are the newest. The data are in close agreement with the older observations made by Darwin and others without the benefit of the newer technology. Molecular techniques have
been applied to thousands of species of plants and animals, and the
data all support the theory of evolution.

The fact that we can develop a scientific hypothesis that is predictive and can be tested suggests that there is no need to resort to

an explanation based on the supernatural to explain the species of finches on the Galapagos. As scientists with faith in God, we personally believe that God created the world but that he employed natural processes to do so, and that we can discover at least some of these.

Most biologists are aware that Darwin was not the only naturalist to develop the theory of natural selection. However, many people who are not directly involved in the biological sciences are not familiar with Alfred Russel Wallace, who independently deduced that change must occur through this process. Wallace wrote, "Every species has come into existence coincident both in time and space with a preexisting closely allied species." Wallace communicated his ideas to Darwin, who presented Wallace's paper, along with an abstract of his own book, to the Linnean Society in 1858. Darwin said of Wallace's work, compared to his own, "I never saw a more striking coincidence" (see "Alfred Russel Wallace," *Encyclopedia Britannica*, 19:530).

Wallace developed his theory while studying the plants and animals of the Malay Archipelago (Indonesia). No more dramatic differences exist anywhere in the world than in these islands. He described what has become known as Wallace's Line, a biological barrier between the islands of Bali and Lombok, only forty miles apart. The line separates two great faunas: one originating in Asia and spreading southeast, the other originating in Australia and spreading northwest. Apparently a deep ocean trench has always separated Bali from Lombok, even when low sea levels opened land bridges between other islands. Asian tigers never crossed the line from Asian Indonesia to Australian Indonesia, and kangaroos never crossed in the other direction. Likewise, *Homo erectus* (human-like primates), spreading out of Asia, were apparently never able to cross that line, but *Homo sapiens*, who mastered seafaring, were able to cross the forty-mile stretch of ocean, and still do on a regular basis (see Gore, "The Dawn of Humans: Expanding Worlds").

A third archipelago that has yielded dramatic data concerning geographic distribution is the Hawaiian Archipelago. There are at least 1,250 species of the "fruit fly" genus *Drosophila* throughout the world, and more than a third of them are found only in the Hawaiian Islands. In addition, there are about 300 species of the closely related genus *Scaptomyza* in Hawaii. Only a few species of *Scaptomyza* are found outside Hawaii. Furthermore, several species between *Scaptomyza* and *Drosophila* are found only in Hawaii. It is very difficult to determine in which genus these intermediate species belong. The 800 fly species belonging to the two Hawaiian fly genera are so closely related that scientists have proposed that they are all derived from a single ancestral species. Many of the Hawaiian *Drosophila* are very specialized to Hawaiian vegetation; they are highly selective in their choice of host plants where they lay their eggs. New islands have continually risen out of the ocean and have been invaded by *Drosophila* from the older islands. *Drosophila* species exist on the new islands that are found nowhere else (see *Biology*, 420-21). In a series of studies conducted in the 1960s and 1970s, H. L. Carson demonstrated that progression of new species of *Drosophila* from the older to the newer islands could be followed by examining changes in the banding patterns of their chromosomes. *Drosophila* chromosomes have distinctive dark and light stripes, which can be viewed as a "species fingerprint." Carson found that the differences in banding patterns between closely related species can consist of the deletion of certain bands, the addition of certain bands, or the inversion of banded regions (as though that region had been reversed end for end) (see "The genetics of speciation at the diploid level").

Darwin concluded his work by stating,

> It is interesting to contemplate a tangled bank, clothed with many plants of many kinds, with birds singing on the bushes, with various insects flitting about, and with worms crawling through the damp earth, and to reflect that these elaborately constructed forms, so different from each other, and dependent upon each other in so complex manner, have all been produced by laws acting around us. ... There is grandeur in this view of life, with its several powers, having been originally breathed by the Creator into a few forms or into one; and that, whilst this planet has gone cycling on according to the fixed law of gravity, from so simple a beginning endless forms most beautiful and most wonderful have been, and are being evolved.

Darwin followed a very logical progression in writing *The Origin of Species*. Beginning with variation and artificial selection, which can be seen all around us and which are undeniable, he progresses to natural selection and speciation. He presents numerous examples to support his theory, and it provides many predictions that can be tested. Darwin's logical progression is similar to Newton's in developing the theory of gravitation. So why are Newton's ideas not challenged to the extent that Darwin's are?

Newton's observing an apple falling from a tree and extending the concept of that observation out into the universe made certain predictions about the speed with which a satellite has to be launched to go into orbit. Darwin's observing artificial selection and extending it to the theory of natural selection made certain predictions about the relatedness of plants and animals that can be examined at the molecular level. Darwin could not have anticipated the molecular revolution that has occurred in biology over the last forty years, since the discovery of the double helix of DNA, any more than Newton could have predicted artificial satellites. Darwin did not even understand basic inheritance, let alone envision its molecular basis. Nonetheless, his theory predicts that given the gradual transition from varieties, to species, to genera, and so on, all of Nature is related. These predictions have been borne out in thousands of observations and experiments. Relatedness at the molecular level means that closely related plants and animals share common DNA sequences, that they have great similarity in the molecules of inheritance. (These similarities will be discussed in the next chapter.)

One perceived dilemma for a belief in God's hand in creation is that many scientists believe Darwin's theory suggests that the process of descent is essentially random. The prevailing scientific view, which has developed over the past 140 years, is that mutations (variations in genes) are more or less random. These random mutations are usually deleterious to the organisms in which they occur. However, largely because many genes are present in multiple copies, a relatively large number of mutations can occur in one or more copies of a given gene without affecting the normal function of other copies. Initially, the mutations in one copy make it non-functional.

However, a series of random mutations in that non-functional gene can occasionally result in a new gene with a new and unique function. The new gene may result in some change in the organism, which may be naturally selected for or against, according to Darwin's theory. The process of natural selection usually does not favor the change; it is selected against, the organism dies, and the new gene disappears. However, the new trait occasionally makes the organism more "fit"; the organism is then selected for, and the new gene is maintained.

This classic view of random mutation followed by natural selection has, for some scientists, eliminated the need for "direction" in the process of common descent. The idea that descent is random has been thought by many scientists to preclude the possibility of laws controlling the process. The preclusion of laws of control or direction seemingly eliminate the need for a law-giver—i.e., God. This notion that there is no need or even room for God in the process of evolution has seemingly placed it at odds with religion. One can argue that the "law of mutation" could be viewed as one of God's laws and the "law of natural selection" as another. One could also argue that natural selection is not a random process. However, it has appeared to many scientists over the past 140 years that there is enough randomness to eliminate the belief in an orderly creation. Without predictability, how could we be "created in the image of God"? Even most scientists who believe in God and who understand the weight of evidence supporting evolution have taken a "wait and see" attitude. The common belief among such scientists has been that God created the earth and everything on it, or that he created the laws and processes by which the earth and all its creatures came to be, and that evolution was the process by which the Creation occurred. However, those scientists have been at a loss to explain how the process of evolution was controlled to produce predictable results. It seemed that one must either accept the scientific explanation of common descent and natural selection or accept the notion that God created the world by some supernatural means that we cannot comprehend. Those two alternatives seemed to be mutually exclusive.

Only recently has a scientific explanation been advanced that could solve the dilemma of a scientific verses a religious view of the Creation. This new explanation suggests that evolution is more than random mutation followed by natural selection. Rather there are many "constraints" on the process of change. This concept, under the title of Constraint Theory, Complexity Theory, or Order Theory, which is based upon principles of physics and mathematics, proposes that evolution is not exclusively random but is bound within definable limits, which makes the process of evolution predictable (see chap. 12).

# 7.
# DNA on the Witness Stand

O ne of the most basic issues dividing science and religion is the notion that our physical bodies are, or are not, related to the rest of nature. Many people believe that if we are the spirit children of God, then our physical bodies must be unique. They believe that if our bodies are in any way related to those of other animals, such a relationship is in some way degrading. We see a striking parallel between this belief and the medieval concept that if humans are the center of God's creation then Earth must be the center of the universe. Even though this notion seems odd today, it was adamantly adhered to in previous generations (up to about 300 years ago). Eventually, the scientific data became so overwhelming that the notion of an Earth-centered universe had to be abandoned, even by religious leaders and the lay public. The idea that because we are at the center of God's attention we should also be at the center of the physical universe was an error of logic which ultimately could not be supported by observation. But the discovery of our world's true position in the universe does not negate God's existence or diminish his love for each of us his children.

Likewise, the modern molecular data, which have accumulated over the past twenty-five years, overwhelmingly support the notion that we are genetically related to other animals and completely contradict the idea that we are genetically unique. As with an Earth-centered universe, the idea that because we are spirit children of God and are created in his image our physical bodies should be unique is an error that is not supported by the data. In fact, there are far more data supporting the concept that humans are related to other animals than to support the idea that Earth is not the center of the universe. As with the evidence that eventually led all people to accept the notion that Earth is not the center of the universe, the evidence that humans are biologically connected to other animals is overwhelming and cannot be dismissed. If humans were created by some means that made us unique (i.e., by "special creation"), then what is the basis of the demonstrable biological connection?

Some of the most powerful data supporting the theory of evolution in general and, specifically, the notion that all of nature, including humans, are related come from the relatively new field of molecular biology, the study of living things at the level of DNA and its associated molecules. DNA, or deoxyribonucleic acid, an acidic molecule within the cell nucleus which contains the sugar deoxyribose, is the genetic material of cells and is the template for protein synthesis. DNA provides the master pattern for the structure of all proteins (this is described in more detail below). In order to understand the magnitude of these molecular data, it is important to understand something about the field of molecular biology itself. Furthermore, in order to contrast our current level of knowledge in biology with that of even the very recent past, a brief overview of the history of molecular biology is necessary.

This chapter deals with these very issues. Many people may worry that they cannot understand molecular biology. However, it is important to realize that much of what is understood in modern biology about evolution requires a basic knowledge of the subject. We believe that some of the most elementary concepts of biochemistry and molecular biology can be readily grasped by the non-scientist.

We have designed or borrowed analogies which we believe will help readers understand some of the fundamental and important issues.

All living things are made up of cells, the basic functional units of life. It is important to know that the life of a single cell does not necessarily depend on its presence in the body. Cells can be removed from the body and kept alive for days, weeks, or even years.

Cells are very tiny. Approximately 10,000 of them could fit comfortably, in a single layer, on the head of a pin. As small as they are, each cell is a virtual microcosm of activity and contains millions of individual molecules, whose interactions are the basis of the cell's function. Molecules are composed of atoms and range in size from 1/1000 to 1/200,000, the diameter of the cell. At the very heart of the cell, within the nucleus, is a group of relatively large molecules, the DNA, the master controls of the cell. Functional DNA is what distinguishes living things from non-living things. DNA is also the basis of inheritance of genetic information from one generation to the next.

The nucleus may be thought of as a library containing hundreds of books (the DNA) with information about the cell, including much of its structural and functional information, that will be passed on to the next generation. The books in this library also contain information about the history of the cell and about its relatedness to other cells in other animals. This recorded history has been stored in the cell's library for thousands of generations, just waiting to be read and comprehended. Today, for the first time, those books are being opened and read at an incredible pace.

When Darwin published *The Origin of Species* in 1859, biologists knew nothing about DNA or the other molecules making up the cell. They knew very little about the cell itself. The "cell theory," which states that all living things are made up of cells, was just emerging. Biologists of that time did not know how traits are inherited. Darwin realized that a major obstacle to his theory of natural selection was explaining how these are passed from one generation to the next.

The problem of inheritance was partly solved when the work of Gregor Mendel was discovered at the turn of the twentieth century. His work established the field of genetics but, at the same time, brought to light another mystery: What was the basis of the genetic code? What was a gene made of? What molecules were responsible for storing and transmitting the encoded information; what was the nature of the code itself? And, of critical importance to Darwin's theory, can genes change?

One of the objectives of biology in the first half of the twentieth century was to "crack" the genetic code. By mid-century, it had been established that genes are made of DNA, but critical questions remained: what is the structure of DNA and how does it replicate? During the early 1950s, James Watson and Francis Crick were working from x-ray diffraction photographs taken by Maurice Wilkins and Rosalind Franklin. They deduced that DNA molecules form a double helix, referring to their shape which resembles a minute ladder twisted into a spiral. The discovery of this structure allowed Watson and Crick and others to establish how the genetic code works at the chemical level, thus "cracking" the elusive code and ushering in a whole new era for biology. The "molecular age" was born. For their discoveries, Crick, Watson, and Wilkins shared the 1962 Nobel Prize for "Physiology or Medicine." (Sadly, Franklin had died of cancer before the prize was awarded, and did not share in the success her work had made possible.)

In 1965 Watson wrote a book entitled *Molecular Biology of the Gene*. This influential work outlined the new field of molecular biology. Before its publication, the term "molecular biology" was seldom used. By the time his book was published, the codes for a few small proteins had been deciphered, but few comparisons between the encoded sequences (similar to the order or sequence of letters making up words) for proteins had been made between species or classes of plants or animals. Furthermore, the techniques for rapidly sequencing DNA (discovering the sequence of the base units) were not developed until the early 1970s. Therefore, essentially all of what we know about animal interrelatedness at the molecular level has been discovered since 1970. It is important to remember that most of the books that have been written concerning the Mormon church and the theory of evolution were published before any of the molecular data, which are some of the most convincing supporting the theory of evolution, were available.

The first gene was isolated from a bacterium in the summer of 1970, and no genes had yet been sequenced. We have now sequenced thousands in hundreds of species of plants and animals. The entire DNA sequence is known for the bacterium *E. coli*, from which the first gene was isolated. The complete DNA sequence is also known for several other species. More rapid techniques are being developed all the time, such as the polymerase chain reaction (PCR) which has allowed us to produce millions of copies of a given stretch of DNA in a matter of hours. We have gone so far in the past quarter of a century that by the year 2003, less than thirty-three years after the first gene was sequenced, we will have sequenced the entire human genome (a genome is the entire complement of genes contained in every cell in the body), comprising approximately 80,000 genes in all. Every normal human has the same number of genes, but differ in the precise details of their DNA sequence. That is what makes each of us unique.

DNA is composed of basic building blocks called nucleotides. Only four types of nucleotides exist in DNA, represented by the letters A, G, C, and T. Early researchers thought that DNA, with an alphabet consisting of only four letters, was not sufficiently complex to store all the information needed by a living cell. However, with the advent of computers, we now recognize that even a binary code (consisting of only two numbers, 1 and 0) can store and transmit tremendous amounts of information.

The DNA alphabet spells out a code (codon) for particular amino acids. They combine to form proteins, which are in turn the building blocks and machinery of the body. A gene is a portion of DNA that codes for a particular protein product, something like a single word in a sentence or an ingredient in a recipe. Other sequences of DNA serve a regulatory function, controlling the expression of the recipe. (A gene, like the recipe in a book, may remain untranscribed. When it is transcribed and translated, like making a cake from a recipe, the process is called expression.) Also present are stretches of non-coding DNA, which may be thought of as blank spaces between the genes.

As cells continually grow and divide, the DNA library is replicated. During the process of copying millions of nucleotides every time a cell divides, errors are introduced into the new sequences. Such errors may simply be the substitution of a single nucleotide (say an A for a T), or the deletion of a portion of the sequence (e.g., the sequence ATACCGTT being reduced to ATACCG), or the duplication of a segment of DNA (e.g., the sequence ATAC becoming ATACATAC). These errors are called mutations. Most mutations are repaired by enzymes in the cell with that specific function; not all errors are repaired, however. Some occur within genes, whereas others occur in non-coding DNA and are inconsequential. Some occur in the cells of the body, which result in diseases such as cancer. When a mutation occurs in reproductive cells, it may be passed on to the offspring, making it different in some way from its parent. A mutation in a gene involved in the pathway for producing color may result in a person who does not produce skin and eye color. Most mutations reduce survival—but some are beneficial to the organism in the face of changing conditions. For example, mutated insects can become resistant to pesticides, prompting the development of more powerful and more toxic chemicals. Mutations in bacteria may make them resistant to antibiotics. In fact, the overuse of antibiotics has precipitated the emergence of resistant bacteria—posing an international medical crisis.

Mutations that occur in the non-coding regions of DNA (in the blank spaces) have little or no effect on the individual or his or her offspring (i.e., such mutations do not change structure or function of the individual). However, the pattern of accumulated mutations within the non-coding regions results in a relatively unique identity in the DNA of each individual and his or her close relatives. To illustrate, imagine yourself in a shooting gallery. There are targets and blank spaces between the targets. When a bullet hits a target, the target falls over, but if the bullet misses and strikes the space in between, nothing happens. However, the pattern of hits in the space between the targets leaves a unique record of the shots fired. The back walls of no two shooting galleries are exactly alike. In the same way, mutations that "hit" genes can directly affect the individual or his or her offspring; but in the non-coding regions between genes, or "targets," they have no effect on the individual. Still, the "hits" in the non-coding regions, the "spaces between the targets," are recorded, with no two individuals having exactly the same pattern. The pattern of hits in the non-coding regions is passed on to the offspring, providing a unique record of the offspring's heritage.

The discovery that DNA sequences are unique among individuals and families has led to the development of a technique for identification. This technique, called DNA fingerprinting, permits a profile of key "landmarks" to be compared between samples. The procedure takes advantage of the fact that many cells are equipped with a defense mechanism to protect against invasion by foreign DNA. This defense consists of proteins, called restriction enzymes, that recognize specific short sequences of DNA, attach to those sites, and snip the invading foreign strand into two. By exposing a sample of DNA to a select battery of restriction enzymes, the strand will be snipped into a collection of variable-length fragments. The resulting fragments are applied to an electrophoresis gel and the electrical current causes the fragments to spread along the gel, the shorter fragments moving farther than the longer ones. Once this gel is labeled with a dye, it produces a characteristic "fingerprint" of the individual, a relatively unique banding pattern produced by the restriction fragments.

The use of DNA fingerprint evidence has become an important forensic tool in criminal investigation. DNA samples collected from a crime scene can be used to virtually establish the presence or absence of a suspect at the scene. Such evidence is also employed to settle questions of paternity, as in the cases of infants switched at birth in a hospital.

Questions of family relatedness can also be determined. Recently, the DNA of an unknown Vietnam soldier in Arlington National Cemetery was tested and compared to blood samples of presumed family members, the dead soldier was identified, and his remains were returned to his family. As a result of this case, the Pentagon plans to take DNA samples from every soldier to create a registry. This future registry will make it nearly impossible for there ever again to be an unknown soldier.

Similarly, when nine skeletons were found in a shallow grave in July 1991, it was possible to identify the remains of the tsar, his wife, three of their five children, the royal physician, and three servants. Even though the cells had been dead for seventy-five years, DNA

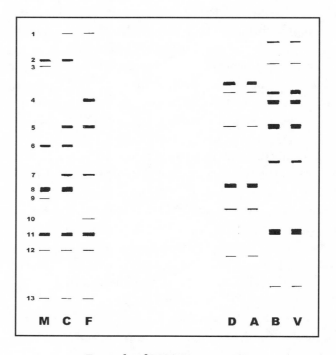

### Example of DNA Fingerprints

*By examining the patterns of bands, molecular geneticists can infer relation-*
*ships. The first series of bands depicts a mother (M), child (C), and father (F).*
*The child's DNA fingerprint exhibits some bands in common with the mother*
*(bands 2, 6, 8, 11, 12, and 13). Other bands are common with the father (1, 5,*
*7, 11, 12, and 13). The second series of bands depicts the DNA fingerprint of a*
*murder victim (V) and that of a defendant (D) accused of the murder. The*
*bands in the center two lanes (A and B) are DNA fingerprints from blood*
*collected at the murder scene. The fingerprint in lane A matches that of the*
*defendant, placing him or her at the scene of the murder.*

fragments were still intact. Analysis revealed an exact match between the wife, the three children, and a living maternal relative. Similar results were achieved with the remains of the former tsar and two living maternal relatives. This forensic evidence supported the hypothesis that the remains were those of the executed Romanov family. On the other hand, DNA analysis refuted the claim of a woman who had claimed to be the surviving Anastasia Romanov.

Similar techniques are currently being used to identify family relations among the ancient pharaohs, who lived 5,000 years ago. DNA has been extracted from 10,000-year-old human bones and teeth, and from 135 million-year-old amber-imbedded insects. DNA from Neandertal fossils, 30,000-100,000 years old, has also been sequenced. The data from this study suggest that Neandertals, although human-like in appearance, were not direct ancestors of modern humans (see Krings, "Neandertal DNA sequences," 19-30).

This new science has taken the witness stand in cases of homicide, paternity, and issues of family relatedness. DNA fingerprinting can identify an individual and tie him or her to living or dead relatives. These same techniques are used by biologists to investigate the interrelatedness of various species. For example, a controversy has existed among botanists for most of this century as to whether yews, which have flat needles and berry-like fruit, should be classified with conifers, which are needle-bearing evergreens with typical cones, or whether they should be classified as a separate class or even as a separate phylum. Until recently, this controversy was unresolvable. However, molecular data collected within the past ten years clearly indicate that yews, for all their apparent morphological differences, are closely related to the other conifers (see Li, *Molecular Evolution,* 160-63).

What do the molecular data reveal about humans' closest relatives in the animal kingdom? The question of which, if any, African apes share a common ancestor with humans has also been investigated using DNA sequencing. Mounting evidence indicates that humans and chimpanzees are the most closely related (see Bailey, "Hominoid trichotomy," 100-108). These findings have independently borne out the conclusions of earlier comparative anatomists that humans are more closely related to the chimp and gorilla than either the chimp or gorilla are related to the third great ape, the orangutan. When the DNA sequences of two humans selected at random are compared, they may differ on average by as much as one out of every 200 nucleotides. In other words, they are about 99.5 percent similar. If the DNA sequences of a human and a chimpanzee are compared, 1.45 out of every 100 nucleotides are found to be different—about 98.5 percent similar. Human DNA is 97 percent similar to that of orangutans and 92.5 percent similar to that of rhesus monkeys. Likewise, chimpanzees are only 92.5 percent similar to rhesus monkeys but 97 percent similar to orangutans. Animals that are more distantly related have even greater DNA sequence differences.

These differences can be seen not only in the DNA but in proteins as well. Proteins are made from the DNA template by a process which we will describe later in this chapter. Because of this relationship, amino acid (amino acids, incidentally, are carbon-containing acids that have an amine group [NH2] and a "side group," which ranges from a single hydrogen atom to larger, more complex groups of atoms) sequences in proteins can be used for comparisons across species. We can compare, for example, the human protein cytochrome $c$ amino acid sequence to that of any other plant or animal. We find that all 100 amino acids in human cytochrome $c$ are identical to those of the chimpanzee, 99 percent are identical to those of monkeys, 90 percent to those of a dog, 88 percent to a horse, 85 percent to a chicken, 83 percent to a snake, 82 percent to a frog, 79 percent to a fish, 72 percent to a fly, 57 percent to wheat, and 52 percent to yeast. The list goes on, confirming the validity of the hypothesis that more closely related plants and animals have more closely related amino acid sequences and that more distantly related plants and animals have less similar sequences. Even though there are up to 50 percent differences in amino acid sequences in cytochrome $c$, the cytochromes from one plant or animal can substitute for those of another. (See, for example, Ernst, "Substitutions of proline 76," 13,225-36; and Tanaka, "Amino acid replacement studies," 477-80.)

When he wrote *The Origin*, Darwin did not know the basis of inherited variation. He knew nothing about DNA, cytochrome *c*, or amino acid sequences. Nonetheless, the theory of descent by natural selection predicted in 1859 the relationship in DNA and amino acid sequences that we observe today. No more powerful evidence exists for any scientific theory than that it clearly and precisely predicts the data obtained from future experiments and observations, especially in fields of science that do not yet exist.

The use of DNA data in forensic science and questions of animal interrelatedness have only become possible in the past three decades and, on a larger scale, only within the past ten years. However, in spite of the relative youth of the molecular biology field, the data which have accumulated are:

(1) **Massive.** There are literally thousands of volumes of DNA sequences now available. It is also equally important to know that the human genome contains huge regions of non-coding DNA. The sequence similarities and differences in these non-coding regions provide the most powerful information about relatedness among humans (such as in homicide and paternity cases) and between humans and other animals.

(2) **Rapidly accumulating.** Newer and faster sequencing techniques are being developed all the time, cutting by factors of hundreds or thousands the time required to sequence a gene compared to the early days of sequencing. Several new genes are being sequenced every day. By the year 2003, the entire human genome, consisting of approximately 80,000 genes will be sequenced, and large portions of the genomes of other plants and animals will be known. The entire DNA sequences of several viruses, bacteria, and yeast are already completely known.

(3) **Consistent.** The DNA sequences discovered for similar genes in different plants and animals have been found to be remarkably alike, demonstrating that there is an impressive similarity in structure and function at the molecular level.

(4) **Supportive of the concept of relatedness.** When we examine DNA sequences to determine how closely or distantly two

plant or animal species are related, it is not the conserved (similar) portion of the DNA sequence that is important; rather it is the portion of the sequence that is different (variable, often non-coding regions) that matters most. In every organism studied to date there is a remarkable correlation between the amount of similarity in those variable regions of DNA and the proposed relationship between the plants or animals examined. The differences between sequences apparently reflect the accumulation of mutations in separate biological lineages derived from a common ancestor. It is important to emphasize, once more, that this information, which is the most powerful information available for examining questions of interrelatedness between living things, was not available twenty-five years ago. This same type of information is used in courts of law to determine DNA matches in paternity or homicide cases. Some people readily accept DNA data as evidence for relatedness among humans yet reject the *same* data indicating our relatedness to other animals.

These data powerfully support the theory of evolution and its prediction that closely related species exhibit closely related DNA sequences. Because of the consistency of these data, we can confidently predict that anyone reading this book can go to any college or university library, pick up any scientific journal containing published DNA sequences, and verify the relatedness of the species presented. These data are powerful because they directly address the forces of creation, the motive cause that forms each plant and animal. They are also powerful because they are objective and do not depend on the subjective comparisons of early systematics.

We present here a demonstration you can try yourself, which is an analogy of the relatedness of DNA sequences among species. All you need for this demonstration are four different colors of paper clips, about thirty of each. From a mixed box with all four colors, select ten paper clips at random and link them together to form a chain. This chain will be made up of the four colors of paper clips in random order. Lay this chain of ten paper clips onto a table so that you can see the pattern.

Now construct a second chain of ten paper clips that is identical to the first. After this second chain is constructed, pick one additional paper clip at random from the box of assorted colors. Then pick at random one link in the second chain. This may best be done by laying out the chain, closing your eyes, and pointing to one link. Once that link has been identified, replace it with the new link you selected from the box. There is a 25 percent chance that the link you are replacing will be the same color as the new link.

Now construct a third chain identical to the second and repeat the process of replacing one link. Once more the link and color of the replacement will be random. There is a 10 percent chance of replacing the same link and a 25 percent chance of replacing the same color as was there before. That does not matter; go ahead and complete the exercise. Repeat this process until you have a total of ten chains of ten paper clips each, with slight color variations. Once all ten chains are formed, place them into a box or some other container, and mix them up. Now dump out the ten paper-clip chains onto a table and sort them out by degree of similarity (it works better if one person makes the chains and another person sorts them out). Organize the chains according to some order that you decide upon. How did you organize the chains? What was the basis of your decision to organize them the way you did? What are the implications of the organization you chose? There may be some chains that are identical and cannot be distinguished. What factors might result in identical chains?

The results of this demonstration are similar to what molecular biologists obtain in examining DNA sequences. We can consider these data relative to at least two alternative hypotheses: (1) The theory of evolution predicts that species are related to each other by descent; or (2) each species was created independently and uniquely, and therefore the species are not related. The DNA sequence data powerfully and consistently support the theory of evolution by indicating that species are related and just as powerfully and consistently refute the hypothesis of special creation. If each species was created independently and uniquely, and the species are not related, then some reasonable explanation must be advanced to explain the apparent relationship in DNA sequences. Science does not preclude the advancement of such an alternative hypothesis; rather, alternative hypotheses are encouraged. There is no conspiracy in science to suppress reasonable alternative hypotheses. The fact is, no reasonable alternative hypothesis has yet been proposed.

The DNA sequence data do not disprove creation, they simply help us explore possible mechanisms and patterns in the course of evolution. One of the most beautiful parts of God's creation is the elegantly simple DNA molecule. That graceful spiral contains the possibility for storing almost infinite amounts of information. DNA is copied and transferred from one generation to the next with *almost* perfect fidelity. Hence, in the short term, likes beget likes. The "almost" part of the process of DNA replication allows for the variation that is a critical part of the creative process. Variation permits species to adapt in the face of a changing environment. That variation is certainly one of God's most profound laws.

Some people argue that it comes as no surprise that the "blueprints" for similarly appearing organisms are likewise similar. That would be a fair assertion if the DNA of an organism was anything like an architect's blueprint, but such is not the case. Rather than a blueprint, an organism's complement of DNA is more like a "recipe" in a scrapbook of family history. In addition to the instructions for the unfolding development of the organism, there are bits and pieces, souvenirs and memorabilia, from far-flung predecessors. Stretches of noncoding DNA—interons, tandem repeats, satellite DNA—have little or no effect on the outcome of development. Mutations accumulate in these stretches of DNA that are invisible to natural selection and therefore provide a relatively unskewed evolutionary record of the lineage like the pattern of bullet holes on the wall of the shooting gallery. When examined in conjunction with more conservative genes that code for functional proteins, these provide a means for determining which organisms share a most recent common ancestor.

The information contained in DNA may be compared to a cake recipe. Suppose you want to bake a very special cake using a recipe available in only a very limited number of cook books. Suppose, also, that the only cook book you can find containing the recipe is in the reference section of the local library and cannot be checked out. The recipe book could be thought of as the DNA sequence for a given plant or animal and the cake recipe itself would be the DNA sequence of a gene for a given protein. The library can be thought of as the nucleus of a cell within the plant or animal. Just like a reference book, which cannot be removed from the library, DNA is too large a molecule to leave the nucleus.

If you want a copy of the cake recipe, your only choice is to copy it from the recipe book. You may choose to copy it onto a card, which you can then take home and use to make the cake. You *transcribe* the recipe from the recipe book onto the card. In the nucleus of an actual cell, a given stretch of DNA is transcribed as a sequence of ribonucleic acid (RNA), a molecule closely related to DNA. The RNA used to transcribe information from DNA that will be used to make proteins is called messenger RNA (mRNA). You may not choose to copy the recipe exactly as written in the book, but may choose to abridge some passages. For example, the recipe may state, "Add one cup of sifted all purpose flour." You may write on your card, "Add one cup of flour." In molecular terminology, the phrase that you transcribed is called an *exon*. An exon is the part of the DNA actually used to make a protein. That portion of the recipe you did not copy, "sifted all purpose," is called the *intron*. An intron is the portion of a given DNA sequence not used to make the protein.

Once you have transcribed the recipe onto a card, you are ready to leave the library and go to your kitchen. You place the card on your kitchen counter or table, which may be thought of as the ribosome of the cell, where proteins are assembled. You then gather up all the ingredients for the cake and place them onto the counter. These are the amino acids from which the protein is to be made. You put the ingredients together according to the instructions in the recipe. Because you are now changing from a written recipe to a cake, the process is called *translation*. In molecular biology, translation is the process of making proteins from an mRNA template. The cake recipe provides the information for whether this will be a chocolate or lemon cake. Likewise, the DNA and mRNA sequences provide the information for the amino acid sequence in a given protein, and this sequence determines the structure and function of it.

Now let us consider changing the letters of the recipe, much like we did the paper clips in the previous demonstration. The original recipe states:

Add one cup of *sifted all purpose* flour.

The italicized words are the intron. Now change one letter, as though a typo had occurred in the recipe book:

Add one **pup** of *sifted all purpose* flour.

This change in the exon is referred to as a functional mutation, which makes the recipe nonfunctional as it can no longer be read correctly. Mutations occur randomly in nature, much like in the exercise of randomly replacing colored paper clips in a chain. Plants or animals with functional mutations rarely survive because the mutation tends to destroy some critical function. However, let us consider a change in the intron:

Add one cup of *sifted all porpose* flour.

In this case, the functional meaning of the recipe is not changed. This type of mutation is called a neutral mutation because function is retained. Neutral mutations can continue to accumulate (in nature, they accumulate at measurable rates). Let us say that the cook book goes through several editions without the accumulated errors being corrected. The page containing the publication date is lost from each book and you want to reconstruct the publication order of five editions of the book. Here is the phrase from each of the five editions:

Add one cup of *sifted all pompose* flour.
Add one cup of *sufter all pompose* flour.
Add one cup of *sifted all porpose* flour.
Add one cup of *sufted all pompose* flour.
Add one cup of *sifted all purpose* flour.

Assuming that no errors were corrected from edition to edition, which phrase came from the oldest, original cook book? Which came from the second edition, which from the third, fourth, and fifth? What is the basis of your conclusions?

Biologists use the same logic to determine not only relationships between plants or animals but also to determine the order of descent. Data obtained from such observations strongly agree with similar data obtained from other sources, such as the fossil record. All of the data combine to powerfully support the theory that all plants and animals are related by descent with modification from common ancestors.

The "witnesses" have testified; the evidence has been presented; the merits of the case rest upon the accumulated data. The fingerprint of our common biological heritage with animals appears self-evident. The same techniques employed in courts of law to settle disputes of paternity, or to research the history of genetic diseases in family genealogies, demonstrate our close relations to the rest of nature. Their validity as tools to elucidate genealogical relationships is unquestioned; why would their application to elucidate relationships between animal species be disputed?

We believe that these data provide insights into the processes used by God to create the plants and animals on this earth, including our own bodies. We must remember again that in science there is always the opportunity for alternative hypotheses to be advanced which better explain the observed data. However, in nearly 150 years of exhaustive study, no one has advanced a testable alternative hypothesis to explain the data that even begins to demonstrate the predictive power of evolutionary biology.

We believe one other aspect of these data is important to remember. We agree with the brother of Jared, who stated, "I know that thou speakest the truth, for thou art a God of truth, and canst not lie" (Ether 3:12; cf. Titus 1:2). As scientists who have faith in the God of truth, we believe that God did not, indeed could not, create apparent relationships between living things to deceive us into believing in the theory of evolution. We believe that, using logical, deductive reasoning, we can determine the publication order of the recipe books and which editions are closest to each other. We do not believe that the author or publisher purposely inserted errors in the manuscript to deceive readers concerning the order of publication. We believe that through the process of science many of the truths of God can be revealed, including truths relating to the process of creation.

# 8.
# Our Place in Nature

Each of us possesses a physical body that, regardless of how intellectualized, sanitized, deodorized, or depilitated, bears the indelible stamp of our continuity with Nature, specifically the animal kingdom. Like all organisms, we are born, grow, consume, metabolize, eliminate wastes, sleep, reproduce, and ultimately die. The writer of Ecclesiastes noted: "I said in mine heart concerning the estate of the sons of men, that God might manifest them, and that they might see that they themselves are beasts. For that which befalleth the sons of men befalleth beasts; even one thing befalleth them, as the one dieth, so dieth the other; yea they have all one breath; so that a man hath no preeminence over a beast: for all is vanity" (3:18-19).

This passage seems to suggest that to consider ourselves superior to animals, at least in the *physical* sense, is simply vane. The issue of human beings' relation to the animal kingdom has its beginnings in Genesis, where the Lord commanded Adam to *subdue* the earth and have *dominion* over every living thing that moveth upon it (1:28). Hugh Nibley has discussed the nuances in meaning of the original Hebrew terms, whose derivatives range from *trample* and *plow* to *violate* and *cherish* ("Man's Dominion," 47-48). Through revelation to Joseph Smith, we understand this charge to be one of stewardship—to care for and nurture the Lord's creation, as his representatives during his absence. "I the Lord ... make every man accountable as a steward over earthly blessings which I have made and prepared for my creatures" (D&C 104:13).

Normative Judaism and early Christianity maintained a strict dichotomy between humans and animals, a tradition whose roots can also be traced to Aristotle (see Olroyd, *Darwinian Impacts*, 247). Aristotle believed in three distinct principles of life (which he called "psyches") that animate all living things. He proposed that every living thing possesses the "vegetative psyche," which carries out functions such as growth and reproduction. Animals are added upon with an "animal psyche," which facilitates body movements. Humans alone are distinguished by possession of the third or "rational psyche," which bestows rational behavior and thought. Based on a belief in this tradition, early Christians rejected the idea that animals might in any degree be classed with men, who alone enjoy the powers of speech and reason, the mark of divinity that sets them uniquely and absolutely apart ("Man's Dominion," 50).

In 1858 Richard Owen, Britain's leading paleontologist and anatomist at the time, published a classification of mammals in which he placed humans apart from all primates, not merely in a separate order, but in a separate subclass (see Gross, "Huxley versus Owen," 493-98). His justification rested on three minor distinctions in the anatomy of the brain, most importantly the presence of a structure known as the hippocampus minor. The hippocampus minor is a small convolution in the floor of one of the fluid-filled cavities in the brain. Owen placed undo significance on this structure based on a now obsolete notion of the function of brain spaces or ventricles. He declared that the hippocampus minor eliminated any possibility of continuity between man and the animal kingdom.

In response, Thomas Huxley, the foremost protagonist for Darwinism, brought forward extensive comparative data to correct Owen's assertion. His findings were published in the now classic booklet, *Evidences as to Man's Place in Nature*. Therein he "endeavored to show that no absolute structural line of demarcation, wider than that between the animals that immediately precede us in the scale, can be drawn between the animal world and ourselves" (152). He pointed out that the similarities between the brains of apes and humans are far greater than those between apes and monkeys.

In commenting on the significance of this contest of classification, noted American scientist Stephen J. Gould wrote in 1975, "The Western World has yet to make its peace with Darwin and the implications of evolutionary theory. The hippocampus debate merely illustrates in light relief the greatest impediment to this reconciliation—our unwillingness to accept continuity between ourselves and nature; our ardent search for a criterion to assert our uniqueness" ("Man and Other Animals," 24f).

In the meantime, other criteria for uniqueness have been proposed. A list of those criteria appears impressive on the surface. It includes such things as erect posture, tool use, self-awareness, language, reason, compassion, and the possession of a soul or spirit. However, close examination of the list in the light of increasing knowledge and understanding of ourselves and of other animals quickly undermines the absolute nature of these supposed distinctions.

Consider erect posture. The Judeo-Christian traditions placed particular significance on the upright posture of humans. "God formed man in his own image and made him to be Lord over them [animals]. Whenever man stands upright and lifts his eyes towards heaven, then all the animals raise their heads too and look to man, fearing and trembling in his presence" (qtd. in "Man's Dominion," 48). Obviously the ancients, who held these views, had little if any knowledge of such things as ostriches, kangaroos, gerbils, or for that matter the imposing *Tyrannosaurus rex*. Bipedalism, or the habit of walking on two feet, has evolved independently in a number of reptiles, birds, and mammals. The fossil record of early human ancestors indicates no less than ten species of bipedal hominids, which stood fully upright, some with a brain no larger than a chimp's. The most direct evidence of early bipedalism is a fossilized trackway preserving the passage of three upright hominids across an ash-strewn plain in the aftermath of a volcanic eruption in Tanzania, Africa, 3.6 million years ago (see Leakey, "Pliocene Footprints," 317-23). That we are currently the only living species of primate that walks upright is an

outcome of extinction. (The persistent reports of sightings and human-like footprints of giant upright apes from various regions of the
world may indicate the survival of a fellow bipedal primate, as yet un-
classified by science [see Krantz, *Big Footprints*; and Bindernagel,
*North America's Great Ape*].)

Consider tool use. The employment of tools to modify the surrounding environment has long been considered an ability solely attributed to humans. "Tools maketh the man" was a common maxim
in anthropology. In more recent years, field studies of chimpanzees
have revealed the construction and employment of simple tools. Jane
Goodall recalled the excitement with which she informed her men-
tor, Louis Leakey, of her observations of chimps selecting and *modifying* blades of grass in order to "fish" for termites in their mounds.
Leakey responded, "Now we must either redefine *tool*, redefine *Man*,
or accept chimpanzees as humans" (Goodall, *Through a Window*,
19). Continued naturalistic and laboratory studies have added to the
repertoire of tools wielded by the three species of ape, including le-
vers, props, sops, wipes, hammer and anvils, clubs, and missiles (see
Tuttle, *Apes of the World*, 147-70). The first consistent appearance of
simple flaked stone tools dates to 2 million years ago in the archeo-
logical record and appears to coincide with the first appearance of the
genus *Homo*. These were not modern humans, however. The skeletal
remains associated with these tool artifacts are of a bipedal hominid
with a brain half the size of a modern human. Tools equivalent in so-
phistication to those made by modern human populations still sub-
sisting with a "stone-age" culture have been present in the archeolog-
ical record for over 50,000 years.

Consider language. The fictional Dr. Doolittle epitomizes our
fascination with the prospect of communicating with animals. Early
attempts to teach chimpanzees to speak were unsuccessful. Lucy, a
chimp raised in a human home as a "human child," was never capable of more than a few simple utterances, such as "mama." It was concluded that apes simply lacked the vocal mechanism or neural centers for articulate speech. Then, in 1966, Allen and Beatrice Gardner
made an astounding breakthrough by teaching the chimp Washoe
American Sign Language (Ameslan). In just four years Washoe

learned 132 symbols and could use them in combinations similar to those of a human child in the first stages of language development ("Teaching Sign Language to Chimpanzees," 76-82). Not long after this, David Premack began working with a chimp named Sarah, using plastic symbols ("Language in Chimpanzees?" 808-22). In turn, David Rumbaugh taught a chimp, named Lana, to use a computerized typewriter to communicate ("Reading and Sentence Completion by a Chimpanzee," 730-33). Then Penny Patterson began work with a female lowland gorilla, Koko, who by 1978 had mastered 375 signs of Ameslan ("Conversations with a Gorilla," 438-65). Koko currently has a working vocabulary of over 500 signs and has a tested IQ of between 70 and 95 on a human scale (www.gorilla.org). The once common notion that language sets us uniquely apart from the animals appears to be just another vanity.

Consider self-awareness. In 1953 A. I. Hallowell stated: "The attribute of self-awareness, which involves man's capacity to discriminate himself as an object in a world of objects other than himself, is central to an understanding of the ... psychodynamics of the individual. ... Man, unlike his animal kin, acts in a universe that he has discovered and made intelligible to himself as an organism not only capable of consciousness, but also self-consciousness" (qtd. in *Anthropology Today*, 597-620). Gordon Gallup Jr. conducted experiments with primates involving mirrors. While monkey subjects generally ignored their reflections or reacted to them as if they were a rival monkey to be challenged, chimps employed the mirrors to examine themselves, clean their teeth, make faces, etc. All indications were that they fully recognized their reflections and indeed had a concept of self-identity ("Chimps and Self-Concept," 59-61). Studies of ape language mentioned briefly above also indicate a deeper awareness of self and surrounding. When Koko, the signing gorilla, was once asked if she was an animal or a person, she replied without hesitation, "Fine animal gorilla" ("Conversations," 465).

Consider compassion. Few dramas have so captivated the public interest as that involving a female gorilla named Binti, at Illinois's Brookfield Zoo. A three-year-old boy had climbed over a fence and careened into the mote surrounding the gorilla enclosure. Binti, her own infant clutched to her chest, approached the unconscious child without hesitation and attempted to rouse him. She then gently scooped him up and cradled him to her chest as her own, fending off the curious attentions of the other gorillas. She laid him near the door to the enclosure where the keepers were able to retrieve him (Hirshberg, "Primal Compassion," 78-92). Long-term field studies have revealed much about the complex social interactions in ape communities. These reveal strong family relationships, maternal and sibling bonds, humor, grief, and other emotions formerly considered uniquely human (see Goodall, *Window*).

This is but a brief exploration of a few examples of the criteria ostensibly distinguishing humans from animals. We suggest that upon closer examination, each of the foregoing criteria fails to establish a distinct line between humans and the animals, especially the apes. Instead it appears that the noble qualities of humankind are essentially differences of degree, not kind.

This leaves us to consider the soul or spirit of a human being. At this point we must venture from the arena of empirical observation and adopt a philosophical position. On the long-standing question of whether animals possess an *autonomous, preexistent* spirit, we have no definitive answer. The scriptures allude to this. For example, in a commentary on the vision of the four beasts seen by John the Revelator, the prophet Joseph Smith once remarked, "That which is temporal in the likeness of that which is spiritual; the spirit of man in the likeness of his person, as also the spirit of the beast, and every other creature which God has created" (D&C 77:2). This would seem to echo the revelation of Moses, recorded by Joseph Smith, in which the Lord stated, "For I the Lord God, created all things, of which I have spoken, spiritually, before they were naturally upon the face of the earth" (Moses 3:4-6). Do we know what a "spiritual creation" entails, especially as it pertains to plants and animals? Does every living thing contain a soul? Every single virus, every individual bacterium, each algae that has teamed in the oceans for the past 3.5 billion years? If any "lowly" forms of life are to be excluded, where is the line to be drawn? As we shall see in chapter 13, there remains a great deal of uncertainty regarding the nature of the spiritual creation and its relation to the "physical" creation as it may have been carried out on this planet.

Whatever the state of plant or animal "spirits" in this regard, humans do lay claim to a *qualitative* distinction. The position of the LDS church, as declared in a 1909 statement of the First Presidency, asserts that "man, as a spirit, was begotten and born of heavenly parents" ("The Origin of Man," rptd. in *Encyclopedia of Mormonism*, 4:1665-69). Humans, apart from the rest of creation, lay claim to a spirit that is the literal offspring of Deity. It would seem that this alone establishes the only absolute demarcation between humankind and the rest of the animal kingdom, and constitutes the only truly significant link in human spiritual genealogy. Much of the confusion that surrounds evolution results from confounding these two distinct aspects of human nature—the spirit and the body. We will treat this in more detail in chapter 9.

We now return to the evidences that speak for the physical continuity of humans and animals, particularly the apes—chimpanzee, gorilla, and orangutan. In 1699 Edward Tyson, a noted comparative anatomist, was afforded the opportunity to dissect and describe an infant chimpanzee that was captured by a sailor in Africa and subsequently died at sea. His conclusion: the chimp more closely resembled humans than other primates, the differences being reduced to matters of nuance (see Boorstin, *The Discoverers*, 459-63). Never before had there been so public a demonstration of the human kinship with the animals, and attention drawn to our particular similarity to one of the apes (Tyson, *Orang-Outang*, 129). Of course, at this time the similarity was interpreted as proximity on a static scale of nature. Darwin's concept of the descent of species through modification was a century and a half away. But Tyson's observations and impressive illustrations served to dramatically narrow the perceived "gulf" between humans and animals.

In 1735 Linnaeus, the father of our modern scheme of classification of plants and animals, published his *Systema Natura*. He took a bold step and included humans as a species of the order Primates—the "First or Top Ones." He christened man as *Homo sapiens* but confessed that he "could not discover the difference between man and the orangutan." (In Europe of this period, the term "orangutan" referred to any great ape.) Nor did he ever find a single "generic character" to distinguish humans from apes. "It is remarkable," he concluded, after comparing their anatomies, that "the stupidest ape differs so little from the wisest man, that the surveyor of nature has yet to be found who can draw the line between them" (qtd. in *The Discoverers*, 463). This move precipitated strong objections from many quarters, such as the remark by Thomas Pennant, who in his *Synopsis of the Quadrupeds* (1771) commented, "I reject [Linnaeus'] first division, which he calls Primates, or foremost in Creation, because my vanity will not suffer me to rank mankind with apes, monkeys and bats" (qtd. in Richards, *Ape, Man, Apeman*, 16).

By Darwin's time, significant advances had been made in the comparative anatomy of humans and apes. Thomas Huxley's *Evidences as to Man's Place in Nature*, published as a popular booklet in 1863, summarized his anatomical observations comparing humans and apes. In it he concluded that humans were more closely related to the African apes—the chimp and gorilla—than were either of the latter to the third ape, the Asian orangutan.

Near the turn of the twentieth century, Ernst Haeckel observed, "The comparative anatomy of all the organs of the group of the Catarhine simiae (Old World monkeys and apes) leads to the result that the morphological differences between man and the great apes are not so great as those between the man-like apes and the lowest Catarhinae. In fact, it is very difficult to show why man should not be classified with the large apes in the same zoological family. We all know a man from an ape, but it is quite another thing to find differences which are absolute and not of degree only" ("The Last Link," 26 Aug. 1898). Interest in the comparative anatomy of humans and apes has received renewed impetus as a consequence of recent discoveries of early hominid fossils, discussed in chapter 10.

In the face of over a century of mounting evidence, it is interesting that such a strong reaction was evoked by the suggestion of a close relationship (i.e., shared common ancestor) between apes and humans. During the famous debate between Huxley and Bishop Wilberforce, the bishop breached etiquette when he asked Huxley if he claimed descent from apes on his mother's or his father's side. Following the debate, a member of the audience, whose sensibilities were obviously offended by such a suggestion, reportedly remarked, "Descended from the apes? It certainly can't be true. But, if it is, let us hope it does not become generally known!" (Dobzhansky, *Mankind Evolving*, 5). Darwin's theory linking man to ape was offensive to many. How could humans be the near kin of such creatures?

What is it about Western culture that precipitated such an intense reaction? Perhaps it was because medieval Christians had regarded monkeys and apes as synonymous with the devil. Their sin was that they resembled, or were in the *similitude*, of man, hence the nomen *Simian*. This is a good example of the medieval obsession with the final cause. They were seen as a caricature and a mockery of humankind. In a twelfth century Latin bestiary (a "field guide" to animal life), the devil is equated with the primates, for apes had no tail (*cauda*) and the devil has no scripture (*caudex*). "The whole of monkey is disgraceful, yet their bottoms really are excessively disgraceful and horrible. In the same way, the Devil had a sound foundation when he was among the angels of heaven, but he was hypocritical and cunning inside of himself, and so he lost his cauda-caudex as a sign that all of him would perish in the end" (34-35). The metaphysical significance of the tail can even be traced farther still to early Christian tradition: "It was assumed that the tail was a necessary appendage of all animals (*cf.* Leviticus 22:23); indeed it was thought that human beings had once also sported a tail. The subsequent removal of Adam's tail by God, and the now tailless condition of all human beings was rationalized as a symbol of our species' unique character and place in nature. The tailless ape on the other hand was regarded as an impostor, whose acaudate condition was indicative of its presumptuous desire to rise above its natural station and that, unlike human beings, its deprived state was a symbol of Divine disgrace" (Spencer, *Pithekos to Pithecanthropus*, 14). As late as the sixteenth century, Martin Luther employed the word "ape" and "demons" interchangeably.

It should be recognized that Western public exposure to apes was limited to exhibits at menageries under conditions very different from most of today's progressive zoological gardens. The animals that were unfortunate enough to survive a violent capture and the long, arduous ocean voyage were kept isolated in small, monotonous, unsanitary enclosures, and were often provided with an unsuitable diet. Removed from their natural environment and social groups, their behavior was neurotic and their health poor. They were often lethargic and exhibited little in the way of natural behavior.

Added to this was the Western literary characterization of the ape as a savage monster. In 1861 the exploits of Paul Du Chaillu, an American adventurer/explorer, were published under the title *Equitorial Africa*. Du Chaillu, in recounting his four years hunting gorillas, describes one fatal encounter: "At this distance the hunters could see the gorilla's face—it was distorted with rage ... a face so evil it suggested the devil himself. The animal roared again. He beat his breast with his immense hands, each beat sounding like the firing of a cannon. Then he began his final rush at the hunters." The influence of Du Chaillu's demonization of the gorilla can be seen in the *Tarzan* epics of Edgar Rice Burroughs and the ever popular remakes of *King Kong*. Du Chaillu's embellished descriptions gave birth to the conception of the gorilla as a fierce, violent creature that lusted after human women (see Bourne, *The Gentle Giants*, 17-18). In the 1930s Barnum and Baily still exhibited in their circus a gorilla, called Gargantua the Great, billed as "*the world's most terrifying living creature*" (Ducros, "From Satyr to Ape," *Ape, Man, Apeman*, 338).

In contrast stand the perceptions of primates by Eastern cultures and religions. In repeated examples, ranging from Egypt to Japan, monkeys and apes occupy roles as deities, heroes, reincarnated ancestors, or even surrogate children. For example, in Egyptian mythology, Anubis, the god of the underworld, is represented by a baboon. Baboons adorn numerous monuments, and embalmed baboons accompanied royalty in their tombs. Hanuman, the monkey-god and loyal servant to King Rama, is revered in Hindu mythology and his exploits are compiled in the epic *Ramayana*, written in the fifth century B.C.E. To this day, langur monkeys are considered sacred and allowed to range freely in towns and major cities (see *A Complete Guide to Monkeys, Apes, and Other Primates*, 125-26). In a traditional Oriental epic, the hero monkey, Osaru, is a fearless and loyal character and a devoted follower of Buddha. He sees through the guise of demons and rescues the monk Hsuan-tsang (Wang, *Monkey Subdues the White-Bone Demon*). To the Japanese, the monkey has a great deal of affinity to humans, even so far as serving as a *mirror* of humans, playing a powerful role in deliberations about who they are as humans and humans' relation to nature (see Asquith, "Of Monkeys and Men," in *Ape, Man, Apeman*, 309). In southeast Asia numerous legends persist of people turning into orangutans, acknowledging a close relationship between humans and apes. In some instances, Indonesians adopt infant orangs to replace lost children. The Mende, a native people of West Africa, believe that humans and chimpanzees belong to a single class of forest-dwelling primates, sharing a common origin (see Richards, "Local Understandings of Primates and Evolution," in *Ape, Man, Apeman*, 271).

Modern Western appreciation of the history and behavior of the great apes has been advanced by exposure to numerous documentaries on television and video. The media have brought apes into our homes and afforded a new understanding of primates. These documentaries have been made possible by pioneering field studies, which, amazingly, were first conducted as recently as the past three decades. They include landmark studies of the mountain gorilla by George B. Schaller (*Mountain Gorilla*) and Dian Fossey (*Gorillas in the Mist*); the common chimpanzee by Jane Goodall (*Chimpanzees of Gombe*); and the orangutan by John MacKinnon (*In Search of the Red Ape*) and B. M. F. Galdikas (*Reflections of Eden*).

A remark by Gordon G. Gallup Jr. in 1977 is all the more pertinent in light of recent molecular data. "Over the centuries man has talked himself into feeling a world removed; now he suddenly feels himself hard pressed to come up with a single, substantial self-definition which excludes the encroaching chimpanzee" ("A Mirror for the Mind of Man," 311). Does a close biological or physical relationship with these grand animals in any way lessen our spiritual relationship with God or diminish our eternal potential, or have some individuals simply fallen prey to their vanity?

# 9.
# The Body
# as a Temple

"K now ye not that ye are the temple of God, and that the Spirit of God dwelleth in you?" (1 Cor. 3:16; see also D&C 93:35). This scripture compares our physical bodies to the holy temple of God. The temple symbolizes a link to eternity, a sanctuary for the Spirit. Just as the temple is the abode of God, the spirit of God dwells in our bodies. What makes the temple hallowed: the stones of which it is constructed or the spirit within?

Probably the two most famous temples for Latter-day Saints are the Temple of Solomon and the Salt Lake temple. God commanded Solomon to build a temple (1 Chron. 22: 6-10). He also gave Joseph Smith, Brigham Young, and other latter-day prophets the same command (D&C 57:3; 97:10-16; 105:33; 109; 124:25-55; 124:39; 138:54). Solomon's magnificent ediface was built of stone and decorated with carved wood overlain with gold. Solomon dedicated the temple in 1005 B.C.E., but its glorious condition hardly lasted beyond his death in 975 B.C.E. During the reign of his son, some of the gold was stripped from the temple by Shishak of Egypt. It was subsequently spoiled many times by both foreign and domestic kings, and then rebuilt. It was polluted several times, then cleansed and rededicated. Finally, it was burned to the ground and completely destroyed by Nebuchadnezzar in 587 B.C.E. (*Bible Dictionary*, 100). Were the stones from which Solomon built his temple sacred? Was it still sacred even after it was polluted? Were the pieces of the temple carried off by foreign rulers and other vandals still holy?

On 28 July 1847, only four days after arriving in the Salt Lake Valley, Brigham Young identified the site for the Salt Lake temple (Roberts, *Comprehensive History of the Church*, 3:280). Ground was broken on 14 February 1853, and the cornerstones were laid and dedicated that 6 April (ibid., 4:16-17, 21-23). The Saints in the valley spent the next nine years laying the massive foundation. (The walls were 16 feet deep and 16 feet wide; the building being 186 feet long and 99 feet wide.) However, in the summer of 1862, they discovered that the foundation had been set on "chinky, small stones" and that many of the foundation stones had cracked. The original foundation of red sandstone was discarded and was replaced by granite quarried from the mouth of Little Cottonwood Canyon. In 1874 the quarry was moved about 1½ miles farther into the canyon where the stone was of better quality. Some of the stones intended for the temple apparently never made it to the temple site but were lost along the side of the road as wagons broke down (see Holzapfel, *Every Stone a Sermon*, 22). At last, the massive temple was dedicated on 6 April 1893, forty years to the day from the time the cornerstones were first laid. Can any physical difference be discovered between the stones incorporated into the temple and those left behind or lost on the way down the Little Cottonwood Canyon? Are the temple stones themselves hallowed or special?

What makes the temple special is the spirit of God which dwells in it. Even though the stones were dedicated as part of the temple, if the building is defiled or the stones removed, they are no longer hallowed. After the Saints had been driven out of Nauvoo and the temple there was destroyed, many of its stones were used to construct other buildings. Are those stones, which form the walls of common buildings in Nauvoo, still hallowed because they were once dedicated as part of the temple? Clearly, a temple is hallowed by the Spirit that resides in it, not by the physical materials from which it is built.

Likewise, our bodies are said to be hallowed by the spirits within us, not by the flesh of which we are composed. Elder James E. Talmage said, concerning this issue, "In speaking of the origin of man we generally refer to the creation of man's body; and, of all the mistakes that man has made concerning himself, one of the greatest and the gravest is that of mistaking the body for the man. The body is not more truly the whole man than is the coat the body" ("The Earth and Man," 476). Even though we are the spirit children of God, there is no reason to believe that our physical bodies are any more than a temple made of stone. Many church members believe that because we are the spirit children of God, there must be something distinctive, something "special," about our physical bodies as well. The thought seems to be, "How can the spirit children of God dwell in bodies descended from beasts?"

Several ideas have been advanced as to the "supernatural" origin of our physical bodies. The most common among LDS people are that Adam and Eve were resurrected beings transplanted here from their celestial realms, or that they were our Heavenly Father and Mother, or that they were physical children of our Heavenly Father and Mother, or that they were mortal beings transplanted by God from some other terrestrial planet. None of these ideas is supported by official pronouncement. Indeed, some of these have been explicitly condemned by church leaders. (Questions concerning Brigham Young's teachings on God eventually resulted in the First Presidency's Doctrinal Exposition on the Father and the Son in 1916. See Buerger, "The Adam-God Doctrine," 14-58; and Bergera, "The Orson Pratt-Brigham Young Controversies," 7-49.)

The unsupported notion that our physical bodies must be in some way special, i.e., apart from nature, and directly descended from God's immortal body is a major source of conflict with evolution theory. There are no scientific data to support any of these supernatural hypotheses; in fact, the body of accumulated scientific evidence stands against them. If our physical bodies are in some way "special," in that our ancestors' physical bodies came from some other planet or directly from God, then we could predict that the *physical nature* of our bodies should be in some way different from those of life forms originating on this earth. If we are indeed *aliens*, then our bodies should reasonably exhibit *alien* characteristics. One would predict, for example, that the nucleotide sequences in our DNA, especially in the non-coding regions, would have no particular relationship to, and no continuity with, the nucleotide sequences of plants and animals native to this planet. That prediction has been tested, thousands of times, and just the opposite has been found. Our DNA nucleotide sequences are remarkably similar to those of other living things on this planet. There are no greater sequence differences between humans and other species than between those species. In fact, our DNA is more similar to chimpanzee and gorilla DNA than theirs is to the orangutan.

We are clearly told that Jesus Christ was the only begotten of God: "For God so loved the world, that he gave his only begotten Son, that whosoever believeth in him should not perish, but have everlasting life" (John 3:16). Some have equivocated by stating that Christ was the only begotten "in the flesh," that is, born to a mortal mother. This in some way allows the claim that Adam and Eve were also physically begotten of God. According to this notion, they were not begotten "in the flesh" because they were begotten by exalted parents as *immortal beings. Neither* the statement that Christ was "the only begotten son in the flesh" *nor* the statement that Adam and Eve were created in an immortal state is given in the scriptures. Therefore, the idea that our physical bodies are in some way unnatural and not part of this earth has been perpetuated by tradition rather than scripture or other revelation.

The only scripture cited in support of the notion that Adam and Eve, as well as all the animals, for that matter, were *inherently* immortal and incapable of reproduction is 2 Nephi 2:22, where Lehi stated, "And now, behold, if Adam had not transgressed he would not have fallen, but he would have remained in the garden of Eden. And all things which were created must have remained in the same state in which they were after they were created; and they must have remained forever, and had no end." The central part of this scripture is the phrase "all things ... must have remained in the same state in which they were after they were created; and they must have remained forever, and had no end." What does the term "all things" refer to? Verse 23 appears to refer to Adam and Eve only, and verse 24 uses the term "all things" twice to refer to concepts. Can we be certain that "all things" in verse 22 means Adam, Eve, all the animals, and all the plants? Could the term "things" simply mean conditions? And what is "the same state in which they were after they were created"? That statement still does not indicate what that condition was. If the phrase "all things" is to be interpreted as literally *all things*, then what about the fruit that Adam and Eve were eating. There is no way that the fruit could have been eaten and still remained in the same state in which it was created. Apparently, Lehi's comments were not meant to include *all things*. Could it have referred to conditions? If Adam had not transgressed, his *condition*, of immortality, in the garden would have continued indefinitely. A passage in the *Encyclopedia of Mormonism* may be of interest here. Under the section on the Fall of Adam, Robert J. Matthews stated, immediately after quoting 2 Nephi 2:22, "Various interpretations have been suggested concerning the nature of life on the earth before the Fall and how the Fall physically affected the world, but these go beyond the clearly stated doctrine of the Church. The Church and the scriptures are emphatic, however, that the Fall brought the two kinds of death to Adam and his posterity" (2:485-86).

An interpretation of 2 Nephi 2:22 that is compatible with the huge, accumulated volume of scientific data is that the prevailing conditions would have continued indefinitely, as they had for millennia. On the other hand, Adam and Eve would have continued in a state of immortality as long as they had access to the Tree of Life. Elder Bruce R. McConkie has presented a different interpretation of this scripture:

> The initial creation was paradisiacal; death and mortality had not yet entered the world. There was no mortal flesh upon the earth for any form of life. The Creation was past, but mortality as we know it lay ahead. All things had been created in a state of paradisiacal immortality.

> It was of this day that Lehi said: "And all things which were created must have remained in the same state in which they were after they were created; and they must have remained forever, and had no end" (2 Ne. 2:22). If there is no death, all things of necessity must continue to live everlastingly and without end. ("Christ and the Creation," 9-15.)

Again, 2 Nephi 2:22 is the only scripture that we can identify as coming close to suggesting that there was an inherent, worldwide immortal condition before the Fall. We agree that Elder McConkie's is one possible interpretation, but find it less reasonable in light of the new scientific data. Nor has it received official sanction as a doctrine; and it has no explicit foundation in scripture. Furthermore, it is inconsistent with the fossil record and other well-established scientific data indicating a very old earth in which natural processes (life and death) have been at work for billions of years. With the presentation of two alternative interpretations, should we not at least consider one that does not require us to ignore millions of individual pieces of evidence supporting it?

Although the scriptures do not affirm that Adam and Eve's bodies were *inherently* immortal, they *do* tell us that our resurrected, immortal bodies will be *different* from our current, physical ones. The apostle Paul, in his famous essay on the resurrection of the dead, answered his own question, "How are the dead raised up? and with what body do they come?" (1 Cor. 15:35). He stated, "Thou sowest not that body that shall be. ... It is sown a natural body; it is raised a spiritual body. There is a natural body, and there is a spiritual body" (vv. 37, 44). We are told in D&C 88:15-28,

> The spirit and the body are the soul of man. And the resurrection from the dead is the redemption of the soul. And the redemption of the soul is through him that quickeneth all things, in whose bosom it is decreed that the poor and the meek of the earth shall inherit it. Therefore, it must needs be sanctified from all unrighteousness. ... They who are of a celestial spirit shall receive the same body which was a natural body; even ye shall receive your bodies, and your glory shall be that glory by which your bodies are quickened.

Until the time of the resurrection, we are all subject to death; our physical bodies are separable from our spirit bodies and are corruptible; some day the body and spirit will be inseparably united. When Christ was resurrected, he took up the same body that had been laid in the tomb to demonstrate the reality of the resurrection. Will we? As our pioneer forebears crossed the ocean, some of them died and were buried at sea. Great sharks often followed the ships until the body of the deceased silently slipped into its watery grave. The sharks were not seen thereafter. Will those pioneers have the same body in the resurrection that was eaten by the sharks? Six thousand Mormon pioneers died on the plains en route to Zion. Packs of wolves followed the wagon and handcart companies and devoured the bodies of the deceased—in some cases, before the pioneer company was even out of site. The bones of many pioneers were scattered over the plains. Will those pioneers receive every part of their original body in the resurrection? When you are resurrected, will you have those diseased tonsils or inflamed appendix that were removed when you were a child? What about a transplanted heart? Some people propose that there is some physical substance in the body that is never lost, even after cremation. There is no evidence, either from science or from the scriptures, to support this concept.

Four hundred years ago, people believed that if we are the children of God and if we are the primary objects of his creation, then we ought to be in the center of his creation. This notion made perfect sense at a time when the earth was thought by both scientists and theologians to be the center of the universe. However, the scientific evidence to the contrary became so overwhelming that the concept had to be abandoned, first by scientists and eventually by theologians. Today no one has a problem with the idea that placing us on a small planet, orbiting an average sun, on the edge of a common galaxy, in any way diminishes God's love for us. One hundred and fifty years ago, many scientists and theologians believed that because we are the spirit children of God, our physical bodies must in some way be special and unrelated to those of the beasts around us. Today the scientific evidence overwhelmingly supports the idea that our physical bodies are closely related to all of nature. This concept is now accepted by the vast majority of scientists and by a large number of theologians, including many members of the church.

James Talmage stated concerning the origin of humankind, "We are told that scientists and theologians are at hopeless and irreconcilable variance. I regard the ... claim ... as an exaggeration. Discrepancies that trouble us now will diminish as our knowledge of pertinent facts is extended" ("Earth and Man," 475). Over the past thirty years, those facts have expanded by several fold. Henry Eyring said, "Questions involving pre-Adamic man, organic evolution ... are interesting and important questions. They will all receive adequate answers in accord with the truth in due course. Whatever the ultimate answers are, the gospel will remain. ... the truth of the gospel does not hinge on such questions, interesting as they are" (*Faith of a Scientist*, 60-61). He also stated,

> Organic evolution is the honest result of capable people trying to explain the evidence to the best of their ability. ... The physical evidence supporting the theory is considerable ... It would be a very sad mistake if a parent or teacher were to belittle scientists as being wicked charlatans or else fools having been duped by half-baked ideas. ... That isn't an accurate assessment of the situation, and our children ... will be able to see that when they begin their scientific studies. (Ibid., 62.)

Brother Eyring made that statement thirty years ago. Tremendous advances have been made in "due course" during those intervening years. Science has, in many instances, provided "adequate answers." And the gospel *does* remain, as he predicted. We share Brother Eyring's sentiment when he stated, "Some people object to the slightest hint of being related to the rest of the animal kingdom, particularly the hairy apes. ... I've kind of enjoyed what little I've seen of them. ... Animals seem pretty wonderful to me. I'd be content to discover that I share a common heritage with them, so long as God is at the controls" (*Reflections of a Scientist*, 60).

# 10.
# Written in Stone

The chronicle of past ages is unfolded to our view in the orderly, stratigraphic record exposed at many locales around the world, like the pages of a textbook left open on a library table. Stratigraphy is the study of the layers (strata) of rock at Earth's surface. Not only are the effects of past geologic events (e.g., volcanic eruptions, erosion, sedimentation, and faulting) preserved in the record of stone, but, under the appropriate conditions, traces of past life remain preserved as fossils. These are often limited to the more enduring parts of an organism—shells, bones, and teeth—but occasionally conditions are such that impressions of hair, skin, scales, and feathers also remain.

In September 1987, responding to mounting questions from church members about the meaning and significance of fossils, the editors of the *Ensign* published an essay in the "I Have a Question" column entitled, "Do we know how the earth's history as indicated from fossils fits with the earth's history as the scriptures present it?" The author was Morris Petersen, Professor of Geology at Brigham Young University and president of the Provo East Stake. Brother Petersen stated,

> Among the life forms that God created were apparently many species now extinct. Fossil-bearing rocks are common on the earth, and these fossils represent once-living organisms, preserved now as part of the earth's crust. ... The existence of these animals is indisputable. ... What eternal purpose they played in the creation and early history of the earth is unknown. The scriptures do not address the question and it is not the realm of science to explore the issue of why they were here. We can only conclude, as Elder Talmage did, that ... "These lived and died, age after age, while the earth was yet unfit for human habitation."

The fossil record certainly provides one of the most compelling corroborations of evolution by descent. It also demonstrates the fact that plants and animals lived and *died* long before humans walked the face of the earth. In fact, many species became extinct long before "Adam was placed in the garden." Furthermore, fossils provide direct evidence for the chronological sequence of evolutionary history. Scientists may infer relationships between living organisms based on features ranging from anatomical to molecular. They may discover the processes by which variations were introduced into living plant and animal populations and by which natural selection and speciation occured. But it is the evidence of fossils that attests to the chronology of these processes by recording the sequential passage of life forms throughout Earth's history.

The orderly succession of strata, evident around the globe, yields fossils of increasing complexity and diversity through time. Elder John A. Widtsoe cited this as the first of several "well-established observations" that support evolution. He said, "The fossil remains of prehistoric life on earth show that in the oldest rocks are remains of the simplest forms of life; and as the rocks become younger [i.e., higher up the geologic column], more complex or more advanced life forms seem to appear. The scale of life seems to ascend from amoeba to man, as the age of the particular part of the earth's crust diminishes" (*Evidences and Reconciliations*, 159; "amoeba" here refers to a unicellular form of life, similar to, but not necessarily the same as, the living *Amoeba amoeba*). The notion that the earth was created in a paradisiacal state in which the effects of death were absent until after the Fall receives no support from the fossil record or from the scriptures, ancient or modern.

The accumulated evidence does not support the suggestion that fossils are the traces of past life on other worlds, parts of which were used in the "organization" of this earth. This notion has been a popular one since Joseph Smith, commenting on the eternal nature of the elements, remarked, "This earth is organized or formed out of other planets which were broken up and remodeled and made into the one on which we live" (qtd. in *Discourses of the Prophet Joseph Smith*, 207). At the turn of the century, B. H. Roberts speculated further:

> Accepting this statement of Joseph Smith relative to our planet in its present state being created or formed from the fragments of a planet which previously existed, one may readily understand how the supposed differences between scientists and believers in revelation have arisen. Scientists have been talking of the earth's strata that were formed in a previously existing planet; they have considered the fossilized flora and fauna imbedded in those strata. ... If scientists shall claim that the fossilized remains in the different strata of the earth's crust reveal the fact that in the earlier periods of the earth's existence only the simpler forms of vegetation and animal life are to be found, both forms of life becoming more complex and of a higher type as the earth becomes older, until it is crowned with the presence of man—all that may be allowed. But that this gradation of animal life owes its existence to the process of evolution is denied. ... The claims of evolution as explained by the philosophers of the Darwin school, are contrary to all experience so far as man's knowledge extends. (*Gospel*, 281-82.)

Over the last century, tremendous advances have been made and a great deal has been learned in the fields of paleontology and geology. Much of this new knowledge has been disseminated through magazine articles and television documentaries. The popularity and interest in dinosaurs, for example, continues to be enlivened by dramatic discoveries in Africa, South America, and Mongolia. Given what is now known regarding the pattern of distribution of fossils, together with what has been learned about the formation and movement of the earth's crust (plate tectonics, etc.), the proposition that pieces of disassembled planets, with fossil-bearing sedimentary rocks, were reassembled to form this earth in such a way as to appear as if this planet was of great antiquity is no longer tenable. Henry Eyring observed: "The orderly structure of these horizontally lying layers, with their fossils, argues strongly against the notion that the earth has been assembled, relatively recently, from the wreckage of other worlds" (*Reflections of a Scientist*, 55).

If the "remains of other worlds" had been used to build this one, the heat involved would have melted everything. That a 1968 Volkswagen was melted down to provide some of the metal for a 1999 Volvo does not mean that you can see pieces of the Volkswagen sticking out of the Volvo. The earth's crust is only 30 km thick in the areas of dry land and 15 km thick in the ocean. Below the thin crust are approximately 2,200 km of hot "plastic" mantle, 2,900 km of superheated molten liquid, and a 1,200-km solid core. Any part of any other planet helping to form the earth would presumably have been completely melted down in the process, including fossil remains.

The pattern of distribution and orderly succession of life recorded in the fossil record is too consistent to validate an extraterrestrial explanation for it. In any case, such a proposal simply sidesteps the issue—if these plants and animals could have existed on other planets, presumably created by God through some process, to become extinct and fossilized on another planet or planets, why is it so unreasonable to think they could have been created by God and become fossilized on this planet, as the overwhelming evidence attests? If it is a matter of choosing between two interpretations of the fossil record: an extraterrestrial versus a terrestrial origin, neither of which is clearly addressed in the scriptures, it seems more reasonable to adopt the interpretation that does not contradict the scientific data.

The fossil record is well correlated around the globe and consistently reveals the orderly succession of simple life to more complex and more diversified organisms. Traces of life, in the form of crystal-encased grains of carbon of a type usually produced by living organisms, were recently discovered in sedimentary rocks in Greenland and date to 3.85 billion years ago (see "Older, not Better," 20). The earliest fossils of the oldest and simplest forms of life are found in rocks in Australia, dated to 3.5 billion years ago (see Monastersky, "The Rise of Life on Earth," 75). These life forms are similar in appearance to the bacteria of today. The first eukaryotes (cells with membrane-bound nuclei) appeared as fossils about 1.5 billion years ago. Multicellular organisms followed, 700 million years ago (see Schopf, "Evolution of the Earth's Earliest Ecosystems," 214-39). The first animals with backbones, the vertebrates, appeared 500 million years ago; the first tetrapods (four-legged animals) about 400 million years ago; the first reptiles 310 million years ago; the first true mammals 225 million years ago; the first birds 180 million years ago; first primates 65 million years ago; first hominids (human-like apes) 6 million years ago (see Pough, *Vertebrate Life*). These data and continuing discoveries consistently support the interpretation drawn by scientists and echoed by Elder Talmage—"these lived and died age after age."

## Fixity of Species

Some may respond that the orderly succession of fossil-bearing strata does not "prove" the descent of one species from another. In 1976 Frank Salisbury, author of *The Creation*, stated, "The paleontologist, in his attempts to establish evolutionary sequences, assumes that morphological similarity implies relationship and descent. Similar form may well *imply* relationship and descent, but it certainly does not prove it. If it did we would have to conclude that Fords and Chevrolets are genetically related and that 1976 Fords descended from 1975 Fords. But each automobile is the product of an act of special creation" (225). A little reflection reveals the fundamental flaw in this analogy, which incorrectly equates cars, that cannot pass on traits, with biological organisms capable of reproduction and transmission of genetic information from one generation to the next. There is simply no basis for a reasonable comparison between the two, and yet this ill-conceived analogy is frequently used against evolution.

Also at the root of this attitude is the overgeneralized notion that "like begets like." Indeed, a *strict* reading of Genesis reveals a subtle distinction between the plant and animal kingdoms. The earth

144 / Evolution and Mormonism

brought forth grass and herb and tree, yielding seed *"after its kind"* (Gen 1:11-12). As for the animals, the earth brings forth various forms of animal life after their kind, which are subsequently commanded to *be fruitful and multiply* (Gen 1:22). It does not explicitly state that the animals were to *reproduce after their kind*, as is so frequently paraphrased, rather they were blessed generally to be fruitful and multiply and fill the seas, etc.

The contradictions resulting from a literal reading of the first chapter of Genesis soon become apparent. If there was no procreation or death of animals prior to the Fall, then "made after their kind" cannot be taken as synonymous with "like begets like." And the charge and blessing to be fruitful and multiply rings hollow. The production or yielding of seed is typically a sexual process of procreation, a process some have asserted was not in action prior to the Fall (2 Ne. 2:23 is often referenced in this context). If there was no procreation or death before the Fall, what was the source and fate of the fruit (the reproductive organs of trees) of which Adam and Eve freely ate?

Some of the difficulty revolves around the application of modern definitions to biblical imagery and phraseology. The term "kind" has become equated in many minds with the modern concept of "species." The meaning of "kind" as rendered from the Hebrew word *Min* has never been satisfactorily defined, but is roughly equivalent to our contemporary taxonomic concept of family. For example, Genesis 1:21 reads, "And God created great whales ..." Whales comprise two suborders of cetaceans, the baleen whales and the toothed whales. A suborder is an even higher taxonomic hierarchical unit than family. Looking at other "kinds" in Genesis 1:20-26, fowl is a class or subclass distinction, cattle is a genus distinction, creeping thing is probably a kingdom designation, and man is a species designation.

The concept of fixed "biological species" was first defined by John Ray (see Boorstin, *The Discoverers*, 432-33) in 1682, and traces its roots to Plato's concept of *eidos*, or the separate *essence* of a class of things. Plato's pupil, Aristotle, applied this concept to the living world of Nature. Species were defined as self-evident units of nature. Linnaeus built upon Ray's concepts and devised the system of binomial nomenclature, the two-part naming system which gives each species a unique label, e.g. *Homo sapiens* (Latin: wise man). This system revolutionized the classification of plants and animals and inspired an unprecedented worldwide program of specimen gathering. "We can count as many species now as were created in the beginning," Linnaeus declared (Boorstin, *The Discoverers*, 446). He initially advocated the immutability of species, that is that all species remained the same as in the day on which they were originally created. However, as collections of thousands of specimens accumulated, there were clear examples of hybridization and transitional variations, and Linnaeus began to doubt the fixity of species. But the genie was out of the bottle and the synonymy of "kind" and "species" had taken root in the dogma of Christianity.

Linnaeus listed 9,000 known species when he published his *Systema Naturae* in 1758. Today there are somewhere between 20 million and 50 million living species. Recent studies of tropical rain forests revealed, in one case, 1,700 species of terrestrial insects, 63 percent of which were previously unknown. Another study suggested that every species of tree in the tropical forest houses 600 *unique* species of insects. With some 50,000 species of tropical trees, there are potentially 30 million species of insects in the tropical forest alone. Perhaps even more astounding is that 1/5 of all recorded species are beetles (that is *all* living species, not just insects). This statistic caused British geneticist J. B. S. Haldane to state that the Creator must have "an inordinate fondness for beetles" (May, "How Many Species Inhabit the Earth?" 42-48; see also Benton, "Mass Extinction Among Non-marine Tetrapods," 811). Are the 50,000 species of tropical trees all one kind, not to mention all the other trees of the world (Gen. 1:12)? What about every thing that creepeth upon the earth after his kind (Gen. 1:25)? Are all the beetle species part of that kind? And are they the same kind as, say, salamanders, which also "creepeth"? Or is each species of beetle a different kind? There are around 150 families of beetles. Vertebrate animals (birds, reptiles amphibians, fish, and mammals) represent one of the smallest taxonomic groups, with only about 45,000 total species. In terms of sheer numbers, it is estimated that insects outnumber humans on the earth by a ratio of 200 million to 1 (see Raven, *Biology*, 793, 825).

There is relatively little commentary by the early leaders of the Mormon church concerning the idea of "kinds" (see Jeffery, "Seers, Savants, and Evolution," 41-75). It was simply not an issue and isolated remarks appear to reflect the prevailing notion "that every species is true to its kind" (Young, qtd. in *Journal of Discourses* 8:30). After all, it was simply common knowledge that like begets like. A revealing remark was made by President John Taylor,

> The animal and vegetable creation are governed by certain laws and are composed of certain elements peculiar to themselves ... each one possessing its own distinctive features, each one requiring a specific sustenance, each having an organism and faculties governed by prescribed laws *to perpetuate its own kind.* ... These principles do not change, as represented by evolutionists of the Darwinian school, but the primitive organism of all living beings exist in the same form as when they first received their impress from their Maker. (*Mediation and Atonement*, 160-61.)

There is no question that distinct species do exist and that there is a basis of continuity from generation to generation within species, otherwise chaos would ensue. It is common knowledge, as perceived during the brief span of an individual lifetime, that like essentially does beget like—hens' eggs do not hatch out crocodiles. However, a precise and uniform definition of "species" remains problematic. The observed boundaries between species, subspecies, and even geographical populations vary considerably in their distinctiveness or ambiguity. Hybrid zones are common. Dr. Jack Sites and his colleagues in the Department of Zoology at BYU have been studying lizard speciation in central Mexico for several years. They have found that lizards of the species *Sceloporus grammicus* exist in several races with significant differences in chromosome number. In one forty-six-acre plot, one *S. grammicus* race had thirty-four chromosomes and another race *of the same species* had forty-six chromosomes (see "Cytonuclear Genetic Structure," 379-92).

In a sense, species go through a life cycle of their own: originating, diversifying, differentiating, multiplying, and eventually going extinct. When comparing individual species, their distinctness may vary depending on their stage in the "life cycle." It is a marvelous system that, on the one hand, insures the orderly transmission of critical genetic information from one generation to the next. This is information the individuals of a species need to thrive in their particular niche. Anything else would result in a loss of integrity and lead to chaos. Natural safeguards of varying effectiveness are in place to insure the relative integrity of the gene pool of the species. On the other hand, the system is flexible enough that it permits the introduction of variation into the genetic information bank, in order that the species might cope with and adapt to an ever-changing environment. What works for one generation of organisms may not be suitable for the next in the face of changing climate, resources, competition, or predation. This inherent capacity for variation and mutation is at the heart of speciation. It is the raw material upon which natural selection acts to insure the survival of those organisms suited to the dynamic conditions and to eliminate those that are not.

Extinction is a fact of biology. It has continued from the time the earliest life forms can be identified in the fossil record. The recent disappearance of numerous species as the result of human encroachment has been well documented. However, this appears to be a natural process in the evolution of life on a dynamic planet. During the earth's history, five major episodes of extinction have been identified. During these times of mass extinction, large portions of the species then living disappeared. During the fourth major extinction period, the Permian Period 248-238 million years ago, 96 percent of all marine species became extinct. It is estimated that there are far fewer living species today than there are extinct species (Raven, *Biology*, 151; Ridley, *Evolution*).

The concept that the environment influences the form and diversity of organisms might be taken to harmonize with latter-day revelation. Commenting on the Abrahamic account of the Creation, Hugh Nibley observed,

The creation process as described in the Pearl of Great Price is open-

ended and on-going, entailing careful planning based on vast experience, long calculations, models, tests, even trial-runs for a complicated system requiring a vast scale of participation by the creatures concerned. ... What they [the Gods] ordered was not the completed product, but the process to bring it about, providing a scheme under which
life might expand: "Let us *prepare* the earth to bring forth grass ..." (Moses 4:11). *Not* let us create grass. "Let us prepare the waters to bring
forth abundantly. And the Gods prepared the waters that *they might*
bring forth great whales, and every living creature that moveth ..." Note
the tense—it is future potential: the waters are so treated that *they* will
have the capacity to bring forth. ("Before Adam," 49-85.)

A sticking point seems to be a reluctance by some to allow for
processes of divine creation other than the stereotype of "special"
creation, or "creation by edict." However, for Latter-day Saints the
ultimate issue is the authorship of creation, not the process, as Henry
Eyring remarked:

> The only important thing is that God did it. I might say in that regard
> that in my mind the theory of evolution has to include a notion that the
> dice have been loaded from the beginning in favor of more complex life
> forms. That is, without intelligent design of the natural laws in such a
> way as to favor evolution from lower to higher forms of life, I don't
> think the theory holds water. I can't see randomly generated natural
> laws producing these remarkable results. So, in my mind, God is behind
> it all whether we evolved or not. (*Reflections*, 62.)

More and more frequently, a similar sentiment is being expressed by scientists who do see the odds stacked in favor of the
emergence of complex life. They recognize that "conditions in our
Universe really do seem to be uniquely suitable for life forms like
ourselves" (Gribbon, *Cosmic Coincidences*, 209). Paul Davies, a professor of mathematical physics, University of Adelaide, observed:
"Suffice it to say that, if we could play God, and select values for these
quantities [laws of physics, etc.] at whim by twiddling a set of knobs,
we would find that almost all knob settings would render the universe uninhabitable. In some cases it seems as if the knobs have to be

fine-tuned to enormous precision if the universe is to be such that life will flourish" (*Mind of God*, 199-200).

## Transitional Forms

The inspiring diversity of life forms, ranging from simple to complex, has been viewed historically as the divine order of God's creation—a *Scalae Natura*, or Great Chain of Being. The work of early naturalists was to discover those living animals that would serve to fill in the gaps in the scale of Nature so that the creative handiwork of God could be more fully comprehended. Travellers' accounts of fanciful creatures occupying those intermediate gaps were often uncritically accepted.

We now know that many of these apparent "gaps" are the result of extinctions of past life forms. And yet critics of evolution repeatedly suggest that the fossil record lacks intermediate forms that would support the premise of transitional evolution. Salisbury's following comment is typical: "And how about the transitions or continua in fossil types that allow us to see how genera, families, orders and phyla come into being by evolutionary pathways? Such series do not appear in the record ... the fact of the matter is, *no* major group has obvious fossil predecessors that inform us as to how the group came into being by evolution" (*Creation*, 224). Even if this statement were accurate in 1976 (when his book was published), which it was not, it has been rendered obsolete by additional discoveries of the past few decades. Yet such misleading statements remain a mainstay in anti-evolution propaganda.

How are we to define a transitional form? Would a fish with legs constitute such a form? How about a reptile with feathers? Or an egg-laying mammal? Or a bipedal ape? In 1861, just two years after publication of *The Origin*, a fossilized feather was discovered in a German sandstone quarry of late Jurassic age (150 million years ago), evidence that birds had lived in the age of dinosaurs. But when the bearer of that feather was discovered later that same year, it was no bird of modern aspect. Rather, it was more a feathered reptile and was named *Archaeopteryx* (meaning "ancient wing") (see Feduccia, *Origin and Evolution of Birds*). Seven European specimens have since been discovered. The most recent, found in 1993, was the first to preserve the ossified furcula (wishbone), which serves as the attachment of flight muscles. The horny claws covering the bony toes were also clearly preserved and are similar to those of modern perching birds. These features, together with the aerodynamic asymmetrical flight feathers, confirm that *Archaeopteryx* was capable of flight. Yet the remainder of its anatomy is that of a small dinosaur. Of approximately fifty anatomical features that can be identified as either bird or reptile, three are bird-like and forty-seven are reptile-like. If *Archaeopteryx* does not meet the criterion of a transitional form, what does? To deny the transitional nature of this animal is to willfully ignore the obvious.

Even more recently a number of spectacular dinosaur-bird transitional forms have been discovered in the Liaoning Province of China (*National Geographic*, July 1998, 74-99). *Caudipteryx* and *Protarchaeopteryx* are both more primitive than *Archaeopteryx*, and are transitional between it and the dinosaurs. *Sinornithosaurus millenii* is even more of a dinosaur, essentially a velociraptor with some feathers. However, some Liaoning fossils may be questionable.

The fact is that numerous examples document the origin of, and transition between, several major groups of vertebrate animals—e.g., fish to amphibian, amphibian to reptile, reptile to bird, and reptile to mammal. Given the rapid pace with which evolution can proceed and the rarity of fossilization, these examples are significant. Clearly it is beyond the scope of this chapter to consider each of these transitions in detail. A perusal of the recent popular literature provides numerous spectacular examples of previously "missing" transitional forms. Instead we will make brief note of two examples in light of some of the most recent discoveries: the transition from water to land, and the reverse, the return to water by aquatic mammals.

A series of new fossil discoveries over the past two decades has contributed significantly to resolving tetrapod origins (four-legged animals with backbones). It has been held for more than a century that tetrapods evolved from lobe-finned fishes during the Devonian period (360 million years ago). However, sufficient transitional

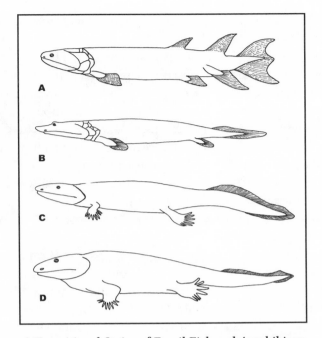

**A Transitional Series of Fossil Fish and Amphibians**

*(A) An osteolepiform fish, Eusthenopteran; (B) a panderichthyid fish, Panderichthys; (C) an amphibian tetrapod, Acanthostega; and (D) an amphibian tetrapod, Ichtheostega.*

forms to test this hypothesis were lacking. Fossils recently discovered in Devonian sediments around the world now provide distinct evidence of this transition (see Ahlberg, "The Origin and Early Diversification of Tetrapods," 507-14). Critics ask what advantage would limbs afford a fish living in water? Why would they evolve limbs in the first place that might later be used to crawl out onto land?

Newly discovered remains of the panderichthyid lobe-finned fish from Canada and Russia reveal an even more tetrapod-like body plan than previously recognized. *Panderichthys* had a rather broad, elongated body with paired pectoral and pelvic fins, lacking dorsal and anal fins. A long, straight tail was equipped with prominent fin rays. It shares a number of derived features of the cranium with tetrapods, confirming the link between earlier lobe-finned fishes and later tetrapods.

Devonian sediments in Greenland, Canada, and Ireland yielded a number of specimens of an important primitive tetrapod *Acanthostega*, including a complete skeleton (see Zimmer, "Coming Onto the Land," 118-27; "From Fins to Feet," 114-27). *Acanthostega* was equipped with an internal gill chamber, indicating it was fully aquatic yet had well-developed limbs. It seems the tetrapod limb evolved as an adaptation for shallow water environments, enabling the possessor to scuttle about on the bottom or lunge from hiding to capture passing prey, and was only later exploited for terrestrial movement. Additional fossil specimens continue to document the transition from water to land.

The past few years have not only seen new, significant evidence for the transition from water to land, but also transitional forms demonstrating something of the reverse—the evolution of aquatic mammals from land mammals. One of the most stunning paleontological stories of the 1990s was the discovery of early fossil whales. Anatomical and molecular evidence had long suggested a link between cetaceans (whales, porpoises, dolphins) and artiodactyls (even-toed hoofed mammals). Cranial similarities to a hyena-sized mesonychid artiodactyl, (55 million years ago), suggested that it may represent a basal stock from which whales evolved; but fossil documentation was meager or altogether lacking. Paleontological investigations in northern Africa and Pakistan have bridged the gap. In 1994 Hans Thewissen and colleagues described a remarkable fossil, *Ambulocetus*, from 52 million-year-old sediments in Pakistan (see Thewissen, "Fossil Evidence for the Origin of Aquatic Locomotion," 210-12). Features of the skull clearly linked it with an earlier mesonychid ungulate and with later cetaceans. The postcranial skeleton exhibits adaptations for an amphibious lifestyle. For example, the limbs were short and flexible, the enlarged hands and feet were paddle-like, yet its toes still ended in small hooves. The vertebral column and elongated tail were capable of dorsoventral (up and down) undulation as in cetaceans, as opposed to the side-to-side undulations of fish and reptiles.

That same year saw the description of another, slightly younger (46 million years ago) early whale, *Rodhocetus* (Gingerich, "New Whale from the Eocene of Pakistan," 844-47). Its remains were found in sediments deposited in deep-water environments. *Rodhocetus* was even more adapted to aquatic life than those of *Ambulocetus*. Most notably, the hindlimbs were one-third smaller than those of *Ambulocetus*. The sacral vertebrae were unfused, thus facilitating whale-like undulatory movements, and the tail vertebrae were greatly enlarged. These combined features indicate greater dependence on the undulating propulsion of a powerful tail, perhaps equipped with flukes.

Full commitment to an ocean dwelling habitat was evident in the fifteen-foot-long *Prozueglodon*, a 40 million-year-old archaecete. In this animal the hindlimbs were reduced to a pair of six-inch vestigial (non-functional) structures, essentially useless for propulsion on land or in sea. The vertebral column and skull exhibit further elongation and specialization. Modern whales today exhibit even more vestigial hindlimb structures, reduced to mere remnants of the pelvis embedded in their flanks, and occasional atavistic (ancestral-like) rudimentary limb bones.

Even early Greek philosopher Aristotle recognized the distinctness of whales and porpoises from the fish. These air-breathing aquatic mammals shared more in common with their land-dwelling kin, despite their lack of legs, than with their scaly, gilled cohorts. The succession of recently discovered fossil primitive whales provides indisputable confirmation of this most unlikely of transitions in form and habitat. These irrefutable transitional forms were precisely predicted by the preceding molecular and incomplete fossil data. They are just what was expected for a transition between land and aquatic mammals. Michael Novachek of the American Museum of Natural History remarked, "This expanding fossil casebook on the origins of whales is one of the triumphs of modern vertebrate paleontology" ("Whales Leave the Beach," 807).

### "Missing links"
Nowhere was the apparent gap in the "Great Chain of Being"

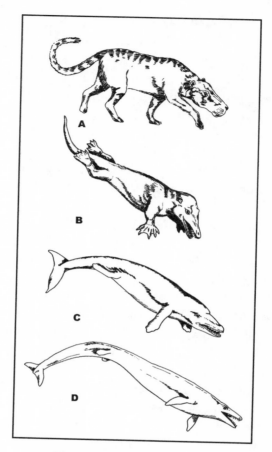

**The Transitional Evolution of
Whales from Terrestrial Quadrupeds**

*(A) Mesonychid artiodactyl; (B) the amphibious Ambulocetus; (C) an early
"quadrupedal" whale, Rodhocetus; (D) the ocean dwelling Prozeuglodon.*

more evident to early naturalists than between humans and the remaining animals. Genesis asserts that humans were created in the
image of God, and early naturalists believed that people possessed
certain unique traits that set them apart from Nature. As noted in the
previous chapter, considerable significance was attached to a number of human characteristics such as upright stance, brain size, tool
use, language, intelligence, and reason.

The idea of a "missing link," spanning the gulf between human-kind and nature, has been a popular one, but was often misconstrued by early naturalists, as it is by some popular writers today. The scale of nature was formerly seen as a static ladder, the *product* of individual acts of special creation, without advancement, or descent, from rung to rung. Furthermore, the possible numbers of "rungs" on the ladder, or links in the chain, were greatly underestimated by early naturalists. It is now known that over 98 percent of all species are extinct. In addition, we now view life as a complex bush instead of as a chain or ladder. Therefore, rather than there being a simple ladder or chain with 10,000 links, a few of which were missing, the "chain" is a complex branching system with millions of links.

Early naturalists believed that if our closest living allies were the apes, then the "missing link" between humans and apes remained to be discovered living in some unexplored corner of the world. Such a creature was perceived to be an intermediate apeman. However, as is evident from recent discoveries in the fossil record, the gap between humans and apes has far more links than previously thought. With the discovery of any one "missing link," two more are created—one above it and one below it.

Although in the nineteenth century little was known from the fossil record, Darwin's theory predicted the existence of *several* extinct links between humans and apes. The only potential specimen at the time was the beetle-browed skull of Neandertal man, discovered in a cave in central Germany, which was dismissed by most authorities as a misshapen contemporary human. In 1863 Thomas Henry Huxley reflected, "Where must we look for primeval man? Was the oldest *Homo sapiens* Pliocene or Miocene, or yet more ancient? In still older strata do the fossilized bones of an ape more anthropoid or a man more pithecoid, than any yet known, await the researches of some unborn paleontologist? Time will tell" (*Evidence as to Man's Place in Nature*). Indeed it has.

Darwin predicted that humans share a common ancestor with the African apes and that eventually fossils of that common ancestor would be found on the African continent. He stated, "In each great region of the world the living mammals are closely related to the extinct species of the same region. It is therefore probable that Africa was inhabited by extinct apes closely allied to the gorilla and chimpanzee; and as these two species are now man's nearest allies, it is somewhat more probable that our early progenitors lived on the African continent than elsewhere" (*Descent of Man*, 520). Darwin's prediction was borne out over half a century later.

In the past few decades, our knowledge of the fossil record of human evolution has exploded. It is fair to say that over three-quarters of the pertinent fossils have been discovered and the ensuing literature written since 1970. Significant discoveries appear annually on the covers of *Time*, *Newsweek*, *National Geographic*, and numerous scientific journals. Again it is impossible within the scope of this chapter to convey the entire fossil record of evolution. It was once asserted that all the fossil evidence of human evolution could be "placed into a single shoe box," with room to spare. This is no longer the case. There now exist tens of thousands of individual specimens in museum collections around the world. Many are single teeth or isolated jaws, but scores are relatively complete skulls and some are largely complete skeletons. The few examples of fossils discussed here serve merely to highlight the ever-increasing body of data that continues to refine our understanding of hominid relationships and adaptations. These examples concentrate particularly on the discoveries of the past few decades and are especially meaningful since they postdate much of the writing by Mormon authors and others on this subject.

Humans are "hominids," but not all hominids are human or even human ancestors. Hominids are members of the primate family *Hominidae*, which encompasses all bipedal (two-legged) primate species that arose since the split from a common ancestor. (This split accounts for the lineage leading to the living African apes [chimps and gorillas] and that leading to humans; it is thought to have occurred sometime between 5-7 million years ago, as also indicated by the accumulated differences in DNA.) This common ancestor has now become the current elusive "missing link." A number of previous "missing links" between the common ancestor and modern humans have already been found and studied.

The common ancestor of apes and hominids may prove difficult to find since it most likely inhabited a tropical forest where conditions for fossilization are poor (no fossil chimpanzee or gorilla has yet been found in Africa). When found, it will likely be difficult to recognize this common ancestor as such since it will share many generalized characteristics with both early apes and early hominids. As long as adaptations for bipedalism are present in a fossil ape, there will be little ambiguity about its membership in the family *Hominidae*. The affiliation of species that predates this evolutionary innovation, to either the African ape lineage or the hominid lineage, will be less obvious.

One potential immediate predecessor of the common ancestor is *Ouranopithecus macedoniensis*, recently discovered in Greek sediments nearly 10 million years old (de Bonis, "New Hominid Skull Material," 712-14). The fossil specimens of this ape include a complete facial skeleton, upper teeth, and several jaws. They share a number of unique features with the living African apes, especially the gorilla. Another candidate, *Dryopithecus laietanus*, was discovered in Spain. The partial skeleton of this 9.5 million-year-old large-bodied ape exhibits arm-hanging adaptations and vertebral column similar to those of living chimps and gorillas (see Maya-Sola, "A *Dryopithecus* Skeleton," 156-59). An even older African specimen of ape displaying similar adaptations was recently discovered in Chad and dubbed *Morotopithecus* (see Gebo, "A Hominoid Genus," 401-404). The emergence of these arm-hanging adaptations is significant, for this mode of locomotion best explains the particular anatomy of the ape chest and shoulder, which distinguishes them from many of the extinct apes. Hominids display a similar anatomy of chest and shoulder.

That critical period from the Miocene epoch, spanning between 4 and 9 million years ago, has a meager representation in the known fossil record of Africa. However, the past decade has witnessed the breach of the 4 million-year "barrier" with the discovery of some of the earliest known hominids. This is a significant advance as it extends the record ever closer to the proposed last common ancestor of apes and hominids, which molecular biologists and morphologists agree probably lived about 5-7 million years ago (see Pilbeam,

"Genetic and Morphological Records," 155-68). These recent discoveries provide clues about some of the earliest members of the hominid lineage.

For many years scientists knew of an isolated fragmentary jaw bone from the locality of Lothagam, in East Africa. Dated to 5.6 million years ago, it was potentially one of the oldest hominid fossils. However, the incompleteness of the specimen and lack of any limb skeleton made it difficult to determine if the specimen was a hominid or a fossil ape. The discovery of additional fossil material from the 4 to 5 million-year range makes it appear more probable that the Lothagam jaw is an early hominid.

Two new and significant species of the earliest known hominids have been described recently. One of these hominids, named *Australopithecus amanensis*, was discovered in Kenya by Meave Leakey in 1994 and dates to 4.1 million years ago. It combines relatively chimpanzee-like jaws with leg bones that indicate adaptations for bipedalism, even at this early date (see "The Dawn of Humans," 38-51). Also in 1994 an additional species of hominid from Ethiopia, *Australopithecus ramidis,* was announced (see White, "*Australopithecus ramidis,*" 306-12). This second hominid dates to about 4.4 million years ago. Subsequent specimens recovered in 1995, including a largely complete skeleton, which is being prepared and has yet to be fully described, prompted the discoverers to assign it to a new genus, *Ardipithecus*. The hands are equipped with long curved fingers and powerful muscle attachments indicative of climbing habits. Eventual description of the pelvis, legs, and feet will reveal if and in what manner *Ardipithecus* was bipedal.

The first fossil of this early group of hominids, called australopithecines, was discovered in South Africa by Raymond Dart in 1924 (hence the name which means "southern ape"), but it was many years before the significance of this controversial discovery was generally appreciated. The second specimen was not found until 1936, by Robert Broom. The australopithecines have been described rather crudely as "bipedal chimps"—in some respects an appropriate description. Their skeleton combines a mosaic of ape-like and human-like traits, clearly satisfying the criterion of a "missing link." In fact, in 1938 the *London Illustrated News* proclaimed, "Missing Link no longer missing!" (310-11). However, acceptance of this discovery by the scientific community was not forthcoming until the late 1940s.

The best known and most complete australopithecine skeleton, dubbed "Lucy," was discovered by Don Johanson in Ethiopia in 1974 (see *Lucy*; "The Dawn of Humans," 96-117). It belongs to the species *Australopithecus afarensis* and dates to 3.7 million years ago. It is of relatively small stature, being just under 3.5 feet tall, and is presumably a female. Males were considerably larger, reaching nearly five feet in height. From the waist up, australopithecines are decidedly ape-like, with a slightly larger than chimpanzee-sized brain (450 cc), large teeth, conical-shaped rib cage, relatively long arms, and rather curved fingers. From the waist down, they are decidedly more human-like, with a shallow broad pelvis, valgus knee (with the feet centered under the body), and less divergent big toe, all evidence of upright bipedal posture. The legs, however, are relatively short and the toes long and curved by comparison to human legs and toes, indicating considerable time spent feeding and/or sheltering in trees. The discovery has now been rivaled by an even more complete skeleton of *Australopithecus africanus* found in a South African cave in sediments more than 3.5 million years old (Clarke, 1999).

The earliest members of the genus "man," *Homo*, also come from Africa (see Gore, "The Dawn of Humans," 72-99). In 1964 Louis Leakey and colleagues announced the discovery of a fragmentary skull of a hominid with an increased cranial capacity of approximately 680 cc. *Homo habilis* was the first known hominid to consistently use simple stone tools and include meat as a large component of its diet. The emergence and dispersal of early *Homo* may have been a response to environmental changes. A major climatic shift, with global cooling and drying, caused dramatic shrinkage and fragmentation of the tropical forests and the appearance of the polar ice sheets about 2.4 million years ago. It was thought that this climatic stress might have caused the divergence and diversification of the first members of *Homo* from the australopithecines, but the oldest fossils of *Homo* were only 1.9 million years old. Then in November 1994, an upper palate with dentition of an early *Homo* was found in Ethiopia just below a volcanic ash layer precisely dated to 2.33 + .07 million years ago (see Kimbel, "Late Pliocene *Homo* and Oldowan Tools," 549-61). It was associated with examples of the earliest simple stone tools and constitutes the oldest well-dated evidence of *Homo*. Such correlations between environmental events and the appearance of new species are gaining corroboration and, for some Mormons, suggest Abraham's account of the Creation in which God manipulated the conditions of the physical environment to facilitate and promote the process of creation by evolution.

In 1984 a virtually complete fossil skeleton of a *Homo erectus* was discovered by Richard Leakey in Kenya. Dated to approximately 1.6 million years ago, this stunning specimen is a sub-adult male estimated to be about twelve years of age. It already stood nearly 5.5 feet tall and had a robust skeleton with prominent muscle markings. Its brain was intermediate in size between a chimpanzee and a human (880 cc)—another "missing link." The proportions of the limbs are human-like, but it retains features of the rib cage, vertebral column, and hips found in the australopithecine skeleton, thus indicating descent from these earlier hominids. Specimens of *Homo erectus* have been uncovered throughout Africa and Asia (see Gore, "The Dawn of Humans," 84-109). Regional variations between Africa and eastern Asia indicate the possibility of two species. In that case, the African species would be referred to as *Homo ergaster*. In addition to the marked shift in anatomy, there was a shift in behavior, including the first controlled use of fire, more complex and consistent tool usage, and big game hunting.

Transitional forms between *Homo ergaster* and modern *Homo sapiens* have been referred to as *archaic Homo sapiens*. Some scientists, however, prefer to designate them as members of a distinct species, *Homo heidlbergensis*. What may appear to be equivocation on the part of some paleoanthropologists simply attests to the obvious transitional nature of these specimens. The fossils display such an intermediate combination of features that opinions split as to how they should be classified. Where does one draw the line between "species" through time when the gradation between them is so continuous?

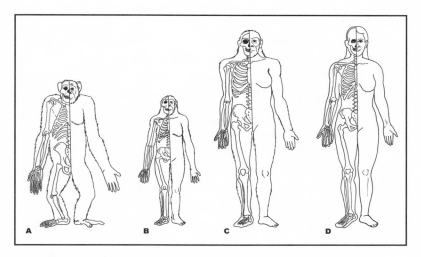

*The fossilized skeletons of a 3.7 million-year-old Australopithecus afarensis (B), a 1.6 million-year-old Homo ergaster (C), contrasted with the skeletons of a chimpanzee on the left (A) and a human on the right (D).*

Shifting opinions in naming do not alter the significance of the specimens as transitional.

*Homo heidlbergensis* first appears about 780,000 years ago. It shows a further increase in brain size (average 1250 cc), somewhat thinner skull bones, but retains a robust, heavily muscled skeleton. Numerous specimens have been found in Africa and throughout Eurasia. One specialized regional side-branch of the *Homo heidlbergensis* lineage is the Neandertal, which appeared in isolated western Europe about 120,000-130,000 years ago (see Gore, "The Dawn of Humans: Neandertals," 2-35). Their disposition of sheltering in caves has resulted in the preservation and recovery of numerous essentially complete skeletons, and originally gave rise to the unfortunate term "caveman." In 1993 Italian spelunkers entered a sealed cave and discovered a very early and apparently complete Neandertal skeleton nestled among the stalagmites, partly encrusted with limestone travertine. These hominids had brains that in size rivaled or exceeded modern human brains, although the organization may have differed somewhat. Physically they remained quite distinct, with rather squat, extremely robust, heavily muscled skeletons, less dexterous hands, low brows, and prominent faces. Culturally they were also distinct, lacking in art objects and adornments.

By as early as 200,000 years ago, modern *Homo sapiens* had emerged, distinguished by their gracile (i.e., more slender) skeletal structure, high foreheads, and small teeth and jaws. In 1988 an absolute date was determined for a site in the Middle East, which in 1965 had yielded several well-preserved modern human skulls. The Qafzeh skulls were 92,000 years old (see Shreeve, "The Dating Game," 76-83). Although the earliest examples of these "anatomically modern" *Homo sapiens* have been found throughout Africa and the Near East, their material culture differed little from that of their more robust and primitive predecessors.

Then somewhat abruptly (archaeologically speaking), a creative explosion occurred. After about 35,000 years ago, sites in Europe yielded modern humans associated with a complex and sophisticated tool kit, varied art objects, bone sewing needles, the use of ochre for adornment, and breathtaking paintings on cave walls. The cover of the October 1988 issue of the *National Geographic* magazine featured a carved ivory bust of a rugged man's face. A self-portrait perhaps? The ivory was dated to 26,000 years ago and originated from a locality in former Czechoslovakia that had long produced neolithic artifacts, as well as in 1986 three complete skeletons in a ceremonial multiple burial.

The frozen corpse and personal effects of the recently discovered "Iceman," preserved for over 5,000 years in the European Alps, captured the public's imagination and provided a virtual window onto the Neolithic way of life in prehistoric Europe (see Roberts, "The Ice Man," 36-67). On the opposite side of the globe, an equally significant discovery received less sensational headlines. A 9,400-year-old Native American mummy was discovered entombed in Nevada ("Oldest American," 26). These were modern human beings, virtually indistinguishable from you and me in bodily form and inferred mental abilities, with a sense of self, an appreciation for aesthetics and possibly religion, and a reverence for their dead. These were of our species, *Homo sapiens*, which has inhabited this earth for nearly 200 millennia.

This has been a brief synopsis of the hard evidence—fossilized bones and teeth, and stone tools—for human evolution. To this must be added the flood of information contributed by paleo-climatolo-

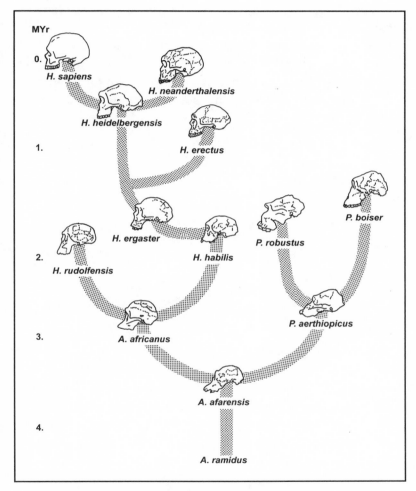

### A Hominid "Family Tree"

*Time ranges of hominid species spanning the past 4.5 million years. Hypothesized relationships are discussed in the text.*

gists, -botanists, -ecologists, -geologists, -archaeologists, and other scientists. The evidence provides a persuasive drama of the evolution of ape-like bipedal hominids, from which a lineage emerged that subsequently evolved into beings physically indistinguishable from modern humans. The search for *the* "missing link" has yielded numerous links, at more and more finely resolved intermediate levels, to a point where boundaries between the types or "species" have become ambiguous. The fossil evidence of human evolution is one of the best examples of transitional evolution in the fossil record. Does this necessarily eliminate the need for a Creator? No. Instead, this implies a natural process by which God carried out his creative design and ultimately prepared suitable physical tabernacles for his spirit offspring.

# 11.
# Genesis Revisited

In some people's mind, the theory of evolution eliminates the need for any other explanation of the Creation. In the face of data that overwhelmingly support evolution, some may even begin to question what they have been taught about religion. Some may say to themselves, "My parents, or my Sunday school teachers, or my seminary teachers didn't know about all the evidence supporting evolution. If it is correct, is the Creation story in Genesis wrong?" For hundreds of faithful LDS biologists, the answer is no. In fact, we believe that the Genesis story is compatible with evolution. Some of the problems that appear to exist arise, not from the scriptures, but from traditions that go beyond what the scriptures state.

Let us examine Genesis and other scriptures concerning the Creation and, in particular, the creation of humankind. We hope to demonstrate that the processes of nature and the scriptures are not at odds. We accept as data the King James version of Genesis and LDS scriptures. We believe that people do not have as much trouble with the actual words in Genesis as with the interpretation of those words.

In this discussion, we will raise many questions, most of which we cannot answer. In raising these questions, we are attempting to follow God's commandments to meditate upon the scriptures (Josh. 1:8) and to "study my word" (D&C 11:22). We intend only to point out that we all read the scriptures differently, and that most people do not search and ponder them, but simply gloss over difficult parts. For believing Mormons, the full meaning of the scriptures is given only by revelation through the influence of the Holy Ghost.

Nonetheless, we realize that there are many unofficial interpretations and that these are often based on tradition. We commonly hear well-meaning people say, "That's your interpretation of the scripture," while also claiming, "I'm not interpreting the scripture, that's what it says." In the first part of this chapter, we attempt to avoid interpreting the passages we cite. Rather, we simply ask questions about their intent. Later in this chapter, we offer some possible interpretations. If a specific scripture can be interpreted at least two different ways, one that contradicts science and one that is compatible with it, we favor the latter. Some of the greatest conflicts between interpretations of Genesis concerning the Creation and the scientific data concerning human origins stem from traditions that are not supported by the scriptures or by official prophetic interpretation. We do not believe that students should be forced to choose between traditions and science. (We have bolded terms or phrases in the following discussion to emphasize certain passages that we want to address.)

In the beginning ...

When we read anything, including the scriptures, personal interpretation—whether intentional or not—occurs at the very outset. What does "In the beginning ..." mean to you? To someone else? Were these three words, in fact, intended to begin the Bible? Clearly, they were not the precise words Moses (or another author) used to start the Bible, because Moses's first words were not in English. The King James version of the Bible has come down to us by several steps of translation. Were all of those accurate? Was the complete story, as intended by the original authors, carried down to us intact or were parts left out? Brigham Young stated, "As for the Bible account of the creation ... that account has been handed down from age to age and we have got it no matter whether it is correct or not" (*Journal of Discourses* 14:115-17).

Fortunately, modern scripture answers many of these questions. Everything appearing in italics in the current King James Bible was not part of the original translation but was inserted—each insertion is thus an interpretation. It is enlightening to read the Bible skipping the italicized words. The meaning sometimes can be quite different.

In the beginning **God** ...

What do we mean by "God"? Does the term mean the same to each of us? Let us examine this by considering a natural law, such as the law of gravity. If we consider God's relationship to the law of gravity, at least four possibilities come to mind. (1) Every time I jump off something, God personally makes sure I land on the ground. He is directly involved in everything I do. What we call "gravity" is actually God pulling me to the ground. Although commonly believed during the Middle Ages, such a view is not held widely today. A slight modification of this view is that God intervenes only when it is really important. (2) God created gravity and gravity has natural consequences for us. This possibility is of modern invention, and may be the most common opinion held by most religious people, perhaps in conjunction with the latter part of possibility 1. (3) God did not create the law of gravity but knows enough about it to work within its confines. Gravity is in some way an intrinsic property of the universe—perhaps even co-eternal with God. Although we suspect that most Mormons would identify with possibility 2, official LDS doctrine is actually more compatible with 3. (4) There is no God at all. If gravity exists and we can understand it, there is not need for God. This last position is taken by many scientists today.

In the beginning God **created the heaven** ...

The creation of the earth has been the subject of much discussion and numerous books, but few people have considered the "creation of heaven." Does the word "heaven" here mean a place where God dwells with his angels? And if this is heaven, how does it differ from the usual objective of a Christian life? Or is heaven here what Mormons call the preexistence? And how does it relate to our concept of the Celestial Kingdom, where we will progress eternally? Or does heaven in this verse mean simply the atmosphere around the earth? (The accounts in Moses 2:1 or JST Genesis 1:3 do not seem to provide additional insights here.) Abraham 4:1 states, "And they went down at the beginning, and they, that is the Gods, organized and formed the heavens and the earth."

In the beginning God **created** the heaven and **the earth**.

Most religious people believe that God, in some way, created the earth, but there is much debate as to *how* he created it. That debate lies at the root of a book like this one. Many people believe that God's creation of the earth and all things upon its face precludes evolution. We do not agree. The scriptures tell us that God created the earth, but they do not tell us how.

And the earth was **without form**, and void; and darkness *was* upon the face of the **deep**. And the Spirit of God moved upon the **face** of the **waters**.

If the earth was without form, then what does the word "deep" mean? And how was there water if there was no form? Was the earth even a sphere? If not, how could there be water, especially water with a "face"? Why "waters" and not just "water"? The waters and land are not separated until verses 6 and 9. Abraham 4:2 states, "And the earth, after it was formed, was empty and desolate ..."

And God said, Let there be **light**: and there was light.

Where did this light come from? There was no sun until verses 14-16.

And God saw the light, that *it was* good: and God **divided** the light from the darkness. And God called the light Day, and the darkness he called Night. And the evening and the morning were the first **day**.

In dividing the light from the darkness, there is still no sun. The term "day" is first mentioned here, even before the sun was made (v. 16). If there is no sun to rise and set, then how was a day calculated? Or was a "day" a period of time of unspecified length? Most "Creationists" insist that the earth was created in six twenty-four-hour days. We do not see the term "day" here to support that view. There are many places in the scriptures where "day" means an unspecified period. Webster gives both definitions. In the book of Abraham, these "days" are called "times" (see Abr. 4:8, 13, etc.).

> And God said, Let there be a **firmament in the midst of the waters**, and let it **divide the waters from the waters**. And **God made the firmament**, and **divided the waters which *were* under the firmament from the waters which *were* above the firmament**: and it was so. And **God called the firmament heaven**. And the evening and the morning were the second day. And God said, Let there be **lights in the firmament of the heaven** to divide the day from the night; and let them be for signs, and for seasons, and for days, and years: And let them be for lights in the firmament of the heaven to give light upon the earth: and it was so. And God made two great lights; the **greater light** to rule the day, and the **lesser light** to rule the night: *he made* the **stars** also. And **God set them in the firmament of the heaven** to give light upon the earth, And to rule over the day and over the night, and to divide the light from the darkness: and God saw that *it was* good. And the evening and the morning were the **fourth day**.

Finally, sun and moon appear on the fourth day. Here, perhaps is an answer, but with more questions. We are told that "God called the firmament heaven" (v. 8). This may answer the question we raised concerning heaven in verse 1. Furthermore, we are told in these later verses that there was water *under* the firmament and water *above* the firmament (v. 6), and that the lights (greater, lesser, and stars) were *in* the firmament (vv. 14-16). (Moses 2:6-16 and JST Gen.1:9-20 give the same account as King James, except to define the terms "greater and lesser lights" as the sun and moon.)

The medieval Hebrew concept of the universe was that of a glass dome, or firmament, stretched over the earth. The word "firmament" means the lid of a pot. The earth and dome constituted the entire universe. The sun, moon, and stars were embedded in this dome; there was water on the exterior of the dome, and "void" beyond that. Most medieval scholars agreed with this model of the universe, which is consistent with Genesis 1:6-19. Then why do we not hold this model today? Because Galileo turned his telescope to the night sky and forever shattered the concept of a solid, domed firmament. He discovered that the moon had shadows (impossible for a "light") and that other moons orbited Jupiter (impossible if all the lights in the firmament were oriented in the dome relative to earth).

Galileo's observations directly contradicted what appeared to be the account in the scriptures. These issues caused a major clash between science and religion 400 years ago. For all his work, Galileo was threatened with expulsion from the Catholic church unless he retracted his interpretation. Only a handful of years ago, the Catholic church finally admitted that Galileo was right.

What has happened to us over the past 400 years? Why does this part of Genesis not cause major conflicts between science and religion today? Unlike the people of Galileo's time, we have had 400 years to live with his data and interpretations. Many other scientists, through the years, have substantiated his observations and confirmed his interpretations. No one today doubts that the moon is a solid sphere orbiting the earth, that the sun is a great ball of burning gas, or that the stars are millions of miles away. In light of what we have learned from science, we no longer accept the medieval interpretation of this scripture. With the greater knowledge we have today, we must admit that we do not know what this scripture was referring to. Perhaps it was simply figurative. Perhaps this was all the people of that time could understand.

> And God said, Let the **waters** under the heaven be **gathered together unto one place**, and let the **dry** land **appear**: and it was so. And God called the **dry** land **Earth**; and the gathering together of the waters called he Seas: and God saw that it was good.

After each phase of the creative process, God saw that "it was good." This statement has been occasionally interpreted to convey the state of perfection in a paradisiacal creation. What is the basis of this interpretation? Could the term "good" simply indicate that the resulting creation was executed as indicated, according to the predetermined plan?

Here is an example of a scripture that agrees more with modern science than with older beliefs. The modern view of the earth's history is that in the remote past all the land was in one place and the water in another. Since then, the continents have been drifting apart. However, we hesitate to suggest that Genesis teaches continental drift and plate tectonics. Notice that the word "land" has been added. The original translation read, "let the dry appear ... And God called the dry Earth ... and God saw that good." Modern revelation confirms that God "called the dry land Earth" (Moses 2:10).

> And God said, Let the earth bring forth grass, the herb yielding **seed**, *and* the **fruit** tree yielding fruit after his **kind**, whose seed *is* in itself, upon the earth: and it was so. And the **earth brought forth** grass, *and* **herb yielding seed** after his kind, and the **tree yielding fruit**, whose seed *was* in itself, after his kind: and God saw that *it was* **good**. And the evening and the morning were the **third day**.

Many people, including some Mormons, believe that there was no reproduction or death of anything, including plants and animals, until after the Fall. How can plants form seeds or fruit without reproduction? How could Adam and Eve eat these seeds and fruit in the garden if there was no death of the cells making up the seeds or fruit? (See v. 29.) This important issue is discussed in greater length elsewhere in this book (see also 2 Ne. 2:22).

> And God said, **Let the waters bring forth** abundantly **the moving creature** that hath life, and **fowl** *that* may fly above the earth in the open firmament of heaven. And **God created** great whales, and **every living creature that moveth, which the waters brought forth abundantly**, after their **kind**, and every winged fowl after his kind: and God saw that *it was* good. And God blessed them, saying, Be fruitful, and multiply, and fill the waters in the seas, and let the fowl multiply in the earth. And the evening and the morning were the fifth day.

These verses do not state that each animal arose from an act of special creation; rather, a process was implemented whereby the elements were to "bring forth" living things. Notice that the fowls fly *in* the firmament, suggesting that the firmament is what we call the sky. Verse 20 states that the "moving creatures," especially the "fowl," came from the water. This seems to be consistent with evolution. The meaning of the word "kind" has been a source of debate between Creationists and scientists for many years. The implication here seems to be some sort of a breeding barrier, which is how modern biologists define, in part, the term "species." However, there is also considerable debate among biologists as to what constitutes a species. Take, for example, the mule. Do mules exist in defiance of God's laws?

> And God said, **Let the earth bring forth the living creature** after his kind, cattle and creeping thing, and beast of the earth after his **kind**; and it was so. And God made the beast of the earth after his kind, and cattle after their kind, and every thing that creepeth upon the earth after his kind: and God saw that *it was* good.

Here the land, not the water, brings forth creatures from the earth. These creatures include the "beast of the earth," "cattle," and "creeping things," which are different from the creatures listed in verses 20-21.

> And God said, **Let us make man in our image, after our likeness**: and let them have dominion over the fish of the sea, and over the fowl of the air, and over the cattle, and over all the earth, and over every creeping thing that creepeth upon the earth. So God created man in his *own* image, in the image of God created he him; **male and female created he them**. And God blessed them, and God said unto them, Be fruitful, and multiply, and replenish the earth, and subdue it: and have dominion over the fish of the sea, and over the fowl of the air, and over every living thing that moveth upon the earth. And God said, Behold, I have given you every herb bearing seed, which *is* upon the face of all the earth, and every tree, in the which *is* the fruit of the tree yielding seed; to you it shall be for meat.

We believe that we are created in the image of God. We also

believe that nothing in the scientific data detracts from this view. These issues are described more fully in the next chapter. It is important to note that there is no mention here (or elsewhere in the scriptures) of Adam and Eve being created as immortal beings or as beings transplanted from another world.

> And **to every beast of the earth**, and to every **fowl of the air**, and to every thing that creepeth upon the earth, wherein *there is* life, *I have given* **every green herb for meat**: and it was so. And God saw every thing that he had made, and, behold, *it was* very good. And the evening and the morning were the sixth day.

No scripture states there was no death before the Fall. Even 2 Nephi 2:22, which some people cite to support the assertion that death did not exist before the Fall, reports simply that "all things ... must have remained in the same state in which they were after they were created; and they must have remained forever, and had no end." What does the phrase "all things" mean? Read verses 23 and 24. Does this one verse really state, or even mean, that there was no death before the Fall? Such a concept is a matter of conjecture and tradition, not doctrine.

Were all beasts and fowls plant-eaters before the Fall? Plants are also living; what about their death before the Fall? If all animals ate plants, the anatomy and physiology of some animals must have changed drastically afterwards. For example, a lion's intestinal tract is only about ten feet long and is well-suited for digesting and absorbing the high-protein nutrients of meat. By contrast, a cow's intestinal tract is nearly sixty feet long and is well-suited for the long, slow process of fermenting and digesting the relatively low levels of nutrients in grasses and hay. A lion fed only grass and hay will soon die of starvation. Notice that the phrases "there is" and "I have given" are both italicized, indicating that they were added after the translation. Moses 2:30 and JST Genesis 1:32 differ from the King James version, although not significantly: "And to every beast of the earth, and to every fowl of the air, and to everything that creepeth upon the earth, wherein I grant life, there shall be given every clean herb for meat; and it was so, even as I spake."

> Thus the heavens and the earth were finished, and all the host of them. And on the **seventh day God ended his work** which he had made, and he **rested** on the seventh day from all his work which he had made.

This is the curtain call for Genesis 1. The Creation is complete, and now God rests. But wait; Genesis 2 gives a *second* version of the Creation. In this one, the earth appears to be a desert waste, watered by misty dews, Adam is made and placed in the Garden of Eden, an oasis, then the beasts are made, followed finally by Eve. The second Creation account begins in verse 4, "These *are* the generations of the heavens and the earth ..." What is going on? We will return to these issues later in this chapter. Verse 5 continues:

> And **every plant of the field before it was in the earth**, and **every herb of the field before it grew**: for **the Lord God had not caused it to rain upon the earth**, and *there was* not a man to till the ground.

This lack of water would be a problem for plants. And what does this partial thought, "And every plant of the field before it was in the earth, and every herb of the field before it grew," mean? What about all the plants before they grew? In this case, modern scripture comes to the rescue, but not without raising more questions. We read in Joseph Smith's translation of Genesis 2:4-6 (see also Moses 3:5), "And now, behold, I say unto you, that these are the generations of the heaven, and of the earth, and every plant of the field before it was in the earth, and every herb of the field before it grew; For I, the Lord God, had created all the children of men, and not yet a man to till the ground, for in heaven created I them, and there was not yet flesh upon the earth, neither in the water, neither in the air." Does this suggest that Genesis 1 describes a spiritual creation and not a physical one? As will become evident, this dichotomy is not so simply resolved. Are most of our questions from that chapter therefore moot? What about the problem of the firmament and the fowls coming out of the water?

But **there went up a mist from the earth, and watered the whole face of the ground**.

Notice that the water comes *up* from the ground, not down from the sky. Does this describe a source of water—wells and oases—more familiar to desert dwellers?

And the Lord **God formed man** *of* **the dust of the ground**, and **breathed into his nostrils the breath of life**: and **man became a living soul**.

Notice that the word "of" has been inserted. The Joseph Smith translation of Genesis 2:8 also uses "of," as well as an interesting phrase at the end of the verse, which is not in the King James version: "And I, the Lord God, formed man of the dust of the ground, and breathed into his nostrils the breath of life; and man became a living soul; **the first flesh upon the earth, the first man also** ..." Moses 3:7 uses the term "from" rather than "of": "And I, the Lord God, formed man from the dust of the ground, and breathed into his nostrils the breath of life; and man became a living soul, the first flesh upon the earth, the first man also; **nevertheless, all things were before created; but spiritually were they created and made according to my word**." Notice that in this version, the statement that man was "the first flesh upon the earth, the first man also" is included. But this is then followed by what appears to be an odd statement: "nevertheless, all things were before created; but spiritually were they created and made according to my word." This is a restatement of verse 5. Why is it inserted, again, at this point?

What does the phrase "the first flesh upon the earth, the first man also" mean, especially when followed by the reminder that all these things were first created spiritually?

And **God planted a garden eastward in Eden**; and there he put the man whom he had formed.

What is the significance of the term "eastward"? East of what? The term "east" or "eastward" comes up several other times in Genesis. Whatever significance it may have once had, that significance has since been lost. Some claim that this means eastward from Canaan, or Israel. But is this not an interpretation based on tradition? What was westward? What was transpiring on the rest of the earth, outside the garden?

> And out of the ground made the Lord God to grow every tree that is pleasant to the sight, and good for food; **the tree of life** also in the midst of the garden, and **the tree of knowledge of good and evil**.

What was the purpose of the Tree of Life? What about the Tree of Knowledge of Good and Evil? Why were these two trees specifically mentioned? These trees will be discussed in more detail later in this chapter.

> And a **river went out of Eden** to water the garden ...

A river went out of Eden to water the garden? Was not the Garden *in* Eden? Apparently Eden was a place or region more extensive than the garden itself. The significance of this has also been lost.

> And the Lord **God took the man, and put him into the garden of Eden** to dress it and to keep it. And the Lord **God commanded the man**, saying, **Of every tree of the garden thou mayest freely eat: But of the tree of the knowledge of good and evil, thou shalt not eat of it**: for in the **day** that thou eatest thereof **thou shalt surely die**.

If God "took" Adam and "put him into the garden," then where was Adam taken from? What was Adam's state or condition before being placed into the garden with its two special trees? Notice that Adam was not given specific instructions about the Tree of Life, even though it had been mentioned in an earlier verse. Did God actually plant the Tree of Knowledge of Good and Evil to create an opportunity for Adam and Eve to sin? ("Let no man say when he is tempted, I am tempted of God: for God cannot be tempted with evil, neither tempteth he any man," James 1:13; see also Omni 1:25, Alma 5:40, and Moro. 7:12.) Maybe God did not specifically plant the Tree of Knowledge of Good and Evil. Maybe he just warned Adam and Eve of the "natural consequence" of eating the fruit, like a parent warning a child: "This tree isn't good for you; it's harmful; don't eat its fruit." We are not suggesting this as an interpretation, only raising the question. However, we must remember that God pronounced everything he created as "good."

> And **out of the ground the Lord God formed every beast of the field, and every fowl of the air** ...

This time we are told that the fowl were made from the ground. Does this contradict Genesis 1:20?

> And the Lord God caused a deep sleep to fall upon Adam, and he slept: and he took one of his ribs, and closed up the flesh instead thereof; And the **rib**, which the Lord God had taken from man, **made he a woman**, and brought her unto the man.

According to modern revelation, this statement is figurative and the event it describes did not actually occur. President Spencer W. Kimball stated, "The story of the rib, of course, is figurative" ("The Blessings and Responsibilities of Womanhood," 70-72). Elder Bruce R. McConkie echoed, "It also says, speaking figuratively, that Eve was formed from Adam's rib" ("Christ and the Creation," 9-15). How much of the entire story is figurative?

The two creation accounts, Genesis 1 and Genesis 2, are similar in plot and characters, yet fundamentally different in staging and sequence of events. The first chapter bears striking similarities to the creation epics of Israel's neighbors in Mesopotamia, except for its emphasis on one god. It depicts the creation of order (life) from chaos (water). The second chapter is set on a stage more familiar to the desert, with a garden oasis watered by mists and springs. Living things, including humans, are created from dust, much as bricks are molded from mud. In the first account, Adam and Eve are the culmination of the creative process. In the second, Adam is the "first flesh," created on day one. These contrasts have not gone unnoticed by other students of the scriptures. Elder B. H. Roberts noted, "What is most perplexing about the Bible narrative of the work of creation is that two accounts are given of it; and apparently there is irreconcilable difference between them" (*Gospel*, 274).

Interpreters of modern scripture have attempted to resolve the apparent conflict between these two accounts. In the Book of Moses we read that "I the Lord God created all things, of which I have spoken, spiritually, before they were naturally upon the face of the earth ... And I the Lord God had created all the children of men; and not yet a man to till the ground; for in heaven created I them spiritually" (3:5). It has therefore been suggested that Genesis 1 recounts a spiritual creation, and Genesis 2 a physical creation. On the other hand, the Book of Abraham suggests that the first account represents the *planning* stage and that the second account is the actual execution of the plan: "And the Gods came down and formed these the generations of the heaven and the earth, when they were formed in the day that the Gods formed the earth and the heavens, according to all that which they had said concerning every plant of the field before it was in the earth" (5:4-5).

We are told that the depiction of Creation in LDS temples relates to the physical creation; yet it generally follows the account of Genesis 1. Elder Bruce R. McConkie stated, "The Mosaic and the temple accounts set forth the temporal or physical creation ... they are not accounts of the spirit creation" ("Christ and the Creation," 9-15). Likewise, a revelation to the prophet Joseph Smith—"We are to understand that as God made the world in six days and on the seventh day he finished his work, and sanctified it, and also made man out of the dust of the earth ..." (D&C 77:12)—suggests that Genesis 1 describes the physical creation. Elder McConkie proposed a novel interpretation of the first two books of Genesis in which the "spiritual creation" pertains to Adam and entails the physical creation of his immortal body in a paradisiacal state, rather than the procreation of his spirit body ("Christ and the Creation," 9-15). In a recent *Ensign* article, Robert Woodward states, "Genesis 1 evidently teaches us about the preparation of the earth for humankind to inhabit and about the creation in heaven of the original plants, animals, and humans—Adam and Eve. Their bodies were physical but not yet subject to death. Genesis 2 evidently teaches us about the placing of these original plants, animals, and humans on the earth in their immortal state" ("In the Beginning," 12-19). Brother Woodford cites no reference to support his unique interpretation.

The *Encyclopedia of Mormonism* suggests that "later revelations make it clear that mankind's spirit creation had taken place long before the events described in any of the accounts of the earth's creation" (1:341). What then is to be done with the two accounts of the Creation? If both accounts in Genesis, as well as the variants in Moses and Abraham, are means to a shared end, then what is that end? What are the common themes?

Bearing in mind that only the prophet can interpret scripture officially for the LDS church, we believe that the scriptures should be considered in the context of the historical and cultural setting in which they were first recorded or received. Nephi relates the difficulty his people had in understanding the words of Isaiah, because they had been removed from their former cultural setting and were no longer familiar with the customs and learning of the Jews (2 Ne. 25:1). How much further removed are we from the ancient setting of Genesis? President Brigham Young stated, "As for the Bible account of the creation we may say that the Lord gave it to Moses or that Moses obtained the history and traditions of the fathers and picked out what he considered necessary and that account has been handed down from age to age and we have got it no matter whether it is correct or not" (*Journal of Discourses* 14:116).

If portions, even large portions, of the Creation story are symbolic or figurative (we have been told that at least part of the story is symbolic), there can be no conflict whatever between symbolism and scientific data. If, on the other hand, most or even part of Genesis is to be taken literally, there still is no conflict between what we read there and the scientific data supporting the theory of evolution.

> ... the **serpent** ... said unto the woman, Yea, hath God said, Ye shall not eat of every tree of the garden? And she said unto the serpent, We may eat of the fruit of the trees of the garden: But of the fruit of **the tree** which is **in the midst of the garden**, God hath said, **Ye shall not eat of it, neither shall ye touch it, lest ye die**. And the serpent said unto the

woman, **Ye shall not surely die: For god doth know that in the day ye eat thereof, then your eyes shall be opened, and ye shall be as gods, knowing good from evil**.

Was this an actual serpent or simply another name for Satan? Moses 4:6-7 states, "And Satan put it into the heart of the serpent, (for he had drawn away many after him,) and he sought also to beguile Eve ... (And he spake by the mouth of the serpent)" (see also JST Gen. 3:7-9). Does the scripture just quoted mean that Satan can actually tempt animals? In contrast to this, we are told in Mosiah 16:3 that the serpent was the devil. Other modern revelation suggests this was not an actual serpent and supports the idea that the serpent was figurative of Satan.

And the Lord God said unto the **serpent**, Because thou hast done this, thou *art* cursed above all cattle, and above every beast of the field; **upon thy belly shalt thou go**, and dust shalt thou eat all the days of thy life:

If this was not an actual serpent, but Satan himself, then what does this verse mean? Other scriptures refer to Satan as a serpent or dragon (Rev. 12:9). Yet the Book of Abraham suggests an actual serpent. If it was, did all serpents walk on legs (this is an interpretation since no such statement is made here) before the Fall, or was it only this one special animal? Which "kind" of serpent was guilty of beguiling Eve? Were all serpentine species cursed because of the act of one, or did new species evolve from the original? Serpents belong to the order *Squamata,* the snakes, which includes over 2,000 species. What about other limbless or nearly limbless reptiles and amphibians, such as skinks, glass snakes, amphiumae, and ceacilians?

And unto **Adam** he said, **Because thou hast ... eaten of the tree**, of which I commanded thee, saying, **Thou shalt not eat** of it: cursed *is* the ground for thy sake ... for **dust** thou *art*, and unto dust shalt thou return. And the Lord **God said, Behold, the man is become as one of us**, to know good from evil: and now, **lest he** put forth his hand, and **take also of the tree of life, and eat, and live for ever**: Therefore the Lord God sent him forth from the garden of Eden, to till the ground from whence he was taken. So he drove out the man; and he placed at the

**east** of the garden of Eden Cherubims, and a flaming sword which turned every way, to keep the way of the tree of life.

At this point we would like to embark upon a more lengthy discussion because the state of Adam and Eve before being placed into the garden is critical to the whole issue of evolution and the Creation. On this issue hinge all others.

First, as Mormons, we believe the Atonement was necessitated by the Fall (see Matt. 20:28; Rom. 5:11; 1 Cor. 15:22; 2 Ne. 2:25, 9:6-7; Mosiah 13:28; Alma 12:22, 42:23; Hel. 5:9; D&C 76:69; Moses 4:7, 6:48, 54; AofF 3). Furthermore, we believe that the Fall changed Adam and Eve from immortality to mortality. However, there are two possibilities concerning the nature of their state. Either Adam and Eve were inherently immortal, that is, created as immortal beings, or they were immortal by their circumstances, i.e., by partaking of the fruit of the Tree of Life. The scriptures do not inform us one way or the other. The common assumption is that they were inherently immortal. Elder Bruce R. McConkie stated, "The initial creation was paradisiacal; death and mortality had not yet entered the world. There was no mortal flesh upon the earth for any form of life" ("Christ and the Creation," 9-15). He then quoted 2 Nephi 2:22, which we have discussed previously. Robert Woodward, speaking of Adam and Eve, stated, "They were placed upon earth as immortal beings" ("In the Beginning," 12-19). His statement has no qualifiers and no references. In spite of the belief that Adam and Eve were placed on earth as immortal beings, we are aware of no scripture or other revelation that makes such a claim. It is our opinion that the notion that Adam and Eve were inherently immortal is one of those commonly held tenants, based on tradition, that has no foundation in officially revealed truth.

If Adam and Eve were not inherently immortal, then they might have been created as mortal beings and maintained in an immortal condition by being placed into the garden, or were placed into a position where they had access to something, such as the fruit of the Tree of Life, that kept them in an immortal state. Do scripture and modern revelation support this possible interpretation? Yes.

If Adam and Eve were inherently immortal, then what was the function of the Tree of Life in the garden? If immortal, they had no need to partake of the fruit of the Tree of Life. Lehi said that the Tree of Life was placed in the garden as an opposite to the Tree of Knowledge of Good and Evil: "And to bring about his eternal purposes in the end of man, after he had created our first parents, and the beasts of the field and the fowls of the air, and in fine, all things which are created, it must needs be that there was an opposition; even the forbidden fruit in opposition to the Tree of Life; the one being sweet and the other bitter" (2 Ne. 2:15). However, if Adam and Eve were *inherently* immortal, choosing between two trees was not the issue. The choice was between choosing to eat of the Tree of Knowledge of Good and Evil and not to eat of that same tree. The Tree of Life, if Adam and Eve were inherently immortal, was not part of the choice. Only if they depended on the Tree of Life to maintain their immortality would it play a roll in their choice. If such were the case, then Adam and Eve were choosing life by partaking of the fruit of the Tree of Life and maintaining their lives or choosing death by partaking of the fruit of the Tree of Knowledge, being cast out of the Garden, and being isolated from the Tree of Life, which was the source of their immortality.

Before the Fall, the Tree of Life was only mentioned as a tree in the midst of the garden, and its significance was never stated: "And out of the ground made the LORD God to grow every tree that is pleasant to the sight, and good for food; the tree of life also in the midst of the garden, and the tree of knowledge of good and evil" (Gen. 2:9). Only after the Fall was the importance of the Tree of Life mentioned, and then the tree was not discussed as a tree of choice but was guarded so that Adam and Eve could not eat of it and live forever *after* the Fall.

Antionah asked Alma in the Book of Mormon about the condition of Adam and Eve after the Fall, "What does the scripture mean, which saith that God placed cherubim and a flaming sword on the east of the garden of Eden, lest our first parents should enter and partake of the fruit of the tree of life, and live forever?" (Alma 12:21) Alma answered: "We see that Adam did fall by the partaking of the forbidden fruit, according to the word of God. ..." Now here is the relevant part of Alma's reply regarding the issues we are addressing: "If it had been possible for Adam to have partaken of the fruit of the tree of life at that time, there would have been no death." Alma went on to say, "If it were possible that our first parents could have gone forth and partaken of the tree of life they would have been forever miserable, having no preparatory state; and thus the plan of redemption would have been frustrated, and the word of God would have been void, taking none effect." But, as Alma pointed out, the Tree of Life was guarded so that Adam and Eve could not partake of the fruit *after the Fall* and live forever. Alma continued, "And we see that death comes *upon mankind* ... which is the temporal death; nevertheless there was a space granted unto man in which he might repent; therefore this life became a probationary state; a time to prepare to meet God. ... Now, if it had not been for the plan of redemption, which was laid from the foundation of the world, there could have been no resurrection of the dead; but there was a plan of redemption laid, which shall bring to pass the resurrection of the dead" (12:21-26, emphasis added; see also 42:1-7, and Moses 4:28-31).

Clearly, the immediate consequence of the Fall was *not* instant mortality. The immediate consequence was that Adam and Eve were expelled from the garden and forcibly separated from the Tree of Life by an armed guard, "lest he put forth his hand, and take also of the tree of life, and eat, and live for ever" (Gen. 3:22; see also Moses 4:28). Why? The scriptures state that *after* partaking of the fruit of the Tree of Knowledge of Good and Evil, Adam could *still* have partaken of the fruit of the Tree of Life and continued to live forever. This explanation for guarding the way to the Tree of Life also suggests its possible function—it offered a means whereby Adam and Eve could maintain their immortality. If it were necessary for them to maintain their immortality, then we may logically conclude that they were *not* inherently immortal. Is it possible that the belief that Adam and Eve were inherently immortal is a tradition that has not yet been discarded in light of the greater revealed truth which we have been given?

Where did this tradition come from if not the scriptures? One possible answer is John Milton's *Paradise Lost*. Even though many people today have not read this classic literary work, it was extremely influential in the seventeenth century and has continued to influence traditional Christian beliefs about the Creation. No Greek myth is more fantastic than Milton's epic Christian drama. No Oriental myth is more fantastic than his image of the earth hanging by a golden chain from the walls of Heaven. Milton proposed that all angels were men, and that women were an anomaly. He introduced the notion that the fallen earthly state is wretched, and that the only way for man to turn away God's wrath is to grovel. He introduced the concept that death was not part of God's creation, but came as the offering from Satan and his female consort, banned from Heaven and consigned to guard the gates of Hell for eternity. Sin and Death, as corporal entities, followed Satan to earth.

The scriptures do not say that Adam and Eve were created in an immortal state, yet Milton has God say, "I, at first, with two fair gifts Created him endowed—with Happiness and Immortality ..." (Book XI). Furthermore, realizing that the concept of the Tree of Life, clearly laid out in the scriptures, did not fit his myth, Milton chose to put these words into God's mouth: "Lest, therefore, his now bolder hand Reach also of the Tree of Life, and eat, And live for ever, *dream at least to live For ever*, to remove him I decree, And send him from the Garden forth, to till The ground whence he was taken, fitter soil. ... And on the east side of the Garden place ... Cherubic watch ... And guard all passage to the Tree of Life; Lest Paradise a receptacle prove to *Spirits foul*, and all my trees their prey, With whose stolen fruit Man once more to *delude*" (emphasis added). Because, in Milton's mind, the Fall was a one-way trip, he could not conceive of Adam and Eve living forever by eating of the Tree of Life. What purpose then for Cherubim to guard the tree? To keep foul spirits, Satan and his consorts, away from the other trees. Thus, for Milton, and his literary descendants, tradition outweighs scripture, which must be made to comply with the former.

Even though no scripture states that Adam and Eve were inherently immortal, and even though Alma's lecture implies that the Tree of Life was a source of immortality, many Mormons accept Milton's view of inherent immortality. This interpretation is plainly at odds with scripture and science, whereas the latter are *not* inherently in conflict with each other. Is the tradition introduced by Milton and others so compelling that we are willing to ignore science, scripture, and the official pronouncements of the church, thereby alienating bright, young students, and others from the church?

Because of modern scripture and revelation, Latter-day Saints have a unique understanding of the nature of Adam and Eve in relation to both science and revealed truth. We, as authors, believe that our scriptures consistently support the notion that Adam and Eve were not created in an inherently immortal state but were maintained in an immortal state by the Tree of Life, and were allowed to exercise their agency. As a result of their decision to partake of the Tree of Knowledge of Good and Evil, they were expelled from the garden and thus denied further access to the source of their immortality. By being cast from the garden, they were separated from God's presence; by being separated from the Tree of Life, they were no longer immortal. Thus came the Fall, both spiritual and temporal.

According to scripture and official LDS doctrine, Adam and Eve represented the first progenitors, or parents, of the human race. According to scientific evidence, human ancestors descended through the hominid line by natural selection. Once having achieved their "human" stature through evolution, Adam and Eve could have been placed into the Garden of Eden where they ate of the fruit of the Tree of Life and were rendered immortal for as long as they partook of its fruits. They were told not to eat of the Tree of Knowledge of Good and Evil. In fulfillment of God's plan that they exercise their agency, they yielded to temptation and ate of the forbidden fruit. They were consequently exiled from the garden, separated from the Tree of Life, and thus reverted to their mortal state.

# 12.
## In God's Image

A major source of contention between science and religion concerning human origins is the idea that evolution is a random process. Several evolutionary biologists have contended that evolutionary outcomes cannot be predicted. Roger Lewin, a science writer, in an interview with Ernst Mayr, a prominent evolutionary biologist, stated, "Evolution is of course a historical process, and its extreme dependence on stochastic [random] ... process makes prediction impossible" ("Biology is not Postage Stamp Collecting," 718-20). Carl Sagan, a well-known cosmologist, said, "Even if life on another planet has the same molecular chemistry as life here, there is no reason to expect it to resemble familiar organisms ... in general the random character of the evolutionary process should create extraterrestrial creatures very different from any that we know" (*Cosmos*, 284). Mark Ridley, author of one of the leading textbooks on the topic, stated, "Evolutionary modification ... is of a particular kind. It depends on external environmental change and on random genetic innovation. At any moment, therefore, the form of future change is unpredictable" (*Evolution*, 4).

In contrast, the scriptures make it clear that there is a plan to our form: "And God said, Let us make man in our image, after our likeness. ... So God created man in his own image, in the image of God created he him; male and female created he them" (Gen. 1:26-27; see also D&C 20:18). The idea that we are created in God's image, from the LDS perspective, proposes that there are limits on human form. If the outcome of human evolution was determined, then there would have to be laws of constraint governing evolutionary processes.

Indeed, recent data support the idea that evolution is not entirely random. As a result, a new paradigm is emerging in biology which is more in line with this concept. Richard Strohman, professor emeritus of molecular and cell biology, University of California, Berkeley, stated, "The neo-Darwinian model of evolution, based on a gradual accumulation of point mutations, appears to be incomplete at best. ... It is not, of course, that one doubts that evolution has occurred. The theory is in trouble because it insists on locating the driving force solely in random mutations. An alternative theory of evolution that emphasizes the importance of nonrandom ... changes during development could explain the problems now being encountered by evolutionary theory" ("The Coming Kuhnian Revolution in Biology," 15:194-200). Strohman suggested that the creation of new forms may arise from epigenetic (influences occurring during the development of an embryo which occur outside the direct control of genes) changes. He noted that this "is a scientific possibility of great merit ... [but it has been] left mostly unexplored." He continued:

> Because a search for boundary conditions at levels above the gene are excluded by the current paradigm, and because that same paradigm is inadequate, we seem to lack any scientific basis with which to explain ... evolution. It is thus often made to appear that the only alternative explanation for evolution and other complexities of life must lie outside of science in some kind of creationist construction. ... The evidence that these boundary conditions must be present is everywhere. Their absence from our current theories of life is at the root of confusion coming from genetic determinism.

The seeds of this pending shift were sewn years ago. Darwin stated in the introduction to *The Origin of Species*, "I am convinced that Natural Selection has been the most important, but not the *exclusive*, means of modification" (emphasis added). If there are other means of modification, what are they? Have any other means been discovered in the past 140 years? Darwin hinted at what some of those might be: "Many laws regulate variation; some few of which can be dimly seen. ... Important changes in the embryo or larva will probably entail changes in the mature animal." In other places in his book, Darwin mentioned that there are as yet unknown "laws of growth" and "laws of development" (*Origin of Species*, 14, 18, 19). Thus in 1859 he alluded to the same possible mechanisms of modification that Strohman proposed in 1997: laws and constraints governing development. As we enter the twenty-first century, an exciting frontier of biology remains the discovery of these "laws of development." François Jacob stated,

> Evolution is described ... as differences between adult organisms. Yet differences between adult organisms merely reflect differences in the developmental processes that produce them. It is mainly through a net of developmental constraints that natural selection works by filtering actual phenotypes out of possible genotypes. (Phenotype: the actual appearance of the individual; genotype: the genetic make-up of the individual.) To really understand the way evolution proceeds, it is therefore necessary to understand embryonic development. Only with this knowledge will it become possible to ... define the rules and constraints of the evolutionary game. Unfortunately, to this day very little is known about embryonic development. (See *The Possible and the Actual*, 43.)

Several scientists, beginning with D'Arcy Thompson in the early part of the twentieth century, have laid a foundation upon which we can build theories of constraint, or bounded variation. Thompson stated,

> Cell and tissue, shell and bone, leaf and flower, are so many portions of matter, and it is in obedience to the laws of physics that their particles have been moved, moulded and conformed ... heredity need not and cannot be invoked to account for the configuration and arrangement of the trabeculae [the internal scaffolding of bone]: for we can see them at any time of life in the making, under the direct action and control of

the forces to which the system is exposed. ... It would, I dare say, be an exaggeration to see in every bone nothing more than a resultant of immediate and direct physical or mechanical conditions; for to do so would be to deny the existence ... of a principle of heredity. ... But I maintain that it is no less an exaggeration if we tend to neglect these direct physical and mechanical modes of causation altogether, and to see in the characters of a bone merely the results of variation and of heredity, and to trust ... to those characters as a sure and certain and unquestioned guide to affinity and phylogeny. (*On Growth and Form*, 7, 237, 265.)

Stephen Jay Gould has said that important trends in the evolution of form may result from "the necessities of architecture ... or ... developmental constraints. ... If there are only a few potential pathways of evolutionary change ... if those potential pathways are set by the structure of the organism, then, even if natural selection is doing the pushing, in a sense the organism pushes back. Its inherited structure exerts very strong constraints on the possible pathways of change. ... Even when natural selection is the driving force, it may not be as universally effective as orthodox Darwinists suppose" (Gleick, "Stephen Jay Gould," 48-64). Gould and Richard Lewontin wrote,

Constraints restrict possible paths and modes of change so strongly that the constraints themselves become much the most interesting aspect of evolution. ... *Developmental* constraints ... may hold the most powerful rein of all over possible evolutionary pathways. ... [Among the most powerful of these constraints are] architectural constraints. ... These arise not from former adaptations ... but as architectural restrictions that never were adaptations, but rather the necessary consequences of materials and designs. ... Architectural constraints can exert far-ranging influence upon organisms as well. The subject is full of potential insight because it has rarely been acknowledged at all. ("The Spandrels of San Marco," 581-89.)

Thompson, quoted above, provided examples of these architectural constraints, which he called the "necessary consequences of materials and design." He pointed out that the trabecular pattern of bone (the internal scaffolding) resembles the steel scaffolding designed by engineers, and that it changes in response to changing pressures placed on the bone, as when a bone is broken and improperly set. He also described many features of the entire animal which comply with constraints of material and design. For example, an animal such as a bison, with a heavy head, has a thick neck and a hump over the shoulders, which are formed by long bony projections of the vertebrae and which correspond to the pillars at the ends of a suspension bridge, and a heavy tendon supporting the head, which corresponds to the cables holding up the suspension bridge. Even though the molecules making up those bones and tendons are encoded by genes, the final structure is constrained by mechanical factors which are controlled by the nonrandom laws of physics. Therefore, which genes are turned on at what time and in what location is apparently determined by mechanical factors.

Thompson described many features of bones and blood vessels that can be ascribed to constraints of material and design rather than to genes. For example, bones grow in response to physical forces applied to them, so that the bones of large animals are relatively larger and thicker than the bones of smaller animals. The branch angles of veins and arteries are directly correlated to the blood pressure at that specific point within the vein or artery. It would be ridiculous to ascribe this precise correlation to the action of genes at each of those sites. Furthermore, if a vein is removed from the leg and grafted onto the heart in place of an artery, in a very short time the microscopic structure of the vessel changes to that of an artery. This is not to say that genes are not turned on in that vessel to produce the proteins involved in the change, but those genes are turned on as a result of *mechanical forces* in the transplanted vessel.

Another Thompsonian concept is that the simplest three-dimensional object in the universe is a sphere. There are literally millions of non-living objects in the universe in the form of spheres, ranging from soap bubbles and oil droplets to planets and stars. There are also numerous living objects in the form of spheres, including the human egg and the human embryo during its first few days of development. Because it is a naturally occurring object which can spontaneously form in non-living matter, there is no reason to assume that it must be determined by genes in living things. Furthermore, if a group of soft spheres, whether living or non-living (for example, soap bubbles), is pushed together, the spheres will be reconfigured into hexagons (six-sided objects) and the angles at each corner will be 120 degrees. Therefore, no hexagon gene or 120-degree-angle gene needs to be invoked for living things to acquire hexagonal shapes, such as can be seen in epithelial cells viewed from the surface, many insect eyes, and honeycombs.

Thompson concentrated his discussions on issues of adult form. If we apply these principles to developing embryos, can we discover some of the laws governing the basis of form, the laws of development alluded to by Darwin and Strohmam? One of us (Trent Stephens) has spent several years applying Thompsonian theory to embryonic development. This research focuses on the question of what determines the position of a limb on the body of a vertebrate animal. The current assumption is that the presence or absence of limbs, their location on the body, and the number of digits they possess is under direct genetic control (see Tabin, "The Initiation of the Limb Bud," 671-74; Tickle, "Vertebrate Limb Development," 121-52).

But Stephens and his students have proposed that the position of the limbs is determined, to a large extent, by biomechanical influences in the early embryo. The early vertebrate embryo can be thought of as a tube (the embryo proper) attached to a sphere (the yolk sac) (see below). Where the tube and sphere come into contact with each other is a groove. As the embryo grows, tissues are pushed away from sites of greatest expansion, such as along the back of the embryo (the top of the tube), and tend to accumulate and thicken in depressions, such as the groove between the embryo and yolk sac. This produces a zone of potential growth along the side of the embryo. Because it is also growing in length, there are sites of expansion along the side of the embryo. As a result, the places where tissues tend to accumulate to the greatest extent, and where potential outgrowth is maximal, are at the ends of the grooves on each side of the embryo. Furthermore, the length of the embryo-yolk sac interface determines the length of the trunk in the adult. If this hypothesis is correct, the most likely number and placement of limbs on a verte-

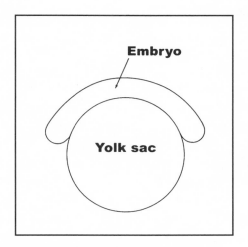

Model of an Embryo on a Yolk Sac

brate animal is two limbs on each side, located at the ends of the trunk. The hypothesis predicts that if the length of the embryo-yolk sac interface is changed, the length of the body and the position of the limbs will be changed accordingly.

This hypothesis was tested experimentally (Stephens, *Journal of Experimental Zoology*, 55-66; see below). The caudal (toward the tail) half of the yolk sac was surgically separated from the body axis of salamander embryos. As a result, the caudal end of the yolk was displaced approximately four segments (future vertebrae) toward the head compared to the control (where no surgery had been performed). The total length of the altered yolk was eight body segments, compared to twelve segments in the control embryo. As a result, the adult salamander trunk was shorter by four vertebrae than that of the control salamander, and the hind limbs formed at the *new* caudal end of the yolk, eight vertebrae from the base of the head rather than the normal twelve.

The fact that the shape of an adult animal can be dramatically changed by simple surgical methods in the embryo, which are mechanical in nature, suggests to us that the basic patterning of vertebrate shape is influenced by mechanical forces at work in the em-

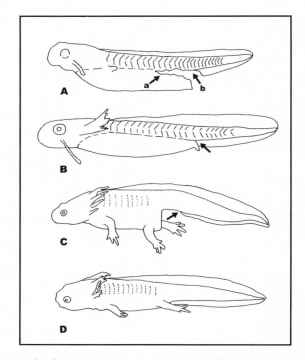

A. Experimental salamander embryo immediately after surgery. The cut (a) was made approximately half the length of the yolk sac from its original end (b). B. Control embryo approximately one week after the surgery in embryo A was performed. The arrow indicates the caudal end of the yolk sac. C. Experimental salamander five months after surgery. There are only nine costal grooves between limbs rather than the normal twelve. Note also the notch posterior to the end of the trunk. The arrow indicates where the trunk would normally end and where the hind limbs would normally form. D. Control salamander approximately four to five months following surgery.

bryo. Stephens and his students suggest that the number and position of vertebrate limbs are constrained by biomechanical forces in the embryo. These constraints are some of the laws of development which we are seeking. For example, we could propose the *law of tissue accumulation* to describe the tendency for embryonic tissues to be pushed out of areas of embryonic growth and accumulate in depressions associated with the embryo, and the *law of enhanced growth* to indicate the tendency for those accumulated tissues to grow out and form appendages. The discoveries of such laws should enable us to predict vertebrate form anywhere in the universe.

This line of research is beginning to uncover many characteristics of vertebrate body form that are relatively independent of the direct action of genes. We predict that many more examples of structural constraint and their governing principles will be discovered. These findings will help reveal laws of development. François Jacob stated, "Complex objects, whether living or not, are produced by evolutionary processes in which two kinds of factors are involved: the constraints that, at every level, specify the rules of the game and define what is possible with those systems; and the historical circumstances that determine the actual course of events and control the actual interactions between the systems" (*The Possible and the Actual*, 31). Jacob then stated that only constraint, and not historical circumstances, can be formalized. Only constraint will be governed by formal laws that will allow us to predict evolutionary outcome. We predict that discovery of such laws, in conjunction with what is already known about genetic forces, will one day demonstrate design in human creation.

One direction in modern science that may lead us to the discovery of laws of mechanical constraint is the theory of chaos. Chaos theory states that events appearing to be completely random are actually bounded by predictable conditions. The scientific theory of chaos, which proposes bounded randomness, is different from the common view of chaos as disorder and confusion. Since the dawn of time, humans have attempted to explain the "workings" of the universe. Throughout history, physicists and mathematicians have formulated laws to explain their observations. Simple phenomena, such as the motion of a pendulum, can be described by what are called "linear equations." A linear equation is a mathematical expression that allows scientists to predict with high degrees of certainty a number of such phenomena. Chemical reactions, the functions of a clock or an engine, the flight of a space ship, and the orbit of a satellite are all predictable and can be described by linear equations, even though the equations may be quite complex. On the other hand, scientists have also discovered even more complex phenomena, which can only be described by means of "non-linear equations." Weather patterns, turbulent water flow, animal population cycles, and biological form are all examples of phenomena that are controlled by less restrictive laws which allow for more variability. This variability makes the phenomena less predictable but nonetheless not totally random. For example, one cannot predict precisely where a tornado will touch down. But it can be predicted within known limits where tornadoes in general frequently occur, thus "tornado alley" in the nation's midsection. The absence of *absolute* predictability comprises the random component of chaos theory, while the *general* predictability defines its boundaries or constraints, thus the term "bounded randomness."

The visual representations of linear equations are lines, the simplest being a straight line; the more complex are hyperbolas, circles, and waves, to name a few. The visual representations of non-linear equations are called "strange attractors," which are complex patterns of never-ending lines (most of which can only be generated by computer).

The visual depiction of linear and non-linear equations provides information about the phenomena being analyzed. Strange attractors (pictures of non-linear equations) provide information about the constraints on the phenomena being observed. The outline of the picture defines the limits of the probabilities; the interior describes what can occur; and the exterior defines what cannot occur. For example, a strange attractor describing the probability of tornadoes touching down somewhere in tornado alley consists of an outline depicting the limits of where tornadoes can touch down (or ever have touched down) versus where they cannot (or do not) touch down. The space defined by the perimeter of the picture indicates that tornadoes will touch down, the outside area indicates that tornadoes will not. However, within the inner space, the probability of a tornado touching down at a specific site is random and not predictable.

The boundaries of strange attractors dictate their predictive limits. For example, the circumference of a circle defines its shape. If the boundary of a circle is lengthened without changing the area, the geometric figure is no longer a circle but becomes an oval or some

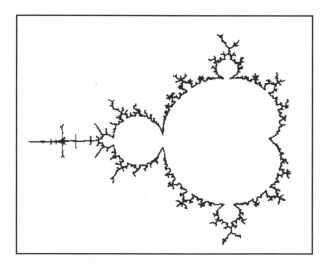

**An Example of a Strange Attractor**
*(see http://dragon.univ-mrs.fr/SCIENCE98).*

other form. As the boundary becomes more and more elongated, the shape of the figure becomes more complex. The more complex the figure, in the case of a strange attractor, the more complex the phenomena it depicts. The boundaries of strange attractors in chaos theory are so complex that they are infinitely long. Their boundaries define their limits and form. According to chaos theory, points within the area of a strange attractor are established randomly, but points at the boundary are deterministic and are controlled by specific, albeit undiscovered, laws.

Chaos theory can provide new insights into evolutionary theory. The evolution of morphology—the form and structure of biological organisms—can be modeled using a strange attractor. The area of the attractor representing evolution is random, but the boundary is deterministic. Referring once more to François Jacob's statement, "Complex objects ... are produced by evolutionary processes in which two kinds of factors are involved: the constraints that ... specify the rules of the game and define what is possible ... and the historical circumstances that determine the actual course of events. ... Only constraints, but not history, can be formalized" (*The Possible and the Actual*, 31). Thus for any given component of biological form, the boundary of the strange attractor sets the *absolute* limits of that component, while the domain of the attractor defines *all possibilities* within those limits. History, which for biological forms is a combination of mutation and natural selection, fills in *part* of that central domain, but not all of it. As a result, we can make many predictions about form but may never be able to predict *all* aspects of biological form.

For example, the tallest human ever recorded was Robert Wadlow, with a height of 8 feet 11.1 inches; the shortest was Pauline Musters, whose height was documented at 21.65 inches (*Guinness Book of World Records* [1990], 1-11). Some people are born with fingers and toes exceeding the usual ten each; others with fingers and toes less than ten each; and still others with no limbs at all. Some people are born completely covered with hair; some remain completely hairless throughout their lives. There are conjoined twins with two heads and one body. The list goes on and on. Clearly, there is a range to the human form, but all are created in the same general image.

The most exciting aspect of Jacob's concept of the interaction of constraint and history is his statement that "only constraints, but not history, can be formalized." Therefore, the boundary is the only part of the attractor that can be "formalized" and is the *only* part for which we can discover laws. Science is not merely the pursuit of history but the attempt to discover the laws of the universe. However, biology, which has been pursuing evolutionary history in the belief that history alone is the driving force in biology, owns few if any of those laws. Biologists have been concentrating on the area of the strange attractor and have largely ignored the notion that the attractor has boundaries. What Jacob implies is that by focusing on the boundaries we can move, in biological theory, from collecting historical information to defining the laws that constrain that history.

Even though Thompson opened the door to exploring those boundaries, few scientists have followed his lead. Richard Strohman said, "Normal science is an approach that reveals genetic maps related to biological function, but the directions for reading the maps are not included in the package. And the real secrets of life are obviously in those missing directions—in the rules and constraints that organize genetic agents into functional arrays. These rules and constraints are more than likely embedded in the organization of life rather than in the catalogue of the organization's agents, and we have mistaken the former for the latter" ("Kuhnian Revolution," 194-200). As modern biologists begin to realize that genetic change alone cannot explain all of what we see in nature, they begin to search for other explanations. As they do so, Thompson's work is being rediscovered.

The results of many observations and experiments indicate that some of the most important aspects of vertebrate morphology are determined by physical rather than genetic factors. Aspects of form under genetic control are subject to natural selection. Darwin pointed out this important aspect of natural selection in *The Origin*. Physical factors, on the other hand, as pointed out by Thompson, are not subject to natural selection.

As described earlier in this chapter, the position of vertebrate limbs may be, to a large degree, determined by mechanical forces. Related research has revealed that the number of fingers or toes (digits) that form on the limbs are correlated with the length of the animal and the number of vertebrae between the limbs. The number of cells available for making limbs appears to be fixed within some range (perhaps by some as yet undiscovered law). More elongated animals apparently have their populations of limb cells scattered over longer distances; as a result, smaller limb buds with less digits are formed in those animals. The mechanism by which limb position and digit number is determined may be described by analogy. If a truck-load of sand (representing the population of cells in a given limb territory) is dumped in a pile, the sand can be used in place to make a sand sculpture. However, if the dump truck is moving five miles per hour while the sand is being dumped, the pile is spread out over a greater distance, the pile is not as deep, and it is more difficult to work with in making a sand sculpture. If the truck is moving twenty miles an hour while dumping the sand, it will be spread out over a very long distance, the sand is very thin, and making a sand sculpture is out of the question.

Taken to its extreme, this model of limb development predicts that very elongated vertebrate animals, with many vertebrae between the limbs (represented by a moving dump truck), will be limbless. In addition to the well-known example of the snakes, there are also elongated, limbless lizards (which, although limbless, are quite different from true snakes). There are also very elongated, limbless amphibians, which resemble giant worms. Extremely elongated fish are nearly finless.

These predictions greatly simplify evolution. For example, if limblessness in snakes were determined strictly by molecular mechanisms, then one series of mutations would be selected for increased body length and another to reduce the size of the limb, ultimately resulting in complete limblessness in very long animals. In addition, a third set of molecular controls would have to exist to coordinate limblessness with the elongation of the body. However, if limb reduction results from biomechanical factors that are affected by the elongation of the body, then only one set of mutations, those influencing body length, would need to be selected for. Because of the biomechanical factors, limb reduction would *automatically* be associated with body elongation. By imposing biomechanical constraints on limb formation, the evolution of snakes and other animals of similar form is simplified by at least an order of magnitude.

In addition, there is another important consideration resulting from constraint. As stated at the beginning of this chapter, one of the greatest points of contention between evolution and religion is the belief that evolution is random. However, if it turns out that evolution is constrained by deterministic, predictable boundaries based on natural laws, then there is plenty of room for God to operate with predictability within evolution's bounded variation.

Many of the structural features of living things are not the result of direct genetic control but of genes interacting with material or design constraints. Those of us who hold this view await the day when the Human Genome Project will be completed, because we believe that once the entire genome is known, the structure of living things will still remain unknown. What we will discover is that many features of our structure are not simply encoded by genes. We will realize that genetic variations fill in a portion of the center of the strange attractors, but that the boundaries of those attractors are largely determined by laws of nature, which necessarily limit the biological form. Indeed, when a more extensive understanding of epigenetic laws is in place, we may realize that the shape and form of nature is not only predictable but is executed under the mandate of God, that humans actually are "created in the image of God."

# 13.
# Eternal Evolution

According to the scriptures and official doctrines of the LDS church, we are on an eternal evolutionary course. The First Presidency has stated, "Man is the child of God, formed in the divine image and endowed with divine attributes, and even as the infant son of an earthly father and mother is capable in due time of becoming a man, so the undeveloped offspring of celestial parentage is capable, by experience through ages and aeons, of *evolving* into a God" (emphasis added) ("The Origin of Man," rptd. in *Encyclopedia of Mormonism*, 4:1665-69). Elder John A. Widtsoe drew a parallel between the church's teachings on eternal progression and secular theories of evolution. He stated, "One of the leading doctrines of the Church resembles the spirit of the law of universal growth so nearly that one is forced to believe that the great truth embodied by this doctrine is the truth shadowed forth by the law of evolution. ... Joseph Smith taught [with regard to humans] a doctrine of evolution which in grandeur and in extent surpasses the wildest speculations of the scientific evolutionists" (*Joseph Smith as Scientist*).

According to this view, we are traveling from one realm to another, never ending, but constantly changing. We progress from intelligence, to spirits, to mortality, and, through death and resurrection, to immortality and eternal lives. In this concluding chapter, we will briefly examine each stage of our existence, as explained by LDS doctrine. Each realm includes distinctive "laws," which fulfill particular purposes. The Lord said, "All kingdoms have a law given; ... and unto every law there are certain bounds also and conditions" (D&C 88:36-38).

## Intelligences

The first realm of our eternal existence for which we have any reference was that of intelligence. "Man was also in the beginning with God. Intelligence, or the light of truth, was not created or made, neither indeed can be" (D&C 98:29). The precise nature of this intelligence is not clear. Whether intelligence consisted of individual, separate identities or was a collective mass of truth and light is not totally understood (see "Intelligences," *Encyclopedia of Mormonism*). But from this matter, this intelligence (D&C 131:7-8), apparently came the substance or essence from which our heavenly parents created spirit children.

## Premortal Spirits

Our heavenly parents, father and mother, are resurrected beings who have obtained Godhood. Through their creative activities, our intelligence became "embodied" as spirit entities, possessing some of the spiritual, if not physical, attributes, characteristics, and potentials of deity. These attributes gave to each spirit the ability to continue to progress eternally, and the potential to obtain Godhood. This potential is predicated upon each individual's agency, knowledge, attitudes, and level of perfection.

As spirit children, we apparently lived together for an unspecified period of "time," learning, growing, and developing, preparatory to mortal life. Did we grow from spirit infants to spirit adults, gaining knowledge, experience, and righteousness, until we were ready for the next station of our existence? We are told that during this time we exercised agency, and the choices we made determined the next step in our progression. "And they who keep their first estate shall be added upon; and they who keep not their first estate shall not have glory in the same kingdom with those who keep their first estate" (Abr. 3:24-25).

## Mortality

God prepared this and other worlds for his children (Abr. 3:24-25). For the first time, our spirit body would be joined with a mortal, physical body. This mortal life is apparently the shortest realm for us but one of extreme importance in our progression. This life is another pivot point of our eternal evolutionary trajectory.

The coming together of our two bodies, spiritual and physical, constitutes the soul (D&C 88:15). This earthly existence is a type of schooling, necessary to prepare, educate, and condition the soul to inherit a resurrected, eternal, exalted state. The conditions and experiences of the soul during mortality are critical to our progression.

So God prepared this earth to provide a meaningful experience. The preparation of the physical earth, including our physical bodies, was conducted by processes that, the authors believe, are continuing and are open to scientific discovery. What we mortals have learned from scientific investigation teaches us that the earth is not the center of the universe and that the human body is not unrelated to the rest of Nature. The data suggest that our physical, mortal bodies were prepared by the process of evolution, from the simple to the complex, ultimately arriving at a point where they could receive our spirits. In the transition to earth life, we left our spiritual home for an earthly one. This transition was affected by our premortal choice, facilitated by our earthly parents, Adam and Eve. In making this decision, we were allowed to experience mortality. The mortal realm introduced us to certain unique conditions, including sickness, pain, struggles, death, separation, infirmities, war, cruelty, hatred, etc., on the one side, as well as health, pleasure, joy, peace, and love on the other (2 Ne. 2:11).

Our exposure to these mortal conditions was made possible by Adam and Eve's disobedience. The Fall was necessary for our eternal progression, but precipitated a need for redemption. For some reason, Adam and Eve's necessary disobedience required reconciliation (Alma 42). Humankind, within a fallen state, cannot satisfy that need. This could only have been accomplished by someone with the ability and power to overcome the limitations of mortality. For this purpose, Jesus was chosen to bear the consequences of the Fall. Our mortal birth, with its veil of forgetfulness, enabled us to work out this phase of our existence through faith, hope, and the pursuit of perfection.

The methods used to satisfy each realm of our existence are relevant to each station of our evolutionary journey. The fact that during mortality our spirits are associated with physical bodies, closely related to the rest of Nature and created by natural processes, should not come as a great surprise. Indeed, one goal of our experience during mortality is to discipline our "natural" appetites (Mosiah 3:19).

Another consequence of the mortal condition is death. For many, death is an unfathomable terminal event. For believers, it is a necessary step along an eternal journey; a birth to a new dimension.

## Postmortal Spirits

At death, the spirit separates from the body to await the resurrection (D&C 88:33). The spirits of the righteous exist in paradise, the spirits of the wicked in prison (Alma 40:11-14). The nature of the next transition, from postmortal spirits to resurrected beings, is not clear at the present time. Nor do we know how the mortal body relates to the resurrected body. We do know that Jesus initiated the resurrection for himself and every one of God's children who has passed through mortality (D&C 138).

## Resurrected Beings

Finally, we arrive at a point on our journey where we can take on a resurrected body and continue to progress eternally. Through the process of resurrection, we are prepared to inherit an eternal kingdom. In sections 76 and 132 of the Doctrine and Covenants, we learn of the celestial, terrestrial, and telestial kingdoms of glory. Virtually every person who has lived on this earth or others will obtain a level of glory (Abr. 3:26).

We are struck by the similarities between the plan of exaltation and natural selection. Natural selection preserves those organisms possessing traits that allow them to survive and reproduce under specific conditions. Those traits are passed on to the next generation, permitting them to "fulfill the measure of their creation." The plan of exaltation preserves those individuals possessing spiritual traits, such as faith, hope, and charity. Those who develop the necessary attributes are endowed with eternal lives and can then pass on the ability to develop the same traits to their offspring.

It is evident that we, as individual entities, are on an eternal journey—an *evolutionary* journey so to speak—of many different realms and states that may ultimately culminate in godhood. Each state has its own set of conditions. We know very little about the particulars of the pre- and postmortal conditions. During mortality we *can* learn much about our present realm. We have been admonished to "teach one another words of wisdom; yea, seek ye out of the best books words of wisdom; seek learning even by *study* and also by *faith*" (D&C 88:118, emphasis added). It is our obligation to understand as much as we can about all phases of our eternal journey, thereby gaining a deeper knowledge and appreciation of our father's plan.

We depend upon the scriptures, as well as upon inspiration and revelation, for insights into the premortal and postmortal realms. Because we now live in mortality, we have the additional advantage of empirical experience concerning it. Therefore, we can learn about our current state by studying what is all around us. In fact, we read: "I give unto you a commandment that you shall teach one another the doctrine of the kingdom ... Of things both in heaven and in the earth, and under the earth ..." (D&C 88:77, 79).

There has been a veritable explosion of scientific knowledge in the past few years. Why, we wonder, would anyone choose to stand hungry in life's great cafeteria? If we take advantage of it, this explosion of knowledge can greatly help us in our quest for understanding. The perceived conflict between science and religion has resulted historically from a lack of knowledge. The new knowledge that is accumulating at an incredible rate will help clarify and resolve past misunderstandings. "How long can rolling waters remain impure?" the prophet Joseph wrote. "What power shall stay the heavens? As well might man stretch forth his puny arm to stop the Missouri river in its decreed course, or to turn it up stream, as to hinder the Almighty from pouring down knowledge from heaven upon the heads of the Latter-day Saints" (D&C 121:33).

# Appendix.
# Three Official LDS Statements on Evolution

## I. "The Origin of Man"

(From the *Improvement Era* 13:75-81, November 1909;
reprinted in the *Encyclopedia of Mormonism*, Appen. 4,
and *Messages of the First Presidency*, 4:199-206)

"God created man in his own image."

Inquiries arise from time to time respecting the attitude of the Church of Jesus Christ of Latter-day Saints upon questions which, though not vital from a doctrinal standpoint, are closely connected with the fundamental principles of salvation. The latest inquiry of this kind that has reached us is in relation to the origin of man. It is believed that a statement of the position held by the Church upon this important subject will be timely and productive of good.

In presenting the statement that follows we are not conscious of putting forth anything essentially new; neither is it our desire so to do. Truth is what we wish to present, and truth—eternal truth—is fundamentally old. A restatement of the original attitude of the Church relative to this matter is all that will be attempted here. To tell the truth as God has revealed it, and commend it to the acceptance of those who need to conform their opinions thereto, is the sole purpose of this presentation.

"God created man in his own image, in the image of God created he him; male and female created he them." In these plain and pointed words the inspired author of the book of Genesis made known to the world the truth concerning the origin of the human family. Moses, the prophet-historian, "learned," as we are told, "in all the wisdom of the Egyptians," when making this important announcement, was not voicing a mere opinion, a theory derived from his researches into the occult lore of that ancient people. He was speaking as the mouthpiece of God, and his solemn declaration was for all time and for all people. No subsequent revelator of the truth has contradicted the great leader and lawgiver of Israel. All who have since spoken by divine authority upon this theme have confirmed his simple and sublime proclamation. Nor could it be otherwise. Truth has but one source, and all revelations from heaven are harmonious with each other. The omnipotent Creator, the maker of heaven and earth—had shown unto Moses everything pertaining to this planet, including the facts relating to man's origin, and the authoritative pronouncement of that mighty prophet and seer to the house of Israel, and through Israel to the whole world, is couched in the simple clause: "God created man in his own image" (Genesis 1:27; Pearl of Great Price—Book of Moses, 1:27-41.)

The creation was two-fold—firstly spiritual, secondly temporal. This truth, also, Moses plainly taught—much more plainly than it has come down to us in the imperfect translations of the Bible that are now in use. Therein the fact of a spiritual creation, antedating the temporal creation, is strongly implied, but the proof of it is not so clear and conclusive as in other records held by the Latter-day Saints to be of equal authority with the Jewish scriptures. The partial obscurity of the latter upon the point in question is owing, no doubt, to the loss of those "plain and precious" parts of sacred writ, which, as the Book of Mormon informs us, have been taken away from the Bible during its passage down the centuries (I Nephi 13:24-29). Some of these missing parts the Prophet Joseph Smith undertook to restore when he revised those scriptures by the spirit of revelation, the result being that more complete account of the creation which is found in the book of Moses, previously cited. Note the following passages:

And now, behold, I say unto you, that these are the generations of the heaven and of the earth, when they were created, in the day that I, the Lord God, made the heaven and the earth;

And every plant of the field before it was in the earth, and every herb of the field before it grew.

For I, the Lord God, created all things of which I have spoken, spiritually, before they were naturally upon the face of the earth. For I, the Lord God, had not caused it to rain upon the face of the earth.

And I, the Lord God, had created all the children of men, and not yet a man to till the ground; for in heaven created I them, and there was not yet flesh upon the earth, neither in the water, neither in the air.

But, I, the Lord God, spake, and there went up a mist from the earth, and watered the whole face of the ground.

And I, the Lord God, formed man from the dust of the ground, and breathed into his nostrils the breath of life; and man became a living soul, the first flesh upon the earth, the first man also.

Nevertheless, all things were before created, but spiritually were they created and made, according to my word (Pearl of Great Price— Book of Moses, 3:4-7. See also Chapters 1 and 2, and compare with Genesis 1 and 2).

These two points being established, namely, the creation of man in the image of God, and the two-fold character of the creation, let us now inquire: What was the form of man, in the spirit and in the body, as originally created? In a general way the answer is given in the words chosen as the text of this treatise. "God created man in his own image." It is more explicitly rendered in the Book of Mormon thus: "All men were created in the beginning after mine own image" (Ether 3:15). It is the Father who is speaking. If, therefore, we can ascertain the form of the "Father of spirits," "The God of the spirits of all flesh," we shall be able to discover the form of the original man.

Jesus Christ, the Son of God, is "the express image" of His Father's person (Hebrews 1:3). He walked the earth as a human being, as a perfect man, and said, in answer to a question put to Him: "He that hath seen me hath seen the Father" (John 14:9). This alone ought to solve the problem to the satisfaction of every thoughtful, reverent mind. The conclusion is irresistible, that if the Son of God be the express image (that is, likeness) of His Father's person, then

His Father is in the form of man; for that was the form of the Son of God, not only during His mortal life, but before His mortal birth, and after His resurrection. It was in this form that the Father and the Son, as two personages, appeared to Joseph Smith, when, as a boy of four-teen years, he received his first vision. Then if God made man—the first man—in His own image and likeness, he must have made him like unto Christ, and consequently like unto men of Christ's time and of the present day. That man was made in the image of Christ, is posi-tively stated in the Book of Moses: "And I, God, said unto mine Only Begotten, which was with me from the beginning, Let us make man in our image, after our likeness; and it was so. *** And I, God, cre-ated man in mine own image, in the image of mine Only Begotten created I him, male and female created I them" (2:26, 27).

The Father of Jesus is our Father also. Jesus Himself taught this truth, when He instructed His disciples how to pray: "Our Father which art in heaven," etc. Jesus, however, is the firstborn among all the sons of God—the first begotten in the spirit, and the only begotten in the flesh. He is our elder brother, and we, like Him, are in the image of God. All men and women are in the similitude of the universal Fa-ther and Mother, and are literally the sons and daughters of Deity.

"God created man in His own image." This is just as true of the spirit as it is of the body, which is only the clothing of the spirit, its complement; the two together constituting the soul. The spirit of man is in the form of man, and the spirits of all creatures are in the likeness of their bodies. This was plainly taught by the Prophet Jo-seph Smith (Doctrine and Covenants, 77:2).

Here is further evidence of the fact. More than 700 years before Moses was shown the things pertaining to this earth, another great prophet, known to us as the brother of Jared, was similarly favored by the Lord. He was even permitted to behold the spirit-body of the fore-ordained Savior, prior to His incarnation; and so like the body of a man was gazing upon a being of flesh and blood. He first saw the fin-ger and then the entire body of the Lord—all in the spirit. The Book of Mormon says of this wonderful manifestation:

And it came to pass that when the brother of Jared had said these words, behold, the Lord stretched forth His hand and touched the stones one by one with His finger; and the veil was taken from off the eyes of the brother of Jared, and he saw the finger of the Lord; and it was as the finger of a man, like unto flesh and blood; and the brother of Jared fell down before the Lord, for he was struck with fear.

And the Lord saw that the brother of Jared had fallen to the earth; and the Lord said unto him, Arise, why hast thou fallen?

And he saith unto the Lord, I saw the finger of the Lord, and I feared lest he should smite me; for I knew not that the Lord had flesh and blood.

And the Lord said unto him, Because of thy faith thou hast seen that I shall take upon me flesh and blood; and never has man come before me with such exceeding faith as thou hast; for were it not so, ye could not have seen my finger. Sawest thou more than this?

And he answered, Nay, Lord, show thyself unto me.

And the Lord said unto him, Believest thou the words which I shall speak?

And he answered, Yea, Lord, I know that thou speakest the truth, for thou art a God of truth and canst not lie.

And when he had said these words, behold, the Lord showed himself unto him, and said, Because thou knowest these things ye are redeemed from the fall; therefore ye are brought back into my presence; therefore I show myself unto you.

Behold, I am He who was prepared from the foundation of the world to redeem my people. Behold, I am Jesus Christ, I am the Father and the Son. In me shall all mankind have light, and that eternally, even they who shall believe on my name; and they shall become my sons and my daughters.

And never have I shewed myself unto man whom I have created, for never hath man believed in me as thou hast. Seest thou that ye are created after mine own image?, Yea, even all men were created in the beginning after mine own image.

Behold, this body, which ye now behold, is the body of my spirit, and man have I created after the body of my spirit; and even as I appear unto thee to be in the spirit, will I appear unto my people in the flesh. (Ether 3:6-16.)

What more is needed to convince us that man, both in spirit and in body, is the image and likeness of God, and that God Himself is in the form of man?

When the divine Being whose spirit-body the brother of Jared beheld, took upon Him flesh and blood, He appeared as a man, having "body, parts and passions," like other men, though vastly superior to all others, because He was God, even the Son of God, the Word made flesh: in Him "dwelt the fulness of the Godhead bodily." And why should He not appear as a man? That was the form of His spirit, and it must needs have an appropriate covering, a suitable tabernacle. He came into the world as He had promised to come (III Nephi, 1:13), taking an infant tabernacle, and developing it gradually to the fulness of His spirit stature. He came as man had been coming for ages, and as man has continued to come ever since. Jesus, however, as shown, was the only begotten of God in the flesh.

Adam, our progenitor, "the first man," was, like Christ, a pre-existent spirit, and like Christ he took upon him an appropriate body, the body of a man, and so became a "living soul." The doctrine of the pre-existence, —revealed so plainly, particularly in latter days, pours a wonderful flood of light upon the otherwise mysterious problem of man's origin. It shows that man, as a spirit, was begotten and born of heavenly parents, and reared to maturity in the eternal mansions of the Father, prior to coming upon the earth in a temporal body to undergo an experience in mortality. It teaches that all men existed in the spirit before any man existed in the flesh, and that all who have inhabited the earth since Adam have taken bodies and become souls in like manner.

It is held by some that Adam was not the first man upon this earth, and that the original human being was a development from lower orders of the animal creation. These, however, are the theories of men. The word of the Lord declares that Adam was "the first man of all men" (Moses 1:34), and we are therefore in duty bound to regard him as the primal parent of our race. It was shown to the brother of Jared that all men were created in the beginning after the image of God; and whether we take this to mean the spirit or the body, or both, it commits us to the same conclusion: Man began life as a human being, in the likeness of our heavenly Father.

True it is that the body of man enters upon its career as a tiny germ embryo, which becomes an infant, quickened at a certain stage by the spirit whose tabernacle it is, and the child, after being born, develops into a man. There is nothing in this, however, to indicate that the original man, the first of our race, began life as anything less than a man, or less than the human germ or embryo that becomes a man.

Man, by searching, cannot find out God. Never, unaided, will he discover the truth about the beginning of human life. The Lord must reveal Himself, or remain unrevealed; and the same is true of the facts relating to the origin of Adam's race—God alone can reveal them. Some of these facts, however, are already known, and what has been made known it is our duty to receive and retain.

The Church of Jesus Christ of Latter-day Saints, basing its belief on divine revelation, ancient and modern, proclaims man to be the direct and lineal offspring of Deity. God Himself is an exalted man, perfected, enthroned, and supreme. By His almighty power He organized the earth, and all that it contains, from spirit and element, which exist co-eternally with Himself. He formed every plant that grows, and every animal that breathes, each after its own kind, spiritually and temporally—"that which is spiritual being in the likeness of that which is temporal, and that which is temporal in the likeness of that which is spiritual." He made the tadpole and the ape, the lion and the elephant but He did not make them in His own image, nor endow them with Godlike reason and intelligence. Nevertheless, the whole animal creation will be perfected and perpetuated in the Hereafter, each class in its "distinct order or sphere," and will enjoy "eternal felicity." That fact has been made plain in this dispensation (Doctrine and Covenants, 77:3).

Man is the child of God, formed in the divine image and endowed with divine attributes, and even as the infant son of an earthly father and mother is capable in due time of becoming a man, so the undeveloped offspring of celestial parentage is capable, by experience through ages and aeons, of evolving into a God.

Joseph F. Smith
John R. Winder
Anthon H. Lund
First Presidency of the Church of
Jesus Christ of Latter-day Saints

## II. "Origin of Man"

### (From the "Priesthood Quorum's Table,"
### *Improvement Era* 13:570, April 1910)

"In just what manner did the mortal bodies of Adam and Eve come into existence on this earth?" This question comes from several High Priests quorums.

Of course, all are familiar with the statements in Genesis 1:25, 27; 2:7; also in the Book of Moses, Pearl of Great Price, 2:27; and in the Book of Abraham 5:7. The latter statement reads: "And the Gods formed man from the dust of the ground, and took his spirit [that is, the man's spirit] and put it into him; and breathed into his nostrils the breath of life, and man became a living soul."

These are the authentic statements of the scriptures, ancient and modern, and it is best to rest with these, until the Lord shall see fit to give more light on the subject. Whether the mortal bodies of man evolved in natural processes to present perfection, through the direction and power of God; whether the first parents of our generations, Adam and Eve, were transplanted from another sphere, with immortal tabernacles, which became corrupted through sin and the partaking of natural foods, in the process of time; whether they were born here in mortality, as other mortals have been, are questions not fully answered in the revealed word of God.

## III. "'Mormon' View of Evolution"

### (From the *Improvement Era* 11:1090-91, September 1925;
### see also *Encyclopedia of Mormonism*, Appen. 5)

"God created man in his own image, in the image of God created he him; male and female created he them."

In these plain and pointed words the inspired author of the book of Genesis made known to the world the truth concerning the origin of the human family. Moses, the prophet-historian, who was "learned" we are told, "in all the wisdom of the Egyptians," when making this important announcement, was not voicing a mere opinion. He was speaking as the mouthpiece of God, and his solemn declaration was for all time and for all people. No subsequent rev-elator of the truth has contradicted the great leader and law-giver of Israel. All who have since spoken by divine authority upon this theme have confirmed his simple and sublime proclamation. Nor could it be otherwise. Truth has but once source, and all revelations from heaven are harmonious one with the other.

Jesus Christ, the Son of God, is "the express image" of his Fa-ther's person (Hebrews 1:3). He walked the earth as a human being, as a perfect man, and said, in answer to a question put to him: "He that hath seen me hath seen the Father" (John 14:9). This alone ought to solve the problem to the satisfaction of every thoughtful, reverent mind. It was in this form that the Father and the Son, as two distinct personages, appeared to Joseph Smith, when, as a boy of fourteen years, he received his first vision.

The Father of Jesus Christ is our Father also. Jesus himself taught this truth, when he instructed his disciples how to pray: "Our Father which art in heaven," etc. Jesus, however, is the first born among all the sons of God, the first begotten in the spirit, and the only begotten in the flesh. He is our elder brother, and we, like him, are in the image of God. All men and women are in the similitude of the universal Fa-ther and Mother, and are literally sons and daughters of Deity.

Adam, our great progenitor, "the first man," was, like Christ, a pre-existent spirit, and, like Christ, he took upon him an appropriate body, the body of a man, and so became a "living soul." The doctrine of pre-existence pours wonderful flood of light upon the otherwise mysterious problem of man's origin. It shows that man, as a spirit, was begotten and born of heavenly parents, and reared to maturity in the eternal mansions of the Father, prior to coming upon the earth in a temporal body to undergo an experience in mortality.

The Church of Jesus Christ of Latter-day Saints, basing its belief on divine revelation, ancient and modern, proclaims man to be the direct and lineal offspring of Deity. By his Almighty power God orga-nized the earth, and all that it contains, from spirit and element, which exist co-eternally with himself. Man is the child of God, formed in the divine image and endowed with divine attributes, and even as the infant son of an earthly father and mother is capable in due time of becoming a man, so that undeveloped offspring of celestial parentage is capable, by experience through ages and aeons, of evolving into a God.

Heber J. Grant
Anthony W. Ivins
Charles W. Nibley
First Presidency of the Church of
Jesus Christ of Latter-day Saints

# References Cited

Ahlberg, P. E., and A. R. Milner. "The Origin and Early Diversification of Tetrapods." *Nature* 368 (1994): 507-14.

Aiello, L., and C. Dean. *An Introduction to Human Evolutionary Anatomy*. New York: Academic Press, 1990.

Aristotle. *Generation of Animals*, with an English translation by A. L. Peck. Cambridge, MA: Harvard University Press, 1953.

—————. *On the Heavens*, with an English translation by W. K. C. Guthrie. Cambridge, MA: Harvard University Press, 1939.

"Ask Marilyn." *Parade Magazine*, 19 Apr. 1998.

Asquith, Pamela J. "Of Monkeys and Men: Cultural Views in Japan and the West." In Raymond Corbey and Bert Theunissen, eds. *Ape, Man, Apeman: Changing Views Since 1600*. Leiden: Leiden University, 1995.

Bacon, Francis. *The Philosophical Works of Francis Bacon*, edited by John M. Robertson. London: Routledge and Sons Limited, 1905.

Bailey, Wendy J. "Hominoid Trichotomy: A Molecular Overview." *Evolutionary Anthropology* 2 (1993): 100-108.

Balaban, Evan. "Changes in Multiple Brain Regions Underlie Species Differences in a Complex, Congenital Behavior." *Proceeding of the National Academy of Sciences* 94 (Mar. 1997): 2001-2006.

Bankhead, Reid E. *The Fall of Adam, the Atonement of Christ, and Organic Evolution*. Levan, UT: Joseph Educational Foundation, 1989.

Begley, Sharon. "You Must Remember This." *Newsweek*, 26 Sept. 1994, 68-69.

Benton, Michael J. "Mass Extinction Among Non-Marine Tetrapods." *Nature* 316 (1985): 811.

Bergera, Gary James. "The Orson Pratt-Brigham Young Controversies: Conflict within the Quorums, 1853-1868." *Dialogue: A Journal of Mormon Thought* 13 (1980): 7-49.

*Bible Dictionary.* Salt Lake City: Church of Jesus Christ of Latter-day Saints, 1990.

Bindernagel, John A. *North America's Great Ape: The Sasquatch.* Courtenay, B.C.: Beachcomber Books, 1998.

Boorstin, Daniel J. *The Discoverers.* New York: Vintage Books, 1983.

Bourne, Geoffrey H., and Maury Cohen. *The Gentle Giants: The Gorilla Story.* New York: Putnam, 1975.

Brodrick, James. *Galileo: The Man, His Work, His Misfortunes.* New York: Harper, 1964.

Buerger, David J. "The Adam-God Doctrine." *Dialogue: A Journal of Mormon Thought* 15 (1982): 14-58.

Burton, Alma P. *Discourses of the Prophet Joseph Smith.* Salt Lake City: Deseret Book, 1956.

Cannon, George Q. In *Collected Discourses*, 5 (4 Oct. 1896) (B.H.S. Publishing, 1992).

————. In *Juvenile Instructor* 9 (31 Jan. 1874): 30. In Bankhead, *The Fall of Adam.*

————. In *Millennial Star*, Oct. 1861.

Carson, Hampton L. "The Genetics of Speciation at the Diploid Level." *American Naturalist* 109 (1975): 83-92.

Cartmill, Matt. "Oppressed by Evolution." *Discover*, Mar. 1998, 77-83.

Clark, J. Ruben. "When Are the Writings or Sermons of General Authorities Entitled to the Claim of Scripture?" *Church News*, 31 July 1954, 2ff.

Clarke, R. J. "First Ever Discovery of a Well-Preserved Skull and Associated Skeleton of *Australopithecus.*" *South African Journal of Science* 94 (1998): 460-63.

Crofts, Paul. "How Old Is the Earth?" *Improvement Era* #67 (Oct. 1964): 828.

Darwin, Charles. *The Descent of Man.* 1871, reprinted by Modern Library, New York.

————. *The Origin of Species,* seventh edition (1872) (first edition: 1859), reprinted by Modern Library, New York.

Davies, Paul. *The Mind of God.* New York: Simon & Schuster, 1992.

Davis, J. D. *Genesis and Semitic Traditions.* Grand Rapids, MI: Baker Book House, 1980.

de Bonis, L., G. Bouvrain, D. Geraads, and G. Koufos. "New Hominid Skull Material from the Late Miocene of Macedonia in Northern Greece." *Nature* 345 (1990): 712-14.

*Discourses of Brigham Young,* selected and arranged by John A. Widtsoe. Salt Lake City: Deseret Book, 1961.

Dobzhansky, Theodosius. "Nothing in Biology Makes Sense Except in the Light of Evolution." *American Biology Teacher* 35 (Mar. 1973): 125-29.

Draper, R. D. "The Remarkable Book of Moses." *Ensign* 27 (Feb. 1997): 15-21.

Du Chaillu, P. J. *Equitorial Africa.* London: John Murray, 1861.

Ducros, A., and J. Ducros. "From Satyr to Ape: A Scandalous Sculpture in Paris." In Corbey and Theunissen, *Ape, Man, Apeman.*

Dunn, Paul. *Truth or Speculation.* Salt Lake City: Covenant Communications, 1990.

Dyer, Alvin R. *Who Am I?* Salt Lake City: Deseret Book, 1973.

Easterbrook, G. "Science and God: A Warming Trend?" *Science* 277 (15 Aug. 1997): 890-93.

*Encyclopedia Britannica,* 15th ed., s.v. "Wallace, Alfred Russel." Chicago, 1978.

Ernst, J. F., D. M. Hampsey, J. W. Stewart, S. Rackovsky, D. Goldstein, and F. Sherman. "Substitutions of Proline 76 in Yeast Iso-1-cytochrome *c.*" *Journal of Biological Chemistry* 260 (1985): 13,225-36.

Evenson, William E. In *BYU Daily Universe,* 12 Nov. 1992.

—————. "Evolution." In Ludlow, *Encyclopedia of Mormonism,* 2:478.

Eyring, Henry, *The Faith of a Scientist.* Salt Lake City: Bookcraft, 1967.

—————. "The Gospel and the Age of the Earth." *Improvement Era* 68 (July 1965): 608ff.

—————. *Reflections of a Scientist.* Salt Lake City: Deseret Book, 1983, 1998.

Feduccia, A. *The Origin and Evolution of Birds.* New Haven, CT: Yale University Press, 1996.

Fossey, Dian. *Gorillas in the Mist.* Boston: Houghton Mifflin, 1983.

Galdikas, B. M. F. *Reflections of Eden: My Years with the Orangutans of Borneo.* Boston: Little, Brown and Co., 1995.

Gallup, G. G., Jr. "Chimps and Self-concept." *Psychology Today,* Mar. 1971, 59-61.

—————. "Self-awareness and the Emergence of Mind in the Primates." *American Journal of Primatology* 2 (1982): 237-48.

Gallup, Gordon G., Jr., et al. "A Mirror for the Mind of Man, or Will the Chimpanzee Create an Identity Crisis for Homo Sapiens." *Journal of Human Evolution* 6 (1977): 311.

Gardner, R. A., and B. T. Gardner. "Teaching Sign Language to Chimpanzees." *Science* 165 (1969): 76-82.

Gebo, D. L., et al. "A Hominoid Genus from the Early Miocene of Uganda." *Science* 276 (1997): 401-404.

Gingerich, Owen. "The Galileo Affair." *Scientific American*, Aug. 1982, 133-43.

Gingerich, Philip D., S. M. Raza, M. Arif, M. Anwar, and X. Zhou. "New Whale from the Eocene of Pakistan and the Origin of Cetacean Swimming." *Nature* 368 (1994): 844-47.

Gleick, James. *Chaos: Making a New Science.* New York: Viking, 1987.

——————. "Stephen Jay Gould: Breaking Tradition with Darwin." *New York Times Magazine*, 20 Nov. 1983, 48-64.

Goodall, Jane. *The Chimpanzees of Gombe: Patterns of Behavior.* Cambridge, MA: Belknap Press, 1986.

——————. *Through a Window: My Thirty Years with the Chimpanzees of Gombe.* Boston: Houghton Mifflin, 1990.

Gore, Rick. "The Dawn of Humans: Expanding Worlds." *National Geographic* 191 (May 1997): 84-109.

——————. "The Dawn of Humans: The First Steps." *National Geographic* 191 (Feb. 1997): 72-99.

——————. "The Dawn of Humans: Neandertals." *National Geographic* 189 (Jan. 1996): 2-35.

Gould, Stephen Jay. "Man and Other Animals." *Natural History* 84 (1975): 24.

——————. "The Panda's Peculiar Thumb." *Natural History* 87 (1978): 20-30.

——————. "Through a Lens, Darkly." *Natural History* 98 (Sept. 1989): 16-24.

——————. *Wonderful Life: The Burgess Shale and the Nature of History.* New York: Norton, 1989.

Gould, Stephen Jay, and R. C. Lewontin. "The Spandrels of San Marco and the Panglossian Paradigm: A Critique of the Adaptationist Programme." *Proceeding of the Royal Society* (London) B, 205 (1979): 581-98.

Grant, Heber J., Anthony W. Ivins, and Charles W. Nibley. "Mormon View of Evolution." *Improvement Era* 11 (Sept. 1925): 1090-91; in Ludlow, *Encyclopedia of Mormonism.*

Gribbon, J., and M. Rees. *Cosmic Coincidences.* New York: Bantam Books, 1989.

Gross, C. G. "Huxley versus Owen: The Hippocampus Minor and Evolution." *Trends in Neuroscience* 16 (1993): 493-98.

Haekel, Ernst. "The Last Link." Address delivered to the Fourth International Congress of Zoology at Cambridge, England, 26 Aug. 1898.

Hallowell, A. I. "Culture, Personality and Society." In A. L. Kroeber, *Anthropology Today.* Chicago: University of Chicago Press, 1953.

Hanks, Marion D. "An Attitude, the Weightier Matters." *Ensign* 11 (July 1981): 70.

Hardy, Sarah B. *The Langurs of Abu.* Cambridge, MA: Harvard University Press, 1980.

Hinckley, Gordon B. "I Believe." *Ensign* 22 (Aug. 1992): 2-7.

Hine, Stuart K. "How Great Thou Art." Valencia, CA: Manna Music, 1953.

Hirshberg, C. "Primal Compassion." *Life,* Nov. 1996, 78-82.

Holzapfel, Richard Neitzel. *Every Stone a Sermon.* Salt Lake City: Bookcraft, 1992.

Huxley, T. H. *Evidence as to Man's Place in Nature.* Williams and Norgate, London, 1863.

——————. *Man's Place in Nature.* New York: Appleton and Co., 1916.

Hyde, Paul Nolan. "Intelligences." In Ludlow, *Encyclopedia of Mormonism,* 2:692-93.

*Illustrated London News,* 1938.

*Improvement Era* 15 (Mar. 1912). See also entry for "Adam" in Ludlow, *Encyclopedia of Mormonism.*

*Improvement Era* 51 (1948).

Jacob, François. *The Possible and the Actual.* New York: Pantheon Books, 1982.

Jeffery, Duane E. "Seers, Savants, and Evolution: The Uncomfortable Interface." *Dialogue: A Journal of Mormon Thought* 8 (1974): 41-75.

Johanson, Donald C. "The Dawn of Humans: Face-to-Face with Lucy's Family." *National Geographic* 189 (Mar. 1996).

——————, and Maitland Edey, *Lucy: The Beginnings of Humankind.* New York: Warner Books, 1982.

——————, and Blake Edgar. *From Lucy to Language.* New York: Simon and Schuster, 1996.

John Paul II. Translation of French-language message to members of the Pontifical Academy of Sciences, 22 Oct. 1996; http://www.origins.

org/mc/resources/pope.html; see also J. L. Sheler, in *U.S. News and World Report*, 4 Nov. 1996.

Kimball, Spencer W. "The Blessings and Responsibilities of Womanhood." *Ensign* 6 (Mar. 1976): 70-72.

Kimbel, W. H., et al. "Late Pliocene Homo and Oldowan Tools from the Hadar Formation (Kada Hadar Member), Ethiopia." *Journal of Human Evolution* 31 (1996): 549-61.

Klein, Richard. *The Human Career*. Chicago: University of Chicago Press, 1999.

Krantz, G. S. *Big Footprints*. Boulder, CO: Johnson Books, 1992.

Krings, Matthias, et al. "Neandertal DNA Sequences and the Origin of Modern Humans." *Cell* 90 (1997): 19-30.

Leakey, M. "The Dawn of Humans: The Farthest Horizon." *National Geographic* 188 (Sept. 1995): 38-51.

——————, and R. L. Hay. "Pliocene Footprints in the Laetoli Beds at Laetoli, Northern Tanzania." *Nature* 278 (1979): 317-23.

LeConte, J. *Evolution: Its Nature, Its Evidence and Its Relation to Religious Thought*. New York: Appleton, 1897.

Lee, Harold B. "Find the Answers in the Scriptures." *Ensign* 2 (Dec. 1972): 2-3.

Lewin, Roger. "Science Is Not Postage Stamp Collecting." *Science* 216 (May 1982): 14.

Li, Wen-Hsiung. *Molecular Evolution*. Sunderland, MA: Sinauer, 1997.

Ludlow, Daniel H., ed. *Encyclopedia of Mormonism*. New York: Macmillan, 1992.

MacKinnon, John. *In Search of the Red Ape*. New York: Holt, Rinehart, and Winston, 1974.

Matthews, Robert J. "Fall of Adam." In Ludlow, *Encyclopedia of Mormonism*, 2:485-86.

May, Robert M. "How Many Species Inhabit the Earth?" *Scientific American* 267 (Oct. 1992): 42-48.

McConkie, Bruce R. "Christ and the Creation." *Ensign* 12 (June 1982): 9-15.

——————. *Mormon Doctrine*. Salt Lake City: Bookcraft, 1958.

——————. *The Mortal Messiah. Book I*. Salt Lake City: Deseret Book, 1979.

——————. "What Think Ye of the Book of Mormon?" *Ensign* 13 (Nov. 1983): 72-74.

McConkie, Joseph Fielding. *Answers: Straightforward Answers to Tough Gospel Questions*. Salt Lake City: Deseret Book, 1998.

McFarlan, Donald, ed. *Guinness Book of World Records.* New York: Bantam, 1990.

Milton, John. *Paradise Lost, 1658-1663.* The Harvard Classics, edited by C. W. Eliot. New York: Collier, 1937.

Monastersky, Richard. "The Rise of Life on Earth." *National Geographic* 193 (Mar. 1998): 75.

Moore, Randy. "Debunking the Paranormal: We Should Teach Critical Thinking as a Necessity for Living, Not Just as a Tool for Science." *American Biology Teacher* 54 (Jan. 1992): 4-9.

Moya-Sola, S., and M. Koehler. "A *Dryopithecus* Skeleton and the Origins of Great-Ape Locomotion." *Nature* 379 (1996): 156-59.

Nibley, Hugh W. "Before Adam." In *Old Testament and Related Studies.* Salt Lake City: Deseret Book, 1986.

—————. "Man's Dominion." *New Era* 11 (Jan.-Feb. 1981): 47-48.

Nielsen, F. Kent, and Stephen D. Ricks. "Creation, Creation Accounts." In Ludlow, *Encyclopedia of Mormonism,* 1:34-43.

Nielsen, Kent. "The Gospel and the Scientific View: How the Earth Came to Be." *Ensign* 10 (Sept. 1980): 66-72.

Novacek, Michael J. "Whales Leave the Beach." *Nature* 368 (1994): 807.

"Older, Not Better." *Discover* 18 (Apr. 1997): 20.

"Oldest American." *Discover* 17 (Sept. 1996): 26.

Olroyd, David Roger. *Darwinian Impacts: An Introduction to the Darwinian Revolution.* Atlantic Heights, NJ: Humanities Press, 1980.

Pack, Frederick J. *Science and Belief in God.* Salt Lake City: Deseret News Press, 1924.

Packer, Boyd K. "The Law and the Light." In *Jacob Through Words of Mormon, To Learn with Joy,* edited by Monte S. Nyman and Charles D. Tate. Provo, UT: Religious Studies Center, Brigham Young University, 1990.

Patterson, P. "Conversations with a Gorilla." *National Geographic* 154 (1978): 438-65.

Paul, Erich Robert. *Science, Religion and Mormon Cosmology.* Chicago: University of Illinois Press, 1992.

Penrose, Charles W. *Journal of Discourses* 26 (16 Nov. 1884): 18-29 (Daniel H. Wells, 1886).

Petersen, Mark E. In Bankhead, *The Fall of Adam.*

Peterson, Morris S. "I Have a Question." *Ensign* 17 (Sept. 1987): 28-29.

Pilbeam, D. "Genetic and Morphological Records of the Hominoidea and

Hominid Origins: A Synthesis." *Molecular Phylogenetics and Evolution* 5 (1996): 155-68.

Pough, F. Harvey, Christine M. Janis, and John B. Heiser. *Vertebrate Life,* 5th ed. Upper Saddle River, NJ: Prentice Hall, 1999.

Pratt, Orson. In *Journal of Discourses* 17 (6 Apr. 1874): 24-36 (Albert Carrington, 1875).

Premack, D. "Language in Chimpanzees?" *Science* 172 (1971): 808-22.

"Priesthood Quorums Table." *Improvement Era* 13 (Apr. 1910): 570.

Raven, Peter H., and George B. Johnson. *Biology.* St. Louis, MO: Mosby, 1992 (3rd. ed.).

Reader, John. *Missing Links.* London: Pelican Books, 1988.

Richards, P. "Local Understandings of Primates and Evolution: Some Beliefs Concerning Chimpanzees." In Corbey and Theunissen, *Ape, Man, Apeman.*

Ridley, M. *Evolution.* Abingdon, Eng.: Blackwell Science, 1996.

Roberts, B. H. *A Comprehensive History of the Church of Jesus Christ of Latter-day Saints, Century 1.* Provo, UT: Brigham Young University Press, 1965.

————. *The Gospel and Man's Relationship to Deity.* Salt Lake City: Deseret Book, 1926.

Roberts, D. "The Ice Man: Lone Voyager from the Copper Age." *National Geographic* 183 (June 1993): 36-67.

Rumbaugh, F. "Reading and Sentence Completion by a Chimpanzee." *Science* 182 (1978): 730-33.

Sagan, Carl. *Cosmos.* New York: Random House, 1980.

Salisbury, Frank B. *The Creation.* Salt Lake City: Deseret Book, 1976.

————. "Science and Religion, Their Basic Positions." *Improvement Era* 56 (Feb. 1953): 80ff.

Santillana, Giorgio de. *The Crime of Galileo.* Chicago: University of Chicago Press, 1955.

Schaller, George B. *The Mountain Gorilla: Ecology and Behavior.* Chicago: University of Chicago Press, 1976.

Schopf, J. W., J. M. Hays, and M. R. Walter. "Evolution of the Earth's Earliest Ecosystems: Recent Progress and Unsolved Problems." In *Earth's Earliest Biosphere*, edited by J. W. Schopf. Princeton, NJ: Princeton University Press, 1983.

"Science and Religion." *Improvement Era* 68 (Oct. 1965): 80ff.

*7th East Press*, 18 Nov. 1981.

Sheler, Jeffery L. "The Pope and Darwin." *U.S. News and World Report*, 4 Nov. 1996 (www.usnews.com/usnews/issue/4evol.htm).

Shreeve, J. "The Dating Game." *Discover* 13 (Sept. 1992): 76-83.

Sites, J. W., Jr., C. J. Basten, and M. A. Asmussen. "Cytonuclear Genetic Structure of a Hybrid Zone in Lizards of the Sceloporus Grammicus Complex (Sauria, Phrynosomatidae)." *Molecular Ecology* 5 (1996): 379-92.

Smith, Joseph, Jr., *History of the Church of Jesus Christ of Latter-day Saints, Period 1*. Salt Lake City: Deseret Book, 1978.

Smith, Joseph F., John R. Windor, and Anthon H. Lund. "The Origin of Man." *Improvement Era* 13 (Nov. 1909): 75-81; reprinted in Ludlow, *Encyclopedia of Mormonism*.

Smith, Joseph Fielding. "Faith Leads to a Fullness of Truth and Righteousness." *Utah Genealogical and Historical Magazine* 21 (Oct. 1930): 145-58.

————. *Man: His Origin and Destiny*. Salt Lake City: Deseret Book, 1954.

————. "The Salt Lake Temple." *Improvement Era* 56 (Apr. 1953): 224, as cited in Holzapfel, Richard Neitzel, *Every Stone a Sermon*. Salt Lake City: Bookcraft, 1992, #292.

Snow, Eliza R. "O My Father." In *Hymns of The Church of Jesus Christ of Latter-day Saints*. Salt Lake City: Church of Jesus Christ of Latter-day Saints, 1985.

Snow, Erastus. In *Journal of Discourses* 19 (3 Mar. 1878): 266-79.

Sorenson, John L. "Origin of Man." In Ludlow, *Encyclopedia of Mormonism*, 3:1053-54.

Spencer, F. "Pithekos to Pithecanthropus: An Abbreviated Review of Changing Scientific Views on the Relationship of the Anthropoid Apes to Homo." In Corbey and Theunissen, *Ape, Man, Apeman*.

Stephens, Trent D., Carolyn J. W. Bunde, and Bradley J. Fillmore. "Non-Molecular, Epigenetic, Physical Factors in Limb Initiation." *Journal of Experimental Zoology* 284 (1999): 55-66.

Strohman, Richard C. "The Coming Kuhnian Revolution in Biology." *Nature Biotechnology* 15 (1997): 194-200.

Tabin, C. "The Initiation of the Limb Bud: Growth Factors, *Hox* Genes, and Retinoids." *Cell* 80 (1995): 671-74.

Talmage, James E. In *Church News*, 21 Nov. 1931, 7-8.

————. "The Earth and Man." *The Instructor* 100 (Dec. 1965): 474-77; 101 (Jan. 1966): 9-15.

—————. As quoted by Hugh B. Brown, in *LDS Conference Reports,* Apr. 1969.

—————. Personal Journal, Archives and Manuscripts, Special Collections, Harold B. Lee Library, Brigham Young University, Provo, Utah.

Tanaka, Y, T. Ashikari, Y. Shibano, T. Amachi, H. Yoshizumi, and H. Matsubara. "Amino Acid Replacement Studies in Human Cytochrome *c* by a Complementation System Using CYD1 Deficient Yeast." *Journal of Biochemistry* 104 (1988): 477-80.

Taylor, David C. *Managing the Serials Explosion.* White Plains, NY: Knowledge Industry Publications, 1982.

Taylor, John. *Mediation and Atonement.* Salt Lake City: Deseret News Press, 1882.

Thewissen, J. G. M., S. T. Hussain, and M. Arif. "Fossil Evidence for the Origin of Aquatic Locomotion in Archaeocete Whales." *Science* 263 (1994): 210-12.

Thompson, D'Arcy Wentworth. *On Growth and Form, 1917.* An Abridged Edition, edited by John Tyler Bonner. Cambridge, Eng.: Cambridge University Press, 1961.

Tickle, C., and G. Eichele. "Vertebrate Limb Development." *Annual Review of Cellular Biology* 10 (1994): 121-52.

Tuttle , R. H. *Apes of the World.* Ridge Park, NJ: Noyes Publications, 1986.

Tyson, Edward. *Orang-Outang, sive Homo Sylvestris: or, the Pygmie compared with that of a Monkey, an Ape, and a Man.* London: Bennet, 1699.

Wang, Hsing-Pei. *Monkey Subdues the White-Bone Demon.* Peking: Foreign Languages Press, 1976.

Watson, James D. *Molecular Biology of the Gene.* New York: Benjamin, 1970.

Weil, Lynne. "Pope: Church Accepts Evolution as Well-Supported Scientific Theory." *Idaho Catholic Register,* 1 Nov. 1996, 2.

Wells, Emmeline B. "Our Mountain Home So Dear." In *Hymns of The Church of Jesus Christ of Latter-day Saints.* Salt Lake City: Church of Jesus Christ of Latter-day Saints, 1985, #33.

White, T. D., G. Suwa, and B. Asfaw. "*Australopithecus ramidis,* A New Species of Early Hominid from Aramis, Ethiopia." *Nature* 371 (1994): 306-12.

White T. H., trans. *The Bestiary: A Book of Beasts.* New York: Capricorn Books, 1954.

Widtsoe, John A. "Evidence and Reconciliations: Were There Pre-Adamites?" *Improvement Era* 51 (May 1948): 305.

————. *Evidences and Reconciliations.* Arranged by G. H. Durham. Salt Lake City: Bookcraft, 1960.

————. *Joseph Smith as Scientist: A Contribution to Mormon Philosophy.* Salt Lake City: General Board of the Young Men's Mutual Improvement Association, 1908.

————. *Science and Your Faith in God.* Salt Lake City: Bookcraft, 1958.

Woodward, R. "In the Beginning: A Latter-day Perspective." *Ensign* 26 (Jan. 1996): 12-19.

Wootton, Richard T. *Saints and Scientists.* Mesa, AZ: EduTech, 1992.

Wordsworth, W. "Ode (Intimations of Immortality from Recollections of Early Childhood), 1803-1806." In *Familiar Quotations*, compiled by John Bartlett. New York: Blue Ribbon, 1919.

Young, Brigham. In *Journal of Discourses* 6 (28 Aug. 1852): 266-70 (Asa Calkin, 1859).

————. In *Journal of Discourses* 2 (23 Oct. 1853): 1-10 (F. D. Richards, 1855).

————. In *Journal of Discourses* 8 (25 Mar. 1860): 27-31 (George Q. Cannon, 1861).

————. In *Journal of Discourses* 14 (14 May 1871): 114-18 (Albert Carrington, 1862).

————. In *Messages of the First Presidency*, 2 (21 Oct. 1865). Edited by James R. Clark. Salt Lake City: Bookcraft, 1965.

Zimmer, Carl. "Coming Onto the Land." *Discover* 16 (June 1995): 118-27.

# Index

## A

Abraham, 3, 34, 147, 160, 179;
    Book of, 178, 180
*Acanthostega*, 151, 152
Adam, 33, 35-38, 44, 45, 51, 52,
    119, 140, 180, 183; and Eve,
    10, 36, 39, 40, 133-36, 144,
    171, 173, 174, 176-78, 181-85,
    205. *See also* Eve.
Adam-God Doctrine, 36, 51
Africa, 95, 125, 129, 155-60
alchemy, 73
aliens, 134
Alma, 67, 72, 182, 183, 185
*Ambulocetus*, 152-54
American Sign Language (Washoe),
    122
amino acids, 105
angels, 168, 184
anthropoid, 155
anthropology, 10, 11, 45, 57
Antionah, 182
Anubis (Egyptian baboon god), 128
ape(s), 51, 122, 124, 126, 128, 138,
    155-57; apeman, 155
*Archaeopteryx*, 149, 150

archeology, 10, 11, 45, 57
archipelago, 94, 97
*Ardipithecus*, 158
Aristotle, 21, 22, 24, 72-76, 144,
    153
arm-hanging locomotion, 157
Armstrong, Neil, 79
Asia, 96, 160
atoms, 103
Atonement, 51, 52, 181
attractors, strange, 196-98, 200,
    201
Australia, 96
*Australopithecus afarensis*, 159, 161
*Australopithecus africanus*, 159
*Australopithecus amanensis*, 158
*Australopithecus ramidis*, 158

## B

baboon, 37, 128
Bacon, Francis, 25, 26, 70
Balaban, 92
Bankhead, Reid E., 50
Barnum and Baily circus, 128
*Beagle*, 82, 83

Bellarmine, Cardinal, 78
bestiary, 127
Bible, 167, 178, 179
Big Bang Theory, 76
binomial nomenclature, 144, 145
Binti (gorilla), 123
biologists, 27, 28, 87, 95, 96, 117, 172, 187, 199
biology, 10, 11, 40, 45, 57, 82, 93, 189, 198; biological form, 196, 198, 201
biomechanical forces, 192, 194, 199, 200
bipedalism, 121, 158
birth, 33, 206
black holes, 72
blind spot, 62
body(ies), physical, 8, 101, 119, 205; of flesh and bones, 35
Book of Mormon, 69; symposium on, 53
brain, size of, 161
Brigham Young University, 41, 55, 139, 146; packet on evolution from, 55
Broom, Robert, 158
Buddha, 129
Burroughs, Edgar Rice, 128

# C

Canaan, 176
Cannon, George Q., 36, 37, 50
Cape Verde Archipelagoes, 94-95
Carson, H. L., 97
Cartmill, Matt, 27
Catarhine simiae, 126
Catholic Church, 78, 79
cauda, 127
caudex, 127
causes, 21-27, 73; efficient, 84; final, 83
Celestial Kingdom, 136, 168

cell theory, 61, 101, 103
chaos, 147, 177, 195; theory of, 195-97
cherubim, 181, 182, 184
chimpanzee, 110, 122, 123, 125, 126, 129, 134, 156, 157, 161
Christianity, 120, 127, 168, 184
chromosomes, 92, 93, 97, 146
Church of Jesus Christ of Latter-day Saints, 9-11; "official" position of on evolution, 38, 55
Clark, J. Reuben, 47
codon, 105
Collins, Francis, 28
Columbus, 76
constraint, 100, 188-91, 194, 195, 197-200
Cook, Melvin, 49
Copernicus, Nicolaus, 77-79, 81
Cracroft, Paul, 49
creation, 3, 8, 11, 33, 37, 38, 49, 52, 56, 82, 83, 87, 98, 99, 100, 133, 135, 137, 142, 160, 165-68, 169, 171, 173, 174, 175, 177, 178, 181, 182, 184, 187, 195; special, 10, 12, 148, 154; spiritual, 38, 124, 175, 178, 179; temporal, 38
Creationist, 46, 169, 171, 188
Crick, Francis, 104
Cro-Magnon man, 46
crocodiles, from hens' eggs, 53
cytochrome c, 110

# D

Dante, 76, 77
Dart, Raymond, 158
Darwin, Charles, 36, 38, 42, 79, 81-99, 103, 111, 155, 188, 189, 192, 199
Darwinism, 32, 44, 120, 146

data, 59, 70, 71, 77, 80, 81, 83, 84, 95, 96, 133, 135, 136, 165, 166, 173, 179, 188
Davies, Paul, 148
Davis, John D., 33
Dawkins, Richard, 18
death, 140, 163, 173, 179, 181, 183, 205; no death before Fall, 45, 144
*Descent of Man*, 36
developmental constraint, 92, 190
devil, 127
Devonian period, 150, 151
dinosaurs, 55, 141
distribution, geographical, 94, 95, 97
DNA, 11, 23, 24, 95, 98, 102-16, 134; fingerprinting, 107-9; noncoding, 114; sequencing, 104, 113, 114
Dobzhansky, Theodosius, 91
doctrine, 32, 48, 56, 173
*Drosophila*, 96
*Dryopithecus laietanus*, 157
Du Chaillu, Paul, 128
Dunn, Paul H., 48
dust, 33, 175

**E**

*E. coli*, 105
earth, 4, 167-79, 184, 205; age of, 34, 49; crust and mantle of, 142
earth-centered universe, 74, 76-79, 101, 137
Eastbrook, Greg, 28
Eden, 176
Egypt, 128
embryo, 8, 24, 38, 43, 189, 192-94
*Encyclopedia of Mormonism*, 7, 9, 10, 44, 56, 135, 179
Eocene, 153

Europe, 155, 162
*Eusthenopteran*, 151
Eve, 37, 180. *See also* Adam
Evenson, William E., 10, 55
*Evidences and Reconciliations*, 42
evolution, 7, 9-13, 17, 18, 27-30, 40-42, 51-53; organic, 57, 59, 79, 81, 89, 91, 93, 98-100, 138, 168, 172, 179, 180, 181, 185, 187-89, 195, 197, 200, 206; theistic, 53; theory of, 11, 13, 17, 26, 29, 60, 83, 91, 92, 94, 96, 133, 165, 188, 197
experimentation, 18, 59, 67, 72, 98, 193
extinction, 55, 91, 140, 147, 154
Eyring, Henry, 15, 29, 30, 32, 49, 54, 79, 138, 141, 148

**F**

faith, 20, 21, 61, 67, 68, 78, 79, 206, 207
Fall, 45, 46, 52, 135, 136, 140, 144, 171, 173, 181-85
firmament, 169-72, 174
First Presidency, 7, 10, 31, 32, 39, 48, 133; statement on "The Origin of Man" (1909), 7, 9, 38, 39, 56
fish, lobe-finned, 150
forms, transitional, 91, 149, 160
Fossey, Dian, 129
fossils, 54, 55, 108-9, 139, 140, 142, 153, 155, 157; extra-terrestrial origin of, 142; gaps in, 149; record/evidence of, 11, 17, 42, 43, 91, 92, 136, 142
Franklin, Rosalind, 104
fruit, 135, 171, 173, 177

# G

Gabala, bishop of, 76
Galapagos Archipelago, 82, 83, 94-96
Galdikas, B. M. F., 129
Galilei, Galileo, 71, 72, 77-81, 170
Gallup, Gordon, Jr., 123, 129
Garden of Eden, 82, 134, 135, 140, 171, 174-76, 180, 182, 185
Gardner, Allan, 122
Gardner, Beatrice, 122
Gargantua the Great (gorilla), 128
general authorities, 32, 52
genes, 92, 99, 104, 105, 147, 191, 192, 195, 200-201
Genesis, 3, 33, 88, 119, 154, 165, 166, 170, 171, 174-79
genetics, 41, 90, 91, 101, 143, 147, 199; code, 104
genus, 88, 97, 98, 144
geology, 10, 11, 45, 57, 94; column, 140
God, 2-5, 9, 11, 13, 20, 26, 28, 30, 35, 40, 67, 68, 82, 83, 99, 100, 131, 133, 134, 137, 138, 142, 160, 167-85, 187, 188, 200, 201; image of, 8, 10, 35, 37, 39, 52, 99, 172, 173, 188, 198, 201
Goodall, Jane, 122, 129
gorilla, 37, 110, 123, 125, 126, 128, 129, 134, 156, 157
Gould, Stephen Jay, 121, 190
Grant, Heber J., 9, 44
Green, Paul R., 44

# H

Haeckel, Ernst, 126
Haldane, J. B. S., 145
Hallowell, A. I., 123
Hanuman (Hindu monkey god), 128
Hanks, Marion D., 48
Hawaiian Archipelago, 96
heaven, 167-69, 174, 178, 184
Hebrew, 144, 170
herb, 171-74
heredity, 189, 190
Hindu, 128
Hine, Stuart K., 3
Hinkley, Gordon B., 4
hippocampus, 120, 121
Holy Ghost, 69, 166
Holzapfel, 132
hominid, *Hominidae*, 143, 156, 157, 163, 164, 185
*Homo erectus*, 160
*Homo ergaster*, 160, 161
*Homo habilis*, 159
*Homo heidlbergensis*, 160, 161
*Homo sapiens*, 122, 125, 145, 155, 159, 160, 162, 163; *archaic Homo sapiens*, 160. *See also* humans; man
Hsuan-tsang, 129
Human Genome Project, 105, 200
humans, 124-26, 140, 156, 161; ancestral origins, 10, 29, 33, 42, 155-56, 166, 187. *See also Homo sapiens*, man
Huxley, Thomas, 120, 126, 155
hybrid, 145, 146
hypothesis, 59, 60, 95, 96, 192, 193

# I

"Iceman," 162
*Ichtheostega*, 151
immortality, 135, 136, 173, 179, 181-85
Indonesia, 96
infallibility, mortal, 32
information explosion, 16, 17

Inquisition, 78
interpretations, 10, 31, 32, 56, 70, 71, 83, 165-67, 171, 176, 178, 180, 185
Israel, 176, 177
Ivins, Anthony W., 9

# J

Jacob, Frabçois, 189, 195, 197, 198
James, King, 33, 169, 173
Japan, 128, 129
Jared, brother of, 68, 69, 117
Jesus Christ, 8, 10, 15, 35, 37, 67-69, 134, 137
Johanson, Don, 159
John Paul II, Pope, 17, 28, 79
John the Revelator, 124
Jupiter, 77, 170
Jurassic age, 149

# K

Kepler, 77
Kimball, Spencer W., 177
King Follett discourse, 35
*King Kong*, 128
Koko (gorilla), 123

# L

Lactantius, 76
Lana (chimpanzee), 123
Larson, Edward, 28
"Law and the Light," 53
laws, 4, 60, 83, 98, 99, 146, 189, 195, 197, 199; natural laws, 40, 148, 167, 200, 206; of development, 194, 195; of gravity, 19, 60, 71, 72, 81-83, 90, 98, 167; of nature, 13, 201; of physics, 189, 191

Leakey, Louis, 122, 159
Leakey, Meave, 158
Leakey, Richard, 160
LeConte, 5
Lee, Harold B., 50
Lehi, 67, 69, 134, 135, 136, 182
Lewin, Roger, 187
Lewontin, Richard, 189
limbs, 192-94, 199, 200
links, missing, 92, 153-54, 155, 164
Linnaeus, 125, 144, 145
Linnean Society, 96
Lucy (australopithecine), 159; chimpanzee, 122
Lund, Anthon H., 10
Luther, Martin, 77

# M

Malay Archipelago, 96
man, 172, 174-78, 180, 184, 187, 188; first, 8, 33, 52, 175; man, origin of, 57, 133; pre-Adamic, 42, 45, 49, 50, 138. *See also* Homo sapiens; humans
Matthews, Robert L., 135
Mayr, Ernst, 187
McConkie, Bruce R., 49, 50, 52, 53, 135, 136, 177, 178, 181
McConkie, Joseph Fielding, 56
McKay, David O., 47, 48
McKinnon, John, 129
Mende, 129
Mendel, Gregor, 70, 71, 90, 91, 103
Merrill, Joseph F., 46
Meservy, Keith H., 51
mesonychid artiodactyl/mesonychid ungulate, 152, 154
Mesopotamia, 177
Michael, the Archangel, 36
Middle Ages, 24-26, 76, 82, 167
Milton, John, 184, 185

*Min*, 144
Miocene, 155, 157
Modern Synthesis, 42, 91
*modus operandi*, 40
molecules, 17, 30, 94, 95, 98, 101,
    103, 191, 200
monkeys, 37, 126, 128, 129
moons, 77, 78, 82, 169, 170
Moore, Randy, 70
Morgan, T. H., 92
*Morotopithecus*, 157
mortality, 40, 181, 183, 207
Moses, 3, 8, 179; Book of, 33, 178,
    210; vision of, 33, 34
Muller, H. J., 91
Musters, Pauline, 198
mutation, 91, 98-99, 106, 147, 198,
    200

N

Natural Selection, 36, 42, 44, 81,
    83, 87, 89-90, 92, 94, 96,
    98-100, 103, 140, 147, 185,
    189, 190, 198, 199
naturalism, scientific, 53
Nature, 21, 26, 80, 83, 85, 86, 98,
    119, 137
Nauvoo, 132
Neandertal, 46, 109, 155, 161
Nebuchadnezzar, 132
neo-Darwinism, 91
Nephi, 69, 179
Newton, Isaac, 71, 75, 81-83, 98
Nibley, Charles W., 9
Nibley, Hugh, 35, 119, 147
Nielson, Kent, 53
Novachek, Michael, 153

O

observation, 18, 20, 59, 61, 62, 67,
    70, 77, 98
offspring, lineal, 9, 39; of Deity, 8,
    10
*On Growth and Form*, 190
orangutan, 110, 125, 126, 129, 134
"Origin of Man," 1909 First Presi-
    dency statement on, *see* First
    Presidency
*Origin of Species*, 36, 81, 83, 98,
    103, 111, 149, 188, 199
Osaru (oriental monkey hero), 129
Osborn, Henry Fairfield, 42
*Ouranopithecus mecedoniensis*, 157
Owen, Richard, 120

P

Pack, Frederick J., 43
Packer, Boyd K., 53
paleontology, 44, 93, 94
*Panderithys*, 151
*Paradise Lost*, 184
paradisiacal, 49, 53, 135, 140, 171,
    178, 181
Patterson, Penny, 123
Paul, E. Robert, 46, 55, 136
Pearl of Great Price, 33, 147
Pennant, Thomas, 126
Penrose, Charles W., 39
Permian Period, 147
Peterson, Mark E., 50
Peterson, Morris S., 54, 139
phylogeny, 190
"Pillars of Faith," 52
Piltdown man, 46
pithecoid, 155
Plato, 144
Pliocene, 155
polymerase chain reaction (PCR),
    105
post-mortal, 206
Pratt, Orson, 37
predictions, 61, 117

pre-existence, 8, 168, 204
Premack, David, 123
Price, George McCready, 46
Primates (order), 120, 125, 143, 156
procreation, 34, 144
prophets, 32, 47, 48, 50, 179
*Prozueglodon*, 153, 154
Ptolemaeus, Claudius (Ptolemy), 75-77

# R

Ray, John, 144
relatedness, 112, 117
relativity, theory of, 19
resurrection, 133, 136, 137, 183, 206
revelation, 9, 20, 21, 32, 133, 166, 177, 179, 181, 182, 185
rib, 34, 177
Ridley, Mark, 187
Rigdon, Sidney, 33
Roberts, B. H., 34, 35, 45, 46, 132, 141, 177
*Rodhocetus*, 153, 154
Romanov, Anastasia, 109
Romney, Marion G., 50
Rumbaugh, David, 123

# S

Sagan, Carl, 61, 75, 187
salamander, 145, 193, 194
Salisbury, Frank B., 48, 50, 143, 149
Sarah (chimpanzee), 123
Satan, 13, 46, 180, 184
scale of life, 43, 149. *See also* Nature
*Sceloporus grammicus*, 146
Schaller, George B., 129

sciences, 18-22, 25-27, 30, 42, 59-61, 70, 71, 78, 79, 93, 137, 166, 171, 185, 198; and religion, 12, 13, 15, 21, 22, 26, 27, 29, 44, 49, 50, 61, 64, 77, 187
scientists, 12, 16, 17, 24, 28, 70, 78, 81, 83, 99, 137, 138, 167, 172. *See also* [individual names of scientists]
Scopes, John, 44
scriptures, 10, 28, 47, 54, 77-79, 133-37, 142, 165-67, 171, 173, 174, 178, 179, 181, 182, 184, 185, 187
seed, 36, 67, 68, 72, 73, 144, 171
serpent, 179, 180
"Seven Deadly Heresies," 52
Seventh-day Adventist, 47
Shishak of Egypt, 131
Simian, 127
*Sinornithosaurus millenii*, 150
Sites, Jack, 93, 146
Smith, Joseph, 32, 33, 35, 69, 124, 131, 141, 178; and translation of Bible, 33, 34, 168, 173-75
Smith, Joseph F., 7, 10, 36, 38, 40
Smith, Joseph Fielding, 45, 46, 50, 52, 54
Snow, Erastus, 37
Solomon, 131, 132
Sorensen, John L., 57
soul, 33, 34, 49, 124, 175, 204
South America, 94
speciation, 98, 140, 147
species, 3, 82-84, 86-90, 92-94, 97, 98, 144-46, 172
speculation, 34, 48
Spencer, Herbert, 89
sphere, 74, 75, 191, 192
spirits, 10, 29, 38, 124, 131, 133, 136, 204, 206; bodies, 137; children, 39, 44, 101, 125, 204
Stephens, Trent, 41, 192-194

stratigraphy, 139
Strohman, Richard, 188, 189, 192, 198
sun, 169, 170
supernatural, 96, 100, 133
survival of the fittest, 89, 90, 94
symbolism, 179

## T

tabernacle, 38, 39, 164
Tabin, Cliff, 192
tail, 51, 127
Talmage, James E., 3, 37, 45, 46, 50, 133, 138, 140
*Tarzan*, 128
Taylor, John, 51, 146
telescope, 77-79, 170
temples, 131-33
tetrapod, 143, 150
theories, 60, 61, 79, 83, 94; of men, 39. *See also* [names of specific theories]
Thewissen, Hans, 152
Thompson, D'Arcy, 189-92, 198, 199
Tickle, Cheryl, 192
tools, stone, 122, 160
traditions, 34, 165, 166, 173, 176, 181, 183, 185
transplantation, 35, 40
Tree of Knowledge of Good and Evil, 176, 177, 179, 180, 182, 183, 185
Tree of Life, 68, 69, 135, 176, 181-85
truth, 13, 15, 21, 27-29, 60, 61, 138, 181, 185
Twelve Apostles, 32
Tycho, 77
*Tyrannosaurus rex*, 121

Tyson, Edward, 125

## U

universe, 98, 148, 167, 170, 195

## V

variations, 44, 84-86, 89-91, 94, 98, 140, 147
vegetation, 36
vertebrates, 143, 145
visions, 70

## W

Wadlow, Robert, 198
Wallace, Alfred Russel, 96
Wallace's Line, 96
water, 34, 35, 168-71, 174, 175, 177
Watson, James, 104
Wells, Emmeline B., 3
whales, 144, 152, 153, 171
White, Ellen G., 47
Widtsoe, John A., 42, 46, 50, 140, 203
Wilberforce, Bishop, 126
Wilkins, Maurice, 104
Winder, John R., 10
Witham, Larry, 28
Woodward, Robert, 34, 178, 181
Wootton, Richard T., 11, 12

## Y

yolk sac, 193
Young, Brigham, 15, 32, 33, 35, 51, 131-33, 166, 179

## About the Authors

*Trent D. Stephens*, Ph.D., is Professor of Anatomy and Embryology at Idaho State University (ISU). Previously he taught anatomy at the University of Washington. He was ISU Distinguished Teacher in 1992, Sigma Xi Jerome Bigalow Award recipient in 1992, and ISU Outstanding Researcher in 2000. He has published over seventy-five scientific papers and books, one textbook, and coauthored nine other books. He currently serves in the LDS church as a ward bishop. He and his wife Kathleen have five children and six grandsons.

*D. Jeffrey Meldrum,* Ph.D., is Associate Professor of Anatomy and Anthropology at ISU and Affiliate Curator of Vertebrate Paleontology at the Idaho Museum of Natural History. Before joining ISU, he was Assistant Professor in the Evolutionary Morphology Group at Northwestern University Medical School, where he also lectured at the Chicago Center for Religion and Science. He is presently investigating the hominoid foot and the emergence of human bipedalism, funded by the L. S. B. Leakey Foundation, and directs a field project in southwestern Montana, funded by the National Geographic Society. He is the scoutmaster and a priesthood instructor in his local LDS ward. He and his wife Terri have six sons.

*Forrest B. Peterson* is a professional writer, theatrical producer, and teacher. He studied marketing and writing at Eastern New Mexico and Idaho State universities, as well as film production at Metro Media Productions in Florida. He has written over fifty stage plays, movie scripts, short stories, and a novel; his film, *Trouble in Oz,* won five Crystal Reel Awards from the Florida Film Festival in 1990. He teaches marketing, drama, and film production. He has served his local LDS ward as elders quorum president, Sunday school teacher, and on both ward and stake activities committees. He is married to Carol Ralston; they have five children.